Max Nettlau's Utopian Vision

Max Nettlau's Utopian Vision

A Translation of *Esbozo de historia de las utopias*

Edited and translated by Toby Widdicombe

ANTHEM PRESS

Anthem Press
An imprint of Wimbledon Publishing Company
www.anthempress.com

This edition first published in UK and USA 2023
by ANTHEM PRESS
75–76 Blackfriars Road, London SE1 8HA, UK
or PO Box 9779, London SW19 7ZG, UK
and
244 Madison Ave #116, New York, NY 10016, USA

© 2023 Toby Widdicombe editorial matter and selection;
individual chapters © individual contributors

The moral right of the authors has been asserted.

All rights reserved. Without limiting the rights under copyright reserved above,
no part of this publication may be reproduced, stored or introduced into
a retrieval system, or transmitted, in any form or by any means
(electronic, mechanical, photocopying, recording or otherwise),
without the prior written permission of both the copyright owner
and the above publisher of this book.

British Library Cataloguing-in-Publication Data
A catalogue record for this book is available from the British Library.

Library of Congress Cataloging-in-Publication Data
A catalog record for this book has been requested.
2022951608

ISBN-13: 978-1-78527-915-7 (Hbk)
ISBN-10: 1-78527-915-7 (Hbk)

Cover Credit: International Institute of Social History, Amsterdam.
Call number: BG D31/404

This title is also available as an e-book.

To Thomas More and Edward Bellamy and Oscar Wilde, who first started me down the delightful path of radical social betterment and change.

CONTENTS

Preface ... ix

Acknowledgments ... xi

Introduction ... xiii

    The Life of Max Nettlau ... xiii

    Nettlau as Anarchist Historian ... xxviii

    Nettlau as Anarchist ... xxx

    Nettlau: Anarchism and Utopianism ... xxxi

    Nettlau's Vision of Utopia ... xxxvii

    The Texts of *Esbozo* ... xli

    Editorial Practices ... xli

Outline of the History of Utopias ... 1

    Biographical Sketch of Max Nettlau ... 1

1. Definition ... 3
2. The Classical and Medieval Ages ... 9
3. The Renaissance and Neo-Classical Periods ... 15
4. The Nineteenth Century (to 1888) ... 27
5. 1888 to the Twentieth Century ... 43
6. The Twentieth Century: 1900–1925 ... 59

Notes ... 75

Appendix A	Select Nettlau Bibliography	91
Appendix B	An Annotated Gazetteer of Nettlau's Utopians	93
Appendix C	List of Intentional Communities in *Esbozo*	131
Appendix D	List of Utopian Newspapers and Journals in *Esbozo*	133

Bibliography 135

Index 161

PREFACE

This is a book that has been three decades in the making. Back in 1992, I wrote a featured essay for *Utopian Studies* on histories of utopia to 1950. Nettlau's book was one of those I listed and briefly discussed. I have persisted with an edition of *Esbozo de historia de las utopías* over the years (despite delays and the creation of many other books and articles) because it profoundly matters that there is a tradition over more than 2500 years of people giving expression to a desire for social betterment—whether by means of written works or the creation and sustaining of intentional communities. It matters now, in particular, as the earth under late capitalism is becoming more and more unlivable. It matters, too, that a little heard voice can, for a moment or two, be heard above the better-known words of Lewis Mumford, Krishan Kumar, Ruth Levitas, and Frank and Fritzie Manuel so as to give to a well-known story an anarchist spin, a spin which began more than 70 years ago with Marie-Louise Berneri's brief account: *Journey through Utopia*. Max Nettlau, as this book will show, is an original.

It matters for one final reason too. I have been struck by this simple fact: of the hundreds of utopian and anarchist thinkers and writers mentioned by Nettlau, I have been unable to provide even the most basic information (birth and death dates, nationality, amateur and professional interests, and so on) for more than 50 and little information for many. They have, even in this age of information, vanished from the historical record as if they never were. Yet, these women and men mattered to themselves, to their families, to their loved ones, to their friends. They devoted themselves to the achievement of ideas. They are gone. Unintentionally, this book is philosophically about transience. The great antidote to egotism is, surely, the realization that oblivion awaits many of us, and that realization makes the cause of social betterment more not less pressing.

As to the organization of this edition, I hope it is reasonably self-evident. I begin with an introduction which presents a chronology of Nettlau's life, Nettlau's ideas about anarchism and utopian thought, the argument of the *Outline* (*Esbozo*), and the copy-texts and editorial principles I have used in this edition. I follow that with the translation of Nettlau's work and provide textual notes intended to aid the reader through some complexities in the work. I finish with four appendices: a select Nettlau bibliography, a gazetteer of Nettlau's utopians, a list of intentional communities mentioned by Nettlau, and a list of utopian newspapers and journals cited by Nettlau. The edition ends with a Bibliography.

ACKNOWLEDGMENTS

This book would never have come to be without the help of four quite disparate groups of people. First, there are the librarians. At the International Institute of Social History (IISH) in Amsterdam, they were always extraordinarily patient and helpful to me as I asked questions both foolish and (I hope) wise. At the Consortium Library at the University of Alaska Anchorage, three librarians deserve special mention: Dawn Berg, Page Brannon, and Ralph Courtney. Next, my students in assorted classes in utopian literature, the utopian novel, American utopianism, and utopian thought. They always challenged me to work hard at the definition of terms and the accuracy of any assertions I made about utopianism. There seems to be no limit to their persistence and politeness. I particularly appreciate the help of my student intern, Ruth Hall, who looked carefully at the typescript with a dispassionate eye. Third, the reviewers of the book proposal and the complete draft of this book. All of them were thorough and helpful in guiding my ideas and my revisions and corrections. The book is so much stronger as a result of the care they showed for Nettlau's ideas. Mistakes will remain, of course, as Nettlau's account is dense and complicated. I have tried to keep them to an absolute minimum.

Last, my friends and colleagues in the Society for Utopian Studies (SUS). I have been talking about this book for a long while, so long indeed that some may have given up hope of its seeing the light of day. A different book or a different idea or a different writer would call me away (Shakespeare, Raymond Chandler, Edward Bellamy, Richard Gooch, and the rest) in part because I am a generalist at heart, but more, in truth, because I knew how challenging an edition of Nettlau's early twentieth-century account would be. I deeply appreciate SUS's critique of my ideas and my strategies of presentation. I thank them for not giving up on me as I grew from a young man (a junior faculty member with long hair and radical ideas) to a much older man with lots of seniority (and still with the same long hair, now grey, and even more radical ideas). For once I can only agree with the Bible: "To every thing there is a season, and a time to every purpose under the heavens" (Ecclesiastes 3.3).

INTRODUCTION

The Life of Max Nettlau

The general view is that Max Nettlau was a vital historian of anarchism, but little is known of his life. "Obscure" might be the fairest term. That is, however, an unfair judgment. While it is true that he is not much heralded, there are more than a score of sources which provide for an adequate understanding of Nettlau's life, enough to provide quite a detailed chronology.

A[rthur]. L[ehning]. "Max Nettlau." *Bulletin of the International Institute of Social History* 5.1 (1950): 25–29. https://www.jstor.org/stable/44601109.

Altena, Bert. "A Networking Historian: The Transnational, the National, and the Patriotic in and around Nettlau's *Geschichte der Anarchie* (History of Anarchy)." *Reassessing the Transnational Turn: Scales of Analysis in Anarchist and Syndicalist Studies*. Ed. Constance Bantman and Bert Altena. New York: Routledge, 2014. [62]–79.

"The Anarchist Encyclopedia: A Gallery of Saints & Sinners." https://web.archive.org/web/20150224043814/http:/recollectionbooks.com/bleed/Encyclopedia/NettlauMax.htm

Becker, Heiner M. Introduction. *A Short History of Anarchism*. By Max Nettlau. Trans. Ida Pilat Isca. Ed. Heiner M. Becker. London: Freedom Press, 1996. ix–xxiii.

Burazerovic, Manfred. "Max Nettlau: Der lange Weg zur Freiheit" (Max Nettlau: The Long Road to Freedom). Dissertation. Universität Bochum, 1995. Berlin: OPPO-Verlag, 1996.

———. "Max Nettlau: Die Verantwortung des freien Menschen" (Max Nettlau: The Responsibility of Free Men). *Anarchisten*. Ed. Wolfram Beyer. Berlin: OPPO, 1993. 88–100.

———. "Nettlau, Max." *Wegbereiter der Demokratie: 87 Porträts* (Trailblazers of Democracy: 87 Portraits). Ed. Manfred Asendorf. Stuttgart: J. B. Metzler, 2006. 162–164.

de Jong, Rudolf. "Biographische und Bibliographische Daten von Max Nettlau, März 1940" (Biographical and Bibliographical Data for Max Nettlau, March 1940). *International Review of Social History* 14 (1969): 444–482.

Enckell, Marianne. "Nettlau, Max." *Les Anarchistes. Dictionnaire biographique du mouvement libertaire francophone*. Ivry-sur-Seine: Les Editions Ouvrières, 2014. 371–372.

———. "Sept theses sur Max Nettlau" (Seven Theses about Max Nettlau). *Bulletin du CIRA (Centre international de recherches l'anarchisme)* (Lausanne) (1972) no. 24: [4]–5.

Hunink, Maria. "Das Schiksal einer Bibliothek: Max Nettlau und Amsterdam" (The Fate of a Library: Max Nettlau and Amsterdam). *International Review of Social History* 27.1 (1982): 4–42.

"Max Nettlau – A Biography." *A Contribution to an Anarchist Bibliography of Latin America*. By Max Nettlau. 1926. Trans. Paul Sharkey. London: Kate Sharpe Library, 1994. [i–ii].

"Max Nettlau historien anarchiste" (Max Nettlau Anarchist Historian). Paris: Centre de Documentation Anarchiste, "Max Nettlau," Dec. 1981. Pamphlet. 15 pp.

Max Nettlau Papers. IISH. 42 metres. www.iisg.amsterdam/en.

Meléndez-Badillo, Jorell. "The Anarchist Imaginary: Max Nettlau and Latin America, 1890–1934." Ch. 10 of *Writing Revolution: Hispanic Anarchism in the United States*. Ed. Christopher James Castañeda and M. Montserrat Feu López. Urbana: U of Illinois Press, 2019. [173]–193.

Muñoz, Vladimiro. *Max Nettlau: Historian of Anarchism*. Trans. by Lucy Ross of *Una Cronologia de Max Nettlau* (A Max Nettlau Chronology). Men and Movements in the History and Philosophy of Anarchism. New York: Revisionist Press, 1978.

———. "Una Cronologia de Max Nettlau" (A Max Nettlau Chronology). *La paz mundial y las condiciones de su realización*. 1950. Second ed. Revised and augmented by Eugen Relgis and V. Muñoz. Montevideo, Uruguay: Ediciones "Solidaridad," 1972. 13–21.

Relgis, Eugen. "Prologo de la primera edicion: Preliminares para una obra de Max Nettlau" (Prologue to the First Edition: Preliminaries for a Work by Max Nettlau). *La paz mundial y las condiciones de su realización*. Second ed. Revised and augmented by Eugen Relgis and V. Muñoz. Montevideo: Edicones "Solidaridad," 1972. 23–36.

Rocker, Rudolf. *The London Years*. Trans. Joseph Leftwitz. London: Robert Anscombe for the Rudolf Rocker Book Committee, 1956. 92–95.

———. *Max Nettlau: Leben und Werk des Historikers vergessener sozialer Bewegungen* (Max Nettlau: The Life and Work of a Forgotten Historian of Social Movements). Berlin: Karen Kramer, 1978. Spanish original ed., 1950. Swedish ed., 1956. French ed., 2015.

Santillán, Diego Abad de (pseud. of Sinesio García Hernández). "23 de julio de 1944: Muerte de Max Nettlau" (23 July 1944: The Death of Max Nettlau). *Reconstruir* (Reconstruction) 19 (July–Aug. 1962): 47–50.

Schrevel, Margreet with Ursula Balzer. "Max Nettlau." https://iisg.amsterdam/en/about/history/max-nettlau.

Tovar, Luis Gomez, and Almudena Delgado Larios. "Max Nettlau." *Esbozo de historia de las utopías*. Colección Investigación y Crítica (series) 8. Madrid: Ediciones Tuero, 1991. 23–30.

Vuilleumier, Marc. "Les sources de l'histoire sociale: Max Nettlau et ses collections" (Resources for Social History: Max Nettlau and His Collections). *Cahiers Vilfredo Pareto* (Vilfredo Pareto Reports) 2.3 (1964): 195–205. https://www.jstor.org/stable/40368656.

CHRONOLOGY

1865

April 30: Max Nettlau born in Neuwaldegg, Austria. At the time, Neuwaldegg was a village; now it is a suburb of Vienna. Full name at birth: Max Heinrich Hermann Reinhardt Nettlau (although another source [Burazerovic, "Nettlau, Max," 26] gives his birth name as Carl Hermann Max Nettlau). He is given a very liberal education by his parents, who were emigrants from Germany, with his father having been born in 1830 in east Prussia. His mother, Agnes Nettlau (née Kast) was a Huguenot; his father, agnostic. His father worked in Potsdam as a royal gardener to the Princess Schwarzenberg.

1866

December: Oskar Hugo Ernst Nettlau, Max Nettlau's younger brother, is born with birth defects, is committed to an institution in 1872, and dies in 1895. Nettlau grows up solitary and—given his father's profession—with a deep love of nature and a fascination with birds. For him, anarchy represents that ideal human relation within society that he finds in nature.

1872

Nettlau encounters the Grimm brothers' *Fairy Tales* as well as Lucian's second-century CE *Dialogues of the Gods*. He is taken with his father's stories of the 1848 year of revolutions. He becomes an atheist after reasoning that the conflict between monotheism (Christianity) and polytheism (Greek myth) meant there probably was no god at all.

1873

The Nettlau family moves to Vienna.

1876

Takes lessons in stenography, the Gabelsberger form of shorthand.

Late 1870s

Encounters newspaper reports of Russian revolutionary activities against the Tsar and begins to consider himself a socialist.

1880

Conceives the idea of writing a biography of Mikhail Bakunin (1814–1876).

1881

Begins to read the anarchist journal *Freiheit* (Freedom), which had only begun to be published in 1879. Becomes an anarcho-communist.

1882

Reads Mikhail Bakunin's *God and the State* (published for the first time in this year). In the autumn, begins to study Indo-European languages and, in particular, Celtic.

1882–1885

Attends the University of Berlin to study philology.

1885

October: Travels to London for the first time to study at the British Museum Reading Room. Meets William Morris (1834–1896) and joins the recently founded Socialist League. (It is the only political organization he ever joined.) During this and subsequent visits, he gets to know many socialists and anarchists such as Andreas Scheu (1844–1927), Josef Peukert (1855–1910), Friedrich Lessner (1825–1910), Eleonore Aveling-Marx (1855–1898), Warlaam Tcherkesov (1846–1925), Vladimir Burtsev (1862–1942), and Jeanne Déroin (1805–1894).

1886

Attends University of Greifswald.

1887

Early in the year, completes his doctoral dissertation in philology at Leipzig University. It is titled *Beiträge zur cymrischen Grammatik* (Studies in Welsh Grammar) and focuses on medieval Welsh. Parts of it are published in *Revue celtique* (Celtic Review) in Paris, and in other journals. Meets the Belgian journalist, editor, and anarchist Victor Dave (1847–1922) in London. They share the same interest in Proudhon (1809–1865) and Bakunin.

1888

Meets Peter Kropotkin (1842–1921) in London. Visits Dublin to work with medieval Irish manuscripts. Meets Auguste Coulon (1845–1923), an agent provocateur hired by the British Metropolitan Police Special Branch to infiltrate the ranks of anarchists. Publishes his first article (on Karl Marx) in *Commonweal* (signed Y. Y.). Begins transcribing the recollections of the old guard of anarchism.

1889

July: Attends the Founding Congress of the Second International (International Socialist Congress) in Paris as a delegate of the Norwich branch of the Socialist League. Due to a mistake on the part of William Morris, he is listed as Max Netlow. In London, Nettlau meets Errico Malatesta (1853–1932); Jean Louis Pindy (1840–1917), a French anarchist; and Auguste Spichiger (1842–1919), a Swiss anarchist (colleagues of Kropotkin). Becomes friends with the Welshman Sam Mainwaring (1841–1907) (a founder of the Socialist League)—because they are both anarcho-communists and because Nettlau's dissertation was on Welsh grammar. Buys the archive of the Socialist League, which its new secretary (who had replaced William Morris) had intended to destroy.

1890

Publishes "Joseph Déjacque—Precursor of Anarcho-communism" (January 25/February 25) and "On the History of Anarchism" (April 19/May 17) in *Freiheit*, an anarchist journal founded, and edited at this time, by Johann Most (1846–1906). These are his first writings on anarchism. *May*: At the Conference of the Socialist League, elected a member of the Socialist League Council but resigns in September to return to Vienna. Also in May: Contributes his first article to *Freedom*, titled "Communism and Anarchy." *May–August*: Edits and finances *The Anarchist Labour Leaf*. The journal produces four issues.

1891

Publishes "Reflections on Social Democracy in Germany" and "Concerning a Biography of Bakunin" (January/April) in *Freiheit*.

1892

March 6: Nettlau's father dies unexpectedly and leaves him a modest fortune (what Rudolf Rocker [1873–1958] in *The London Years* refers to as a "small legacy" [94]). This fortune allows Nettlau to focus for the rest of his life on researching the history of anarchism in general and the life of Bakunin in particular. At times, he collects more than a thousand documents a month. Gives up his philological studies. Meets the French geographer and anarchist Élisée Reclus (1830–1905) in Switzerland. Reads Bakunin's foundational *Revolutionary Catechism* (1866). Meets Gustav Landauer (1870–1919) in Zürich.

1892–1893

Meets the surviving members of the Jura Federation and friends of Bakunin: Adhémar Schwitzguébel (1844–1895), Jean-Louis Pindy, Nicolai Zhukovsky (1833–1895), Jacques Gross (1855–1928), Adolf Vogt (1823–1907), Charles Perron (1837–1909), and Adolf Reichel (1816–1896). Goes to Bucharest to meet Zamfir Arbore (1848–1933), a close colleague of Bakunin in Zürich in 1872–1873.

1893

Publishes "Why We Are Anarchists" in *Commonweal* (Aug. 4, 1893–Jan. 6, 1894), which is later published as a 27-page pamphlet. It cements the journal's move away from socialism.

1894

Begins writing his biography of Bakunin. He works for many years, and not always amicably, with James Guillaume (1844–1916), a friend of Bakunin's. Guillaume was a leading member of the anarchist wing of the First International.

1895

February 28: Nettlau's only brother, Ernst, dies. Now the entire fortune left by his father comes to Nettlau, so it frees him even more to become a collector of anarchist materials. *April/May*: Joins the Freedom Group and helps to fund the *Freedom* journal along with Bernhard Kampffmeyer (1867–1942). *May 1*: Publishes *An Anarchist Manifesto* as a 15-page pamphlet. Reclus encourages Nettlau to produce an extensive bibliography of anarchism. Meets Rudolf Rocker in London. (Rocker would later publish the definitive biography of Nettlau in 1950.) Attends the International Socialist Workers and Trades Union Congress. Writes an introduction to a French edition of Bakunin's *Federalism, Socialism, and Anti-Theologism*. Publishes an early and brief study of Bakunin in New York in the Czech journal, *Denicle Listy*. Publishes the first volume of Bakunin's *Oeuvres* in Paris.

1895–1913

Spends extended periods each year in London living and working. He begins to develop an interest in the history of anarchist and socialist thought.

1896

Publishes essays on the International Congress in London as well as an excerpt in French from his biography of Bakunin. Works with Joseph Presburg (1873–1901?) on possible anarchist alternatives to the International Socialist Congress in London. Organizes (along with Presburg and Malatesta) anarchist meetings after they were expelled from the Congress.

1896–1900

Mimeographs 50 copies of his 281-page biography of Bakunin.

1896–1914

Contributes articles regularly to *Freedom*.

1897

Forms the "Spanish Atrocity Committee" with Presburg and writes a 23-page pamphlet titled *Details of the Tortures Inflicted on Spanish Political Prisoners*. Works tirelessly on *Freedom*, the *Labour Leader*, and other journals and newspapers. In the spring, *Bibliographie de l'Anarchie* (Bibliography of Anarchy) is published by the Parisian journal *Les temps nouveaux* (New Times), under the editorship of Jean Grave (1854–1939). It is his first major work and the first to bear his name. It contains 4,000 titles over almost 300 pages. It is international in scope. Meets Voltairine de Cleyre (1866–1912), an American feminist and anarchist.

1899

December 5: Reads "Responsibility and Solidarity in the Labour Struggle" to the Freedom Discussion Group. This essay would become one of his favorite works. Nettlau visits Italy for the first time to collect anarchist materials about Bakunin. Receives Bakunin's posthumous papers from Bakunin's family in Naples. Meets Celso Ceretti (1844–1909) and Francesco Saverio Merlino (1856–1930).

1900

Publishes "Responsibility and Solidarity in the Workers' Struggle" in *Freedom* (London). Begins spending one month a year in Paris. Begins his next major project—a history of Philippe Buonarotti (1661–1733) and the secret societies of the early nineteenth century.

1901

Nettlau's biographical sketch of Bakunin is published in *Der Syndikalist* (Berlin), with an introduction by Gustav Landauer. Completes, as a manuscript, his "Notes on the History of Secret Societies, from Babeuf to 1830."

1903–1905

Writes a further four volumes as a supplement to his biography of Bakunin, which are never published although he intended they should be.

1904

An Italian edition of his sketch of Bakunin's life is published with an introduction by Reclus.

1906

Begins a correspondence with Fritz Brupbacher (1874–1945)—a Swiss doctor and libertarian socialist. He later becomes friends with him and his second wife, Paulette Brupbacher (née Goutzait-Raygrodski) (1880–1967), in Zürich.

1907

Nettlau's fiancée, Thérèse Bognar, dies. He continues to write to her in his diary until 1920. It is probably at this time that he becomes an ornithologist specializing in the siskin and its 50 subspecies. His anarchist and socialist collection, at this time, comprises 20,500 items.

1909

February 22: Finishes his essay "Panarchy: A Forgotten Idea of 1860." It is first published in Gustav Landauer's journal *Der Sozialist* on March 15.

1910

Edits, writes an introduction, and publishes a French edition of the three-volume *Jours d'exil* (Days of Exile) by Ernest Coeurderoy (1825–1862) as No. 44–46 of the Bibliothèque sociologique series.

1911–1944

Contributes to the *Archiv für die Geschichte des Sozialismus der Arbeiterbewegung* (Archive for the History of Socialism in the Labor Movement) edited by Carl Grünberg (1861–1940) from 1911–1930. In 1931, it becomes the *Zeitschrift für Sozialforschung* (Journal for Social Research) and is edited by Max Horkheimer (1895–1973).

1914

World War I begins. Nettlau lives out the war in Vienna. He is not required to serve in the military as he never became an Austrian citizen but remained a German with strong internationalist sympathies. He lives with a widow who has a 13-year-old daughter. He falls out with James Guillaume over Guillaume's polemics against particular kinds of anarchism and anarchists.

1915

Mourns the death of his friend, the Spanish mathematician and anarchist Fernando Tarrida del Mármol (1861–1915) in London.

1918–1938

Supports the German Free Workers' Union (FAUD).

1919

Loses the rest of the fortune left to him by his father as a result of the hyperinflation that occurred in Germany and Austria after the end of World War I. Lives in a squalid, small room on the Lazarettgasse in Vienna. Grows anxious about his collection of anarchist books, pamphlets, and manuscripts as he can no longer afford to pay for their storage. The collection is scattered around Europe, principally in London, Munich, Paris, and Vienna.

1919/20–1944

Contributes articles regularly to *Freedom*.

1920

Describes how he plans to acquire rare, fragmentary, and unusual forms of documents for preservation and completeness; this becomes the International Institute of Social History's (IISH) policy. Siegfried Nacht (1878–1956)—born into a wealthy Jewish family—and Harry Kelly (1871–1953), communitarian and anarchist, cover the cost of housing his collection. A Russian edition of his sketch of Bakunin's life is published.

1921

Edits parts 2 and 3 of the German edition of the complete works of Bakunin, published by *Der Syndikalist* in Berlin between 1921 and 1924. Contributes an essay on Kropotkin, "A Man and a Life," to a special issue of *Les temps nouveaux* (Paris). By this time, Nettlau's anarchist collection comprises 37,500 items, of which about 10,000 are journals. He describes his principles of collecting as follows:

> I was focused, for quite a while, on the idea of collecting strictly socialist literature, but I saw that it would be appropriate to expand the field in all directions to encompass contemporary social life and to go back as well to earlier eras in the history of ideas. (Vuilleumier 203; my translation)

He collects, among many other documents, utopian works from the eighteenth century. He composes a summary inventory of his collection and says this about "utopists and imaginary voyages":

> One finds that all early socialism as well as that written in the nineteenth century can be seen as utopian. A very fecund part of this literature extends in all directions towards satire, allegory, anti-socialism, adventures, etc. You only find many of these works by chance by leafing through innumerable books; and then there is still: Cabet and his Icaria and his republican and communist propaganda; socialist communities (in America, etc.); Bellamy and the movement brought into being by his *Looking Backward;* early socialism, the medieval period, the eighteenth century—much of it is utopian. The priest Meslier [1664–1729], Abbé Mably [1709–1785], Brissot [1754–1793] etc.: the eighteenth century. (Vuilleumier 204; my translation)

1922

Nettlau's biography of Errico Malatesta (*Errico Malatesta, das Leben eines Anarchisten* [Errico Malatesta, the Life of an Anarchist]) is published by *Der Syndikalist* based on the Italian original (*Vita e pensieri di Errico Malatesa* [The Life and Thought of Errico Malatesta]) by the publisher Il Martello. Editorial Moderna (Barcelona) publishes Nettlau's "Anarchist Critique." *L'idée anarchiste* (Paris) publishes Nettlau's short history of anarchism. Visits Berlin to study anarchist archives and to visit friends. He does so annually until the rise of Hitler makes such visits difficult. Jacques Gross-Fulpius (1855–1928) (an anarchist and later a free thinker) tries to facilitate selling Nettlau's collection to the university and the public library in Geneva for 50,000 Swiss francs in order to provide an income for the nearly destitute Nettlau. However, Nettlau's intransigence on some matters means that the sale falls through.

1922–1932

Corresponds often with Malatesta (whom he had known since 1889) until the latter's death in 1932.

1923

Contributes an essay, "Kropotkin Working," to Joseph Ishill's compilation titled *Peter Kropotkin: Rebel, Thinker, and Humanitarian*. It is privately printed in a limited edition of 75 copies by Free Spirit Press in Berkeley Heights, New Jersey. *La protesta* (Protest) (Buenos Aires) publishes a Spanish edition of his biography of Malatesta. The journal also publishes his first essay in the journal's weekly supplement, on Jorge Herzog.

1924

Makes his first contribution to *La revista blanca* (The White Magazine) (Barcelona), an essay titled "Our Present Struggle." *La protesta* publishes the first volume of Nettlau's edition of Bakunin's complete works. By now, he is becoming well known in Latin America, so much so that the anarchist group Claridad (Clarity) in Buenos Aires arranges a public fund-raiser for the impoverished Nettlau at the Teatro Roma. The Jewish Anarchist Federation publishes an English translation of Nettlau's biography of Malatesta with an introduction by Hippolyte Havel (1871–1950).

1924–1927

Revises his published biography of Bakunin. His intent is to publish the biography in four volumes of about 400 pages each.

1925

Nettlau's *Der Verfrühling der Anarchie* (The Dawn of Anarchism) is published by *Der Syndikalist* (Berlin). It covers the history of anarchism from its beginnings to 1864. Argentinian and Mexican works by Nettlau on Bakunin are published. The first

(*Miguel Bakunin, la Internacional y la Alianza en España (1868–1873)* [Mikhail Bakunin, the Internationale, and the Alliance in Spain (1868–1873)]) is based on a 1913 article by Nettlau. The second, published by "Grupo Cultural Ricardo Flores Magon,'" is a Spanish edition of his biographical sketch of Bakunin. Writes "Esquisse d'un historique des utopies" (Sketch of the History of Utopias), the manuscript for *Esbozo de historia de las utopías*. The latter is published across 10 issues of *La protesta suplemento seminal* (Buenos Aires) between June and August 1925, and in book form in November 1934. Rocker (1873–1958) unsuccessfully tries to arrange a lecture tour of the United States for Nettlau.

1925–1929

Writes long prefaces to the Spanish edition of Bakunin's works, published in five volumes in Buenos Aires. Also annotates the German edition of volumes 2 and 3 (which had been published in 1923–1924).

1926

To commemorate the 50th anniversary of Bakunin's death, *Der Syndikalist* publishes Nettlau's "Our Bakunin." It also publishes the second volume of his history of anarchism under the title *Anarchism from Proudhon to Kropotkin. Its Historical Development in the Years 1859–1880*. Publishes three essays in *La protesta*: "The Place of Fernand Pelloutier [1867–1910] in the Evolution of Syndicalism"; "How to Expand Anarchist Propaganda"; and "Contribution to the Anarchist Bibliography in Latin America." Visits François Dumartheray (1842–1931), arguably the founder of anarcho-communism with his 1876 pamphlet *Aux travailleurs manuels, partisans de l'action politique* (To Manual Workers, Partisans of Political Action). Visits Valeriano Orobón Fernández (1901–1936), who considers Nettlau "the Herodotus of Anarchism" (Muñoz, *Max Nettlau* 12–13).

1927

Publishes in *Der Syndikalist* a critique of the German edition of Bakunin's *Confession*, which had questioned Bakunin's revolutionary zeal. Contributes an essay titled "Élisée Reclus and Mikhail Bakunin" to Joseph Ishill's compilation *Elie and Élisée Reclus, in Memoriam*. Ishill's book is released in a limited edition of 290 copies, 40 of them on Alexandra Japan paper.

1928

Joins a small gathering of sympathetic anarchists in Paris led by Emma Goldman and Alexander Berkman to discuss the future direction of the anarchist movement. Publishes "Élisée Reclus, Anarchist und Gelehrter (1830–1905)" (Élisée Reclus, Anarchist and Scholar [1830–1905]), and "Bakunin and the International in Italy" in *Il risveglio* (The Awakening). Spends some months in Barcelona visiting Federico Urales (pseud. of Juan Montseny Carret) (1864–1942), the editor of *Revista blanca* (which published Nettlau's two-volume study of Reclus).

1928–1936

Nettlau is invited to Spain by the Montseny-Urales (Federica Montseny [1905–1994]) family to use their extensive libraries.

1929

Visits Teresa Claramunt i Creus (1862–1931), an anarcho-syndicalist and editor, in Catalonia.

1930

15 February: Publishes the first volume of his biography of Bakunin in *La protesta*, but the journal is shut down by the military dictatorship in Argentina. He only manages to publish an abridged version of the work in various languages. Publishes his *Unpublished Documents on the International and Alliance in Spain* and praises Federica Montseny—novelist, essayist, and politician—as the symbol of Spanish anarchist youth. Is visited by the Romanian anarchist Eugen Relgis (pseud. of Eugenio Sigler]) (1895–1987) in Vienna.

1931

Goes to the funeral of Teresa Claramunt i Creus. Publishes the third volume of his history of anarchism: *Anarchists and Social Revolutionaries, 1880–1886* with *Der Syndikalist*. Contributes a number of essays to a book celebrating Kropotkin published by Probishdenie in Detroit. Gets an offer from the International Institute of Social History (IISH) to house his complete collection of anarchist materials.

1932

Publishes "Spanish Impressions in the Spring of 1932" in *Die Internationale*. Efforts to publish on anarchism and Bakunin in Germany are stymied by the rise of Nazism there.

1933

Publishes his biography of Errico Malatesta (*La vida de Errico Malatesta, 1853–1932: El hombre, el revolucionario, el anarquista* [The Life of Errico Malatesta, 1853–1932: Man; Revolutionary; Anarchist]) with *Revista blanca* in Barcelona.

1934

Publishes books on anarchism and socialism in Barcelona and Montevideo. His *Esbozo de historia de las utopías* is published in book form by ediciones IMAN of Buenos Aires in November. It is a reprinting of the 1925 *La protesta* publication. Pays tribute to Erich Mühsam (1878–1934), German-Jewish playwright, poet, and anarchist, who was murdered in Oranienburg concentration camp.

1935

Celebrates his 70th birthday in Barcelona with Urales and his family and friends. Sells his collection of anarchist materials to the IISH in Amsterdam. Publishes *La anarquía a través de los tiempos* (Anarchism through the Ages) in Barcelona. It is brought out by Guild of the Friends of the Book. A French edition of his biography of Bakunin fails to appear as the Paris publisher goes bankrupt.

1936

Visits Catalonia for the last time. He had gone there every year from 1928 to 1936. Goes with Federica Montseny on a lecture tour through Catalonia. He makes his last contribution (out of a total of 108 throughout his career) to *Revista blanca*. It is titled "Liberty in the Society of Tomorrow." Works to establish an archive in the Barcelona library in July. In August, he returns to Vienna for the last time. Publishes a pamphlet, *The Fight for Freedom in Spain*, in England.

1937

Supervises the creation of his archive in the IISH in Amsterdam. Writes that he considers Diego Abad de Santillán the best translator of his works. In Zürich is treated for laryngitis.

1938

Publishes six volumes of the Complete Works of Bakunin in Barcelona as well as *Miguel Bakunin, la Internacional y la Alianza en España (1868–1873)* (Mikhail

Bakunin, the Internationale, and the Alliance in Spain [1868–1873]) and an essay on *En torno al pensamiento de Merlino* (On the Ideas of [Francesco Saverio] Merlino). The first two are published by Tierra y libertad (Land and Freedom). Writes his last essay for *La protesta*, a tribute to Tom Keell (1866–1938), the editor of *Freedom*—a journal for which Nettlau had written. Nettlau wrote 46 articles for *La protesta*. Germany takes over Austria by means of Anschluss (or "Joining"). Stays in Amsterdam permanently as a result of this event. IISH succeeds in rescuing Nettlau's anarchist collection in Vienna with the help of the Dutch Embassy there and the tireless efforts of the Institute's librarian, Annie Adama. The Viennese collection consists of hundreds of crates.

1940

The Nazi invasion of the Netherlands closes the IISH. Its collections are taken to Germany. Nettlau moves from a hotel in Amsterdam to an attic. Works on his memoirs. The length reaches 3,500 pages. Ultimately, the various versions total some 6,000 pages. The story is never completed.

1941

Nettlau suffers from chronic bronchitis.

1944

July: Nettlau gets very sick. *July 20*: he goes into hospital and dies there on July 23 of stomach cancer, an inoperable tumor. He is buried in a cemetery in Westerfeld. The IISH director comments: "If we did not find ourselves in the midst of the war, his death would have been mourned as an irreplaceable loss."

1946

The IISH recovers all of Nettlau's anarchist collection. Rudolf Rocker completes his biography of Nettlau.

1950

Rocker's biography of Nettlau is published for the first time in Spanish as *Max Nettlau: el Herodoto de la anarquía* (Max Nettlau: The Herodotus of Anarchism). In Montevideo, Uruguay, the publisher Humanidad (Humanity) brings out an edition of Nettlau's *La paz mundial y las condiciones de su realización* (World Peace and the Conditions for Its Achievement).

1972

Munoz, in *Max Nettlau: Historian of Anarchism* (1978), indicates there are plans by the Revisionist Press to bring out a complete edition of Nettlau's works in English along with an English translation of Rocker's biography. These have not come to fruition yet.

1978

Rocker's biography is published in German as *Max Nettlau: Leben und Werk des Historikers vergessener sozialer Bewegungen* (Max Nettlau: The Life and Work of a Forgotten Historian of Social Movements). It has an introduction by Rudolf de Jong.

To this chronology, I will simply add a few revealing comments from those who knew him well. De Santillán called Nettlau "always a true *gentleman*" ready to help anyone in misfortune ("23 de Julio" 47; my translation), and he goes on to summarize Nettlau's achievement: "60 years of uninterrupted work to raise for libertarian thought the greatest of monuments that a sage, a moral hero, [and] a privileged and acute intelligence could raise" ("23 de Julio" 48; my translation). Rudolf Rocker (in *The London Years*) rather harshly and dismissively says Nettlau "was no public speaker and took no active part in the movement" (92); indeed, "[F]ew were aware of his existence [by 1896]" (92). Relgis summarizes Nettlau's life: "the octogenarian settled down with one foot in the nineteenth century and the other in the twentieth, is a magnificent example of self-abnegation in the interests of the ethical and social freedom of humanity" (24; my translation).

Nettlau as Anarchist Historian

Rudolf Rocker famously termed Nettlau the "Herodotus of anarchism," with the phrase coined (according to Vladimir Muñoz) by Vicente Orobón Fernandez (Rocker, *El herodoto*; Muñoz, *Max Nettlau* 12–13). Others have offered similar praise: Gabriel Kuhn calls him "the famed anarchist historian" (10); Paul Avrich, "the leading anarchist historian" (Introduction x); and Marianne Enckell "the first, the only, the great historian of anarchism" ("Sept theses" 4; my translation). Nettlau's gifts as a historian are many: thoroughness; accuracy; and—perhaps above all—modest skepticism. The last of these shines out from a comment he made in "Erinnerungen und Eindrücke aus meinem Leben" (Memories and Impressions from My Life): "I always believe this: one knows far too little and far too much is lost—so it's absurd to say aloud, and even to believe, what you really can't know" (quoted in Avrich, *American Anarchist* 97; my translation).

The best, succinct (two-page) analysis of Nettlau as anarchist historian is Marianne Enckell's "Sept theses sur Max Nettlau" (Seven Theses about Max Nettlau). According to Enckell, Nettlau wrote an anarchist "history for specialists" (4; my translation). He was not interested in the history of the movement but in the history of ideas and the men who held them. In fact, he only studied the precursors and successors of anarchism. He was "the Great Cataloguer" (4; my translation). He was an individualist anarchist and an internationalist in sympathy although he was always an Austrian in his sympathies. He was a scholar (*"un homme de cabinet"*) and a reader. He was someone removed from the struggles of street anarchists, for he had uncalloused hands ("mains blanches") (4). He had difficulties distinguishing among the main lines of anarchist argument. He was never able to give the big picture or to synthesize as the acquisition of details always got in the way (5). To these characteristics, it is worth adding two others: Nettlau was "the first intellectual to envision and work towards a continental history of anarchism in Latin America" (Meléndez-Badillo, 188), and he was multilingual. He knew well nearly all the European languages he needed for his extensive research into anarchism.

When it comes to Nettlau's qualities as a writer, however, the jury is definitely out. In truth, we have a spectrum of attitudes. On one extreme is Arthur Lehning, who describes Nettlau's style as "lengthy and cumbersome" with his books being crowded with titles, notes, and dates. For Lehning, they are hard to read and sometimes give "the impression of bibliographies raisonées rather than historical surveys" (A. L. 27–28). On the other is M. P. T. Acharya and his essay "Max Nettlau as Biographer and Historian: An Appreciation of His Style, Method, and System." Here, Acharya praises Nettlau for many qualities. His biography of Bakunin is "an art and a permanent monument not to be counted among ephemeral biographies." It is "a scientific investigation, exact and detailed." For Acharya, Nettlau founded the genre of political biography and "nobody has surpassed him in that art" (156). He is objective and his style intense. He works with "true mountains of detailed facts and how they relate to each other" (157). He is serious, accurate, and harmonious. He is *"above the judges"* (159). Between Lehning and Acharya a gulf looms, and the truth lies somewhere in between.

It is not hard to see why as an anarchist historian, Nettlau spent so much energy collecting the frequently ephemeral ideas of other anarchists, material which might so quickly have disappeared but for Nettlau's efforts. Nettlau's doctoral work on the Welsh language shows his love of categorization and nuance for their own sake. He found himself early on with the funds necessary to collect a vast anarchist library. He was fascinated with the sheer variety of ideas presented by anarchism. In this last respect, it is worth touching on Leonard Krimerman and Lewis Perry's invaluable *Patterns of Anarchism A Collection of Writings on the Anarchist Tradition* (1966). The collection consists of eleven pieces on anarchism and education; nine on the soundness of anarchism; seven on defining anarchism; six on the philosophical foundations of anarchism; six on the anarchist critique of society; six on anarchist criminology; six on anarchism and socialism; five on alternative anarchist communities; and, finally, five on contemporary anarchist alternatives. That is surely variety writ large.

Nettlau as Anarchist

Gabriel Kuhn and Siegbert Wolf call Nettlau one of "Europe's best-known anarchists," and rank him with the likes of Kropotkin, Rocker, Malatesta, Louisa, and Reclus (25). A close examination of his ideas shows him to be closest to Spanish anarchists in his sympathies. It has, however, been said that Nettlau was not much of a theorist. That is only part of the truth. If one looks carefully at his life one can see that he does begin with some definite ideas about anarchism, ideas which amount to a theory that is international in its focus and sets freedom at its center. Indeed, it is clear that what attracted Nettlau to Bakunin (the focus of his early work) was the latter's advocacy of freedom (Avrich, Introduction x). Nettlau believed in an anarchism without adjectives as "unique solutions will never do" (quoted in Avrich, *American Anarchist* 158). He wanted a non-sectarian conception of anarchism because "all human life vibrates between [the] two poles" of communism and individualism "in endless varieties and oscillations" (quoted in Avrich, *American Anarchist* 158). His earliest publications are biographical and definitional: "Death of Karl Marx" (1888); "Joseph Déjacque—a Predecessor of Communist Anarchism" (1890); "The Historical Development of Anarchism" (1890); "Notes for a Biography of Bakunin" (1891); and "Communism and Anarchy" (1891). His early publications are programmatic: *Why We Are Anarchists* (1893; 1894) and *An Anarchist Manifesto* (1895). They espouse standing up for a cause. As he says at the end of *Why We Are Anarchists*: "We teach the people by our example to remove all the fetters laid on the free development of Humanity by the State, law, and authority, and the rest: a better state of things will and must come by itself. Our principles are those lying at the bottom of every progress during the past and will be so in the future. *This is why we are Anarchists*" (27).

However, after observing the anarchist squabbles of the 1890s (in which he did his best to stay uninvolved) he loses interest in theory and focuses instead on what had always interested him: the history of the movement and, in particular, the preservation of its ephemeral documents. His interest in Mikhail Bakunin became an interest in anarchist thinkers in general. That said, as late as 1928 in a letter to Emma Goldman, Nettlau is talking about anarchist theory. According to him, there are three phases to anarchism: a "creative educational" phase; a "constructive" phase; and—perhaps—a "destructive" phase (Nettlau, Letter to Goldman). And as well-known an anarchist thinker as Gustav Landauer thought of Nettlau as a valuable anarchist thinker himself (Landauer, Letter to Nettlau). Perhaps the fairest judgment is Manfred Burazerovic's "Max Nettlau's thinking is, therefore, thinking on a small scale" (*Verantwortung* 99; my translation)—albeit without the condescension. It is also surely the case that by circumstance more than intent he "became a nexus in the global cartography of radical ideas at the turn of the twentieth century" (Meléndez-Badillo 188). At any event, the trajectory of Nettlau as anarchist (and historian) is eminently traceable for the reader in Rudolf de Jong's extensive and careful study of the man and his work: "Biographische und bibliographische Daten von Max Nettlau, März 1940" (1969).

Nettlau: Anarchism and Utopianism

Anarchism is one of the hardest of political philosophies to pin down. It sometimes seems as challenging as nailing jelly to the wall. The Oxford English Dictionary (OED) makes it sound so solid and so easy. For that august source, anarchism is simply (as its second definition indicates) "the state or condition of having no absolute ruler or ruling authority; advocacy of this. Later (frequently with capital initial): *spec.* a political philosophy based on the belief that society is best organized according to voluntary cooperation, without any form of governing authority or hierarchy; advocacy of this, esp. as a political movement." However, the OED's first definition indicates how fraught the term has become: "Disorder resulting from the absence or disregard of government or authority; instigation of this; chaos, confusion." Put simply, anarchy's etymology from the Greek (*an* [without] and *arkhos* [ruler]) has become contaminated by the supposed history of "bomb in the pocket" anarchists of the late-nineteenth and early-twentieth centuries.

To this lexicographical definition should be added the encyclopedic approach. For this, we can turn to Sage Publications' *Encyclopedia of Political Theory* (2010), edited by Mark Bevir, and *The New Catholic Encyclopedia* (2003) (with the entry on anarchism written by A. J. Beitzinger). The former defines anarchism by means of multiple choice as "the rejection of authority/ law/government/property/violence/ or domination for the realization of freedom/equality/justice or community" (3). It does helpfully point out, however, that anarchism has in recent years bled over into postmodernist, poststructuralist, situationist, surrealist, and broader activist concerns. The latter (Beitzinger) calls anarchism "a doctrine that teaches the necessity to eliminate political authority in order to realize social justice and individual freedom" (383). He goes on to argue that anarchism is founded on four assumptions (about innate goodness, self-governance, harmony, and corruption), these assumptions leading to four conclusions (about the relation between state control and individual, voluntary actions).

Besides the dictionary and the encyclopedia, there are specialist definitions also. In his classic study, *Anarchism: A History of Libertarian Ideas* (first published in 1962 and revised in 1986), George Woodcock remarks at the beginning of the first part that "Anarchism is a creed inspired and ridden [riddled?] by paradox" (35). He considers it "an element constant in society" (35), one which possesses a "family tree" that is "a magnificent growth" (35). He also defines the term as "a system of social thought, aiming at fundamental changes in the structure of society and particularly—for this is the common element uniting all its forms—at the replacement of the authoritarian state by some form of non-governmental cooperation between free individuals" (14). This is clearly subtler and more useful than the definition provided by the OED. Colin Ward in *Anarchism: A Very Short Introduction* (2004) aims for simplicity with "Anarchism is a social and political ideology which, despite a history of defeat, continually re-emerges in a new guise or in a new country, so that another chapter has to be added to its chronology, or another dimension to its scope" ([i]). Ward, then, adds continuous evolution to the mix as well as situating it within political ideology as a whole: "In the evolution of political ideas, anarchism can be seen as an ultimate projection of both liberalism and socialism, and the differing strands of anarchist thought can be related to their emphasis on one or the other of these" (1). So, to the metaphor of family tree (Woodcock) is added anarchism as weaving project. More recently, Matthew Adams (in "The Possibilities of Anarchist History: Rethinking the Canon and Writing History" [2013]) asks the reader to study anarchism with the emphasis on recent developments in our understanding of cultural history. I suspect some of Adams' argument and the specialist definitions in general would have puzzled Nettlau or, at least, have made him reach for Occam's Razor. Nettlau's own definition, in *A Short History of Anarchism* (1932–1934; 1996), is, then, remarkable for its inclusiveness and the straightforwardness of its expression: The history of anarchism

> starts from the earliest favourable historic moment when men first evolved the concept of a free life as preached by anarchists—a goal to be attained only by a complete break from authoritarian bonds and

by the simultaneous growth and wide expansion of the social feelings of solidarity, reciprocity, generosity and other expressions of human co-operation. (1)

Evolution and growth and the key terms are associated with vital and admirable human qualities.

So much for the reasonably objective efforts. There are others which might be described as rather more partisan. They are to be enjoyed, perhaps, because of their spirit more than for their objective accuracy. So, Leonard Williams, in "Anarchy Revived" (2007) assesses contemporary anarchism from the perspective of several theorists (Chomsky, Bookchin, Zerzan, Bey, and Black) and then sets the ideology within a metaphysical framework. He concludes by asserting that anarchism is focused on "creating and enacting horizontal networks instead of top-down structures like states, parties or organizations; networks based on principles of decentralized, non-hierarchical consensus democracy" (312). So, Aleksandr Stamatov, in "The *Laotzi* and Anarchism" (2014), trenchantly rejects the traditional association between the Asian philosopher and anarchism and declares that anarchism "rejects coercive authority" and "stresses that people alone should govern themselves" (262). And so, Sébastien Faure applies a few adjectives to the anarchist movement itself: "living, flexible, ever-watchful, and always in agreement over libertarian objectives and principles" (*Encyclopédie* 79; my translation from the French).

The reality is that, perhaps, when it comes to defining anarchism everyone has an angle. The history of ideas is actually the history of contested interpretation.

In light, then, of the complexity and importance of the term, scholars, and for that matter anarchists, have adopted several rhetorical strategies in an effort to illuminate its meaning. E. Armand, quoted by Vladimir Muñoz, sees anarchists as offering three sorts of ideals: a human ideal, in which the individual destroys authority; a moral ideal, in which the individual becomes a new person; and a social ideal, where an anarchist society is created in which men determine their own lives through mutual agreement that all are free but will not harm the freedom of others (Muñoz, *Anarchists* 1). Paul Avrich opts for a site-specific focus by mentioning three major collections of anarchist materials: the Landauer Collection at the University of Michigan; the Joseph Fishill Collection at the Houghton Library, Harvard University; and the International Institute of Social History (IISH)—or, more accurately, the Internationaal instituut voor sociale geschiedenis (IISG) (*American Anarchist*). Ward chooses a topical approach: ancestors; nationalism and fundamentalism; prisons; education; and the green movement.

Woodcock offers six types of anarchists and then traces the anarchist movement geographically. In that tracing, he emphasizes Europe, Latin America, and the United States. Alan Carter, in "Anarchism: Some Theoretical Foundations" (2011), looks at anarchism from two theoretical positions—State-Primacy Theory and Quadruplex Theory—with Bakunin as his barometer. He concludes by suggesting the latter theory has particular merit in both "weighted" and "temporarily-weighted" forms (264). Throughout this highly theoretical approach (the essay includes no less than eight explanatory figures), the ghost of Marxism-Leninism explicitly looms large. Nicolas Walter (in *About Anarchism* [2002])—which originally appeared in periodical form in 1969—presents a widely influential definition by function and desire: what anarchists believe, and want, and do, and so on. Finally, Robert Graham, in "(Mis)Conceptions of Anarchism" (2018), uses the insights of deconstruction (albeit without acknowledging a debt to Jacques Derrida) by defining his key term in a largely negative way, so that anarchism as political theory is as much about "anti-authoritarianism, anti-statism, [and] anti-parliamentarianism" as it is about "voluntary association, libertarian methods and direct action" (32).

By contrast, the definition of utopianism is easier but, in its own way, quite as fascinating and challenging. There are two operational definitions that have been adopted by common folk (as it were) and intellectuals. The first is well represented by the descriptive function of the OED, a function which covers how language is used and misused. There utopia is described as specifically "an imaginary island in Sir Thomas More's *Utopia* (1516), presented by the narrator as having a perfect social, legal, and political system" and, much more generally as "an imagined or hypothetical place, system, or state of existence in which everything is perfect, esp. in respect of social structure, laws, and politics." All very true except for the fact that any careful reading of More demolishes the idea that his island is perfect and, along with it, the idea that a system of thought founded on such a model should be or is perfect. Given that utopianism has been misunderstood and/or intentionally misinterpreted for literally half a millennium, those who specialize in utopian studies have tacitly agreed to work with one of a few definitions. Under such a regimen, it is de rigueur to define your operational definition before launching into argument, analysis, or exposition. Half a dozen scholars have mapped the way: Lyman Tower Sargent, George Kateb, Darko Suvin, Ruth Levitas, Roland Schaer, and Fredric Jameson. Sargent (in "The Three Faces of Utopianism" [1967] and "The Three Faces of Utopianism Revisited" [1994]) anatomizes the discipline in a way that has come to be seen as foundational. In the later essay, he defines the term as "social dreaming—the dreams and nightmares that concern the ways in which groups of people arrange their lives and which usually envision a radically different society than [sic] the one in which the dreamers live. But not all are radical, for some people at any time dream of something basically familiar" (3).

One year after Sargent's first stab at definition, George Kateb, in *The International Encyclopedia of the Social Sciences* (1968), gamely offers an essentialist definition based on a "persistent tradition of thought about the perfect society, in which perfection is defined as harmony" (267). According to Kateb, this harmony is that "of each man with himself and of each man with all others," and is dependent on "a number of social conditions, each one of which is a manifestation of harmony" (267). And the definition continues:

> Among these conditions are perpetual peace; full satisfaction of human wants; either a happy labor or a rich leisure, or a combination of both; extreme equality, or inequality on a wholly rational basis; the absence of discretionary authority, or the participation of all in turn in discretionary authority, or the placing of discretionary authority in the hands of those with a clear claim to it; and a nearly effortless virtue on the part of all men. These are the conditions of utopian life in its hypothetical descriptions; these are the conditions that a society must have if it is to be in accord with utopianism (267).

Five years later, Darko Suvin, a scholar whose interests have always been as much focused on science fiction as on utopianism, argued that a utopia can be seen as "The verbal construction of a particular quasi-human community where sociopolitical institutions, norms and individual relationships are organized according to a more perfect principle than in the author's community, this construction being based on estrangement arising out of an alternative historical hypothesis" (132).

Almost two decades pass before a sociologist tries her hand at definition. Levitas, in *The Concept of Utopia* (1990), sees any utopia as being about desire of a specific sort: "The expression of the desire for a better way of being" (8). Schaer, a decade later (2000), sides with Levitas and opts for brevity by asserting "Utopia's first prerequisite" "is *humanitas*, humanity as a virtue" (4). Five years later, Jameson, like Suvin a devotee of science fiction (which has, by the way a fraught relation to utopia which I do not need to explore in this introduction), presents something very original: a diagram which splits utopianism into two camps: program and impulse. The first is the realm of utopian works and intentional communities; the second is the kingdom of theory, reform, architecture, and hermeneutics.

Given how anarchism and utopianism have been generally defined and given, specifically, that Nettlau as an anarchist undertook an outline of the history of utopia, the vital question is surely: What do anarchism and utopia have to do with each other? The interesting answer is twofold: a great deal from a commonsense point of view; and—until quite recently— not a lot from a scholarly perspective. I hope however, that it will become clear that it does matter greatly that Nettlau comes at his discussion of utopia through an anarchist's pathway. I agree with Heiner Becker when he remarks of *Esbozo de historia de las utopías* that it "deepen[s] and extend[s]" Nettlau's "treatment of the subject" of anarchism ("A Short Guide" 361).

To date, there is only one book devoted to the intersection of anarchism and utopia: 2009's *Anarchism and Utopianism*, edited by Laurence Davis and Ruth Kinna. Let me rehearse its compelling argument and add a few flourishes of my own. Most utopias are authoritarian, but a few are libertarian, even anarchic. Davis and Kinna cite more than a dozen: the medieval Land of Cockaigne and the medieval communes of the sisters and brothers of the Free Spirit; oral tradition's Big Rock Candy Mountain; written tradition's Lao Zi (or Tse); Rabelais; Diderot; William Morris; Oscar Wilde; B. Travers; Pierre Clastres; and Ursula K. Le Guin; Ranters and Diggers of the English Commonwealth; the French Revolution's sans culottes; the Paris Commune; the early days of the Bolshevik Revolution; early twentieth-century Argentinian and Mexican anti-capitalist utopias; Republicans in the Spanish Civil War; free schools; free love movements in Britain and the United States, where "speaking/ living/being utopia" is a "manifestation of the anarchist emphasis on the inextricable interrelationship of means and ends" (4); and intentional communities (temporary autonomous zones of the green, peace, and global-justice movements). Anarchist utopias value particular principles: mutual aid; solidarity; personal freedom; autonomy; personal creativity; satisfaction of desire; the transformation of work; unity in diversity; and the struggle against domination, hierarchy, and exploitation.

Utopianism and anarchism have five elements in common, some of which are constantly shifting. First, all anarchist experiments are utopian (albeit utopianism of the evolutionary and not the blueprint variety). Second, utopias and anarchist experiments are both thoroughly impractical and to be valued as such in a world where the practical is overvalued. Third, both philosophies have very little else in common although it is true that state centrism is not a defining or essential characteristic of utopias. Fourth, the relationship between the two has been historically valuable. Last, case studies show the complexity of the relationship: works of literature; anthropological studies; unorthodox or temporary communities; educational experimentation; green communities; and social revolution movements. For Davis and Kinna, "the essence of the anarchist utopia" consists of "transforming the present as part of an organic process in which already existing historical tendencies are actively engaged with, nurtured and built upon" (5). For Davis and Kinna, there are nine elements in utopian thinking, many of which strike me as fundamentally anarchic: domination, elitism, escapism, critique, desire, presence, history, ends thinking, and return.

It may seem Davis and Kinna throw their net rather wide. Nettlau does the same because his argument is that the study of utopianism demands inclusivity. It is worth remembering his categorical, even magisterial, opening to *A Short History of Anarchism* (1932–1934; 1996): "The history of anarchist ideas is inseparable from the history of all progressive developments and aspirations towards liberty" (1). Given his known anarchist views, this inclusivity is always towards freedom. Nettlau would have thoroughly agreed with James Joll's assertions in *The Anarchists* (1964): Anarchism begins with Zeno and the Stoics and includes the Gnostic heretics and the Anabaptists, for it is "both a religious faith and a rational philosophy" (13); anarchists "are the heirs of all the utopian, millenarian religious movements" (13). It is also true that Nettlau's short account of utopia is shot through with a redefinition of anarchism along the lines laid down by Sam Dolgoff in *The Anarchist Collectives* (1974): "It is not the anarchists who are the 'unrealistic day-dreamers,' but their opponents who have turned their back to the facts or have shamelessly concealed them" (xxxix).

Nettlau's Vision of Utopia

To some degree, Nettlau's argument in *Esbozo* should, of course, stand on its own merits, but it is nevertheless useful to rehearse the shape of that argument and point out those places where it is particularly interesting in substance or in rhetorical strategies. Before I do so, however, it is important to point out two outstanding qualities of the work. First (and especially early on in the account) Nettlau offers some wonderful generalizations about utopia from an anarchist perspective. These seem extraordinarily prescient in light of contemporary politics. Second (and especially as the account draws on) Nettlau offers an astonishing number of examples of utopian thought—some of them well known, others worthwhile but quite obscure. All those years of collecting anarchist materials really paid off. Yes, Nettlau availed himself of the resources of the British Museum Reading Room, but he also clearly cites materials which he himself owned.

The first chapter of the work is given over—as one might expect—to definition. Nettlau makes two claims that are particularly interesting: first, that utopianism is universal in its value and its appeal; second, that religion is a "counterfeit coin" and a delusion. To these two claims, Nettlau adds other assertions that are deliberately provocative. For him, utopia should be a "people's utopia." "True utopia" should be grounded in revolution, solidarity, and liberty. Unexpectedly, given his political sympathies, socialism, and anarchism are taken to task for being too dry and theoretical. Both could benefit, implicitly, from the enchanting quality of well-constructed utopias. The last interesting point about this first chapter is that Nettlau (intentionally) eschews citation. Elsewhere, Nettlau mentions scores of utopian works both well-known and obscure. Here, he gives the reader only a simple, clear set of ideas.

The second chapter discusses utopianism in the Classical and medieval ages and, so, begins Nettlau's pursuit of the understanding of utopian thought in chronological terms. Once again, he chides religion—in this case, for castrating popular pagan traditions in order to create income for the Catholic church. He takes a multinational, multilingual approach to utopian thought. He develops a complicated argument about the complicity of the Church and the nobility in exploiting the masses, and offers a crushing anti-clerical comment, the best line in the entire book, perhaps: "Once the Church had tamed the nobility in this way, it sent them off to the Crusades."

The third chapter brings the subject up to the Renaissance (or Early Modern) and Neo-Classical periods. Nettlau offers an enlightening analysis of More's foundational work, *Utopia* (1516), one which focuses not on argument as intellectual game (as is currently fashionable) but on social justice and economics. Overall, Nettlau establishes here a rhetorical strategy that serves him well throughout the entire *Esbozo*: theory and assertion first, followed by extensive examples in many languages but especially French, German, and Spanish (with English something of a given). He continues to show a certain dismissiveness when it comes to particular utopias, finding that one lesser-known instance of utopian writing, for example, has "no social value." He broadens the subject to include educational utopias and utopias in epistolary form. He sees utopias as oases of freedom and, so, sounds a note that rang throughout his entire life: freedom is Nettlau's life's blood. He characterizes intellectual engagement as consisting of periods of energy and periods of decline, and he continues to adopt a markedly honest rhetorical strategy: he readily admits when he has not been able to study a work he nevertheless mentions. *Esbozo* is the work of a man confident in his learning. He knows it is encyclopedic because he has read so much and written about so much of it.

The fourth chapter takes the story into the nineteenth century, up to 1888. As do so many scholars, Nettlau sees the publication of *Looking*

Backward in that year as marking a crucial dividing line. There is pre- and post-Bellamy. The popularity of Bellamy's vision of Boston in 2000 changed everything. Nettlau begins by pointing out that the eclipse in utopian thought in the early nineteenth century derived from the greater political freedom of the masses at that time. He traces the beginning of anti-utopian thought to the same period (the early nineteenth century) and, now, broadens the subject once more by tracing animal fables and fantastical worlds as forms of utopia. He indirectly calls for political and social renewal now (the time of the writing of *Esbozo* in the mid-1920s) and then moves on to look at radicalism and Chartism. He examines the relation between indirect utopias and socialist propaganda and then takes direct aim at Marxism—a philosophy he disliked in theory and in practice. He criticizes Marxist scientific socialism as a form of "atavistic dictatorship." He is equally fierce in his dislike of anti-utopias, which he considers "scurrilous" and as "phobic towards socialism." Once again, albeit in a slightly different form, Nettlau is honest about his limits. He says he knows French and German utopias best, and knows much less about Spanish, North American, and Scandinavian utopianism. Usefully, he ties the absence of Italian utopias in the nineteenth century to that country's protracted political struggles. Implicitly and ironically, if a country is struggling over its identity it does not have the time to create fictional worlds of social betterment.

The fifth chapter takes the story from 1888 to the turn of the twentieth century. As Nettlau sees it, Bellamy deserves much credit for creating a compelling utopian narrative. By contrast, socialists and anarchists (those with whom Nettlau most identifies) deserve strong criticism for failing to develop a coherent anti-capitalist story. Instead, they rejected Bellamy's ideas out of hand, and that rejection led to a total Marxist rejection of utopia—in practice and in theory. He then studies Morris's vision as well as those of Bebel and Hertzka and others as thinkers focused on associationist colonies and the successful bridging of the gap between city and countryside. From a rhetorical point of view, Nettlau impressively combines textual analysis, utopian theory, and a staggeringly broad group of exemplary theorists and practitioners. As he emphasizes the sheer variety of utopian literature post-Bellamy, so he looks at socialist utopias and works of fantasy, feminist utopias, and anti-war literature (with war being understood as the most markedly dystopian of all human activities).

The sixth chapter looks at utopian works from the beginning of the twentieth century to 1925—the present time of Nettlau's *Esbozo*. The account takes an interesting turn from a historical point of view. One might have expected Nettlau to talk of the rise of dystopianism in the twentieth century until one remembers that intensely pessimistic narratives of that sort did not appear until the 1920s with Zamyatin's *We* (1920–1921; trans into English, 1924), and that is too close to 1925 to allow for Nettlau to see or to predict a trend. Instead, he lays into one of the founders of modern science fiction, H. G. Wells. From Nettlau's point of view, Wells wrote too many and varied utopias: "Brilliant author he may be, but he has lowered the utopian genre to the commercial vulgarity characteristic of our times." Nettlau then broadens the critique to an evisceration of the Bolshevik Revolution of 1918: its abject failure in the hands of Marxist fanatics. Movingly because personally, Nettlau talks of "the terrible fall from grace of the modern world." He lost his fortune because of World War I (those years of "homicidal and fratricidal passion") and the hyperinflation in Germany and Austria that followed the end of that conflict. It is hard not to feel the same thing now as a reader, in 2023, in the aftermath of Trump in the United States, of Brexit in Britain, and of Putin's imperialist aims in Ukraine and beyond. Grace is surely as rare now as the ivory-billed woodpecker. Nettlau in this last chapter becomes ever more insistent in trumpeting his aims: liberty, and the reconstruction of society. At the same time, he makes some very shrewd and objective claims about utopian thought in the first quarter of the last century. First, every utopian project is geographically unique. Second, utopias in the countries that were defeated in World War I are very different from those written in the victorious countries. Next, utopias from this period rarely provide solutions to the problems they describe. Fourth, the utopian framework as a narrative device has declined and been replaced with repetitiveness of idea. Last, he complains about the lack of imagination of social betterment in modern fictions. They "do not sing like birds in the winter."

Esbozo does not have a formal, signaled conclusion, but one can see where the work moves from specifics to a broader concern with utopian scholarship. For Nettlau, the utopian element in fiction is essential. Given such vital importance, he sees modern scholarship in the field as inadequate. His example? Lewis Mumford's *Story of Utopias*. That book is generally considered a classic and was *very* contemporary when Nettlau was writing his *Esbozo* even as it may seem rather dated now a century later. Only three years separate Nettlau's manuscript from Mumford's book: 1925 and 1922. It is sobering and illuminating to see why Nettlau dislikes it. For him, Mumford makes two unforgivable errors: he adopts too narrow a focus, and he is ignorant in his coverage of the material. For Nettlau, any work on the history of utopias needs to cover 300–500 works; Mumford covers merely 12–15 in any detail. With Mumford dispatched, Nettlau closes with a stirring call to treat utopianism as the serious genre it is. Nettlau asserts, "Utopia has always existed, and it exists still. It will not die." Nettlau asserts that utopian thought works in subtle ways: "It is the act of creating utopia which is essential; however, utopia does not work directly." Nettlau asserts that what the world needs is a "free and unlimited utopia."

The Texts of *Esbozo*

The manuscript of *Esbozo de historia de las utopías* is written in French and titled "Esquisse d'un historique des utopies." It is 61 folios long, dated January 23, 1925, and signed M. Nettlau. It is housed among the Abad de Santillán papers at the International Institute of Social History (IISH) in Amsterdam. The handwriting is quite legible with few strikethroughs, corrections, and additions marked for placement. The lineation is tight as if to save paper. The newspaper version of the work ran in a Buenos Aires publication, *La protesta suplemento seminal*. The work occupied a section of the newspaper in 10 successive issues (numbers 175 through 184) between June 1 and August 3, 1925. The book edition of the work, published by IMAN in Buenos Aires, is dated November 1934. The title page incorrectly states it was translated from the German by D. Abad de Santillán. The book is in itself a noteworthy artifact. The cover art for the slim volume is printed in light green. It features what looks like a Pacific Islander carrying part of what may be a canoe. He is photographed kneeling down with the object in his grasp. The 101-page book, printed on cheap and friable paper, is part of a series: Cuadernos economicos (Economical Notebooks). It is the eighth in the series, with the earlier volumes being concerned with socialized medicine; Germany then and now; historical socialism; realist cinema; the evolution of modern socialism; the battle of the sexes; and constructive socialism. The publisher was obviously interested in creating an eclectic series for intellectuals of the day. There is a 1991 edition of Nettlau's work edited by Luis Gomez Tovar and Almudena Delgado Larios and published, coincidentally, as the eighth volume in a series titled Colección Investigación y Crítica (Research and Criticism Collection). As it was published long after Nettlau's death, it has no editorial significance. It also simply reprints the 1934 IMAN edition. However, the 30 pages of introductory material (which is heavily illustrated with black and white art) I found useful in preparing this introduction.

Editorial Practices

In light of textual editing's emphasis on authorial intention, I have based my English translation on the French manuscript as this was the only version over which Nettlau had control. (There is no indication that de Santillán consulted Nettlau as he translated the work.) I have consulted the de Santillán Spanish translation for any textual cruxes or illegible words. There were very few of either. Nettlau frequently added bibliographical information to his citations. I have consistently eliminated that on grounds of readability, because online bibliographical resources such as WorldCat, the British Library catalog, and the catalogs of the national libraries of France and Germany render such information unnecessary, and because occasionally Nettlau's information (or his transcription of that information) is inaccurate. I have consistently and silently corrected any bibliographical errors made by Nettlau. (The Bibliography at the end of this volume provides full information about every source to which Nettlau refers.) I have occasionally corrected punctuation. I have sometimes combined paragraphs as Nettlau's use of paragraphs is inconsistent and occasionally confusing. It is noticeable, for example, that the number of paragraphs in the manuscript markedly increases as the account goes on. This increase is in tandem with an increase in the number of citations. It is as if Nettlau's ideas for paragraphing changed as he wrote. It may also be a sign of haste. Overall, when considering any editorial choices, I have always thought of readability as a key criterion. This is in line with another textual-editing principle: textual production is a collaborative act. Readers want to know what Nettlau's views are; they are likely to be less interested in the complexities of how those views were created between 1925 and 1934.

OUTLINE OF THE HISTORY OF UTOPIAS

Max Nettlau

Biographical Sketch of Max Nettlau

A great many well-regarded critical works by Dr. Max Nettlau have helped to define him as the historian of socialism. His work in this field is unique for its interpretive power and the finality of its conclusions. Nettlau has contributed through his research and his ideas to the fight for a better society. Faced, of course, by the forces of hostile authoritarianism, he has promoted the cause of free and harmonious cooperation in society. To this end, he has voiced his sense of the individual and social destiny of humanity in a recent volume published in Spanish: *De la crisis mundial a la Anarquia* [Anarchy and the World Crisis], which he subtitled, in order to define his position: *Eugenesia de la Sociedad libre* [Eugenics in a Free Society]. He has been and is a constant defender of socialist freedom against all the absolutist and exclusionary theories out there and against all the unlikely efforts at achieving equality. For half a century, he has studied the life and times of the best-known free thinkers, and has been an active collaborator in the struggle for freedom against authoritarianism. He has argued for the construction of a new world and has contributed his vast experience to the cause as well as his hard-won knowledge and his noble passion for liberty.

As a writer, he remains largely ignored, not because of the quality of his ideas but because of the ideological limitations placed on thinkers by most editors. His biographies do not follow the party line as far as their critical perspective is concerned, nor do they persistently criticize their subjects as certain well-known historians do today. However, what Max Nettlau has published as a historian is just a very small part of his overall achievement, an achievement which spans many volumes but which lies unedited. He has spent most of his working life in Vienna; however, he has traveled extensively throughout Europe in order to document his work. Of his books, the following deserve notice: *Biography of Mikhail Bakunin*, in five unedited volumes; *Biography of Élisée Reclus*, in two volumes; *Biography of Errico Malatesta, Historian of Anarchism*, in ten volumes (with four published in German); and *Biography of Gustav Landauer*, which includes his correspondence. He has also written histories of the First International and its representative figures. He has, finally, contributed for almost 30 years to the press in the cause of worldwide liberation, primarily to *Freedom* in London and to publications in Spain, Argentina, Italy, and Belgium.

IMAN

Chapter 1
DEFINITION

Utopia. How easily one scorns the genre. It is considered useless, illusory, contrary both to reality and to science. Let us guard against following such dry, utilitarian voices! The world is poor enough as it is right now, and utopia is altogether one of its rarest flowers. Truly poor is the man who doesn't cherish utopia, who can't sustain in his mind an eternal utopia built according to some ideal, as much universal as individual, that he conceives of in his earliest youth. Such a utopia will be very flexible in construction. It will be something he adds to or alters at each step of his intellectual and moral development, something that grows, gets old, and dies with him. What an empty mind it is that doesn't know utopia, that thinks—from pride, resignation, or triviality pure and simple—there is nothing more than the present moment! Not that one has to make an abstraction of the present; on the contrary, *carpe diem* matters. However, those who are absolutely absorbed in what is are as incomplete as those who live in nothing more than a dream, in nothing more than a utopia.

Utopia is a social phenomenon that occurs in every epoch, and is one of the primary and oldest forms in which progress and rebellion are expressed. The desire to lift oneself above a present that seems acceptable only to the power broker or the pleasure seeker; the hope that one day one will triumph when the chance occurs and one becomes transformed into reflecting on the future, into envisioning what one can become. This process alternates in the healthy organism with the impulse to focus on the here and now, on whatever action, work, investigation, or experiment lies to hand. Indeed, because of this impulse, because men would have been truly free and happy by attending to their own affairs, the worst authoritarian clergymen have always tried to prevent them from becoming complete men. In some men, they have cultivated only a liking for the present, for vulgar pastimes, while in others, the dispossessed and the conquered, they have cultivated a belief that the only hope lies in a future under some form of heavenly justice—either the happiness of paradise or the punishment of hell that is found in all religions.

This is not why religions came into being, of course, but once superstitions were believed in, once men were fooled, the priests (who have as their mission the perpetuation of these superstitions and the prevention, at any price, of the intellectual emancipation of the people through science) proclaimed the system then in force to be immovable and totally untouchable. In other words, these men, servants of the rulers of the hour, proclaimed obedience to laws and customs and denied the idea that the people had any power to change the system. People's every hope and every impulse to rebel they relegated to a future dreamed of according to tradition, postponed to a heaven where the poor would come first and a hell where the rich would suffer for their exploitation and their lives devoted to pleasure. This was the counterfeit coin with which the people had to content themselves. They were indoctrinated into absolute submission to the system in force at the time and prohibited from meddling with it. They allowed themselves to be deluded with the hope that in heaven one would find justice and happiness.

So, the utopian impulse has been debased and diverted away from its goal by the priesthood of every age. They have not been completely successful, however, because the roots of utopia run very deep. These roots lie primarily in the traditional belief in the good old days, in a past that was almost always a little less wretched than the present. I know that the very real progress of the second half of the eighteenth century and of all of the nineteenth century has created the impression that the past was bad—it was the dark shadows from which man emerged—and I am far from denying that progress has in some ways been made. However, the first quarter of the twentieth century, which has just gone by, has thrown us into a very pronounced retreat. We would be happy if a little of the thinking of 1848, of the 1860s and the 1880s undermined this authoritarian, nationalistic, and fascist era of ours. Apart from a few unusual periods, the age of Pericles in Athens, for example, the past was commonly a time when some of the exploitation, the repression, the restrictions did not yet exist, a time when one was less confined, when one ate better and worked less hard, a time when scandalous fortunes did not yet exist. From there, the popular fantasy, aided by some traditions and by the spectacle of the lives of more primitive people, found in the past a state of complete and universal justice and happiness, a *golden age*, a *paradise*.

These were the first utopias, and as the human spirit seems to move freely in thought and in dreams and can shift its fantasies without any difficulty from the past to the future, there was no obstacle to people's imagining the continued existence of this golden age and of this paradise in regions inaccessible to the physical body, in regions where spirit, imagination, and dreams could freely go and where, it was concluded, the soul, separated from the physical body, had the power to take them. The imagination certainly created elysium, the raptures of the Christian heaven or the Moslem paradise, the Valhalla of the Teutonic people, and so on. Utopias, with their *golden age*, became for the dead a reality indubitably within the reach of every individual after just a short span of years.

And so, little by little, the priesthood made use of these dreams that masked the desire for justice and happiness and transformed them into instruments of mental submission. From this transformation come the legends that forsake the justice of heaven itself, that declare man a fallen being because he rebelled against God or even because he displayed the least desire to be like God in understanding or knowledge. The Greek priests pointed to Prometheus, who first taught men to master fire instead of leaving it alone as an accidental, destructive force when it would fall suddenly from heaven. For this act of supreme value, Prometheus was enchained, martyred, punished as a rebel. And the Jewish priests point to the man who ate of the "tree of knowledge" and was grossly insulted and brutally expelled from paradise. He and all his descendants were condemned to earthly misery by an incensed and jealous god named Jehovah. And if the gods are capable of spreading horror when confronted by individual rebellion, they can do so as well when faced with collective rebellion. The Greek gods cast down the Giants for their assault on Olympus, and the Hebrew and Christian God repelled quite as violently the assault by devils. Of course, for authority always triumphs. This is how the popular utopia was corrupted and how the people were indoctrinated, brutalized even in their dreams. Man had to resign himself to the fact that not even in heaven could he do what he wanted, that there he would have his small place only if he were absolutely submissive, obedient, and pious on earth. Worse, throughout history, the spirit of the people has been stifled to the point where even when there was a large enough number of rebels and rebellions, the great masses always met them with indifference or even helped in the torture of these harbingers and isolated figures. And we are even now in precisely this condition: we have seen in the last few years more horrors committed than in all of the nineteenth century, but our indifference remains. Because man has been taught the intangibility of the present, he has become lost and has reduced to nothingness the ancient dreams of the future. Here stands the man of today, someone who, it could be said, almost lacks the ability to think. He has much to occupy his mind: the day is filled with all sorts of business or with sports; the night with the cinema. And all the while he is inescapably worried about a job which he is not even interested in, which indeed he hates. So, he resigns himself to it and atrophies, humiliates himself, focuses on himself becoming the master, exploiter, and user.

I do not underrate the tremendous efforts of the worker and humanitarian movements to raise the popular conscience, but evidently all this action amounts to so much less than the reactionary forces at work on the people. And here it has to be said that the obscurantist work done in other times by the priesthood alone is done today by politicians, by the press, by sports, and by entertainment with an efficiency every bit as terrible as that of the priesthood of the past, and for similar reasons: because the people are always paid in counterfeit money, because they are always induced to interest themselves in some illusory objects that have not the least importance to their needs by some manipulative politician or actor or bullfighter or boxer or film star.

From this reasoning, it follows that perhaps the lesson to be learned is that the people need some distant ideal. Without an ideal, it is certain nothing will get done, but *under the impulse of such an ideal*, man will move himself if he can move himself at all. So, we must agree to give ourselves a more powerful, inspiring ideal than our current empty idols. It is crucial that *our utopia*, which continues the ancient dream of justice and happiness that in another time was so valuable to the people, *becomes once again the people's utopia*, and that mankind rids himself of the unhealthy, insignificant, and petty idols of today. We must examine whether we do not share some of the blame for socialism, and anarchism too, having become too dry, too lifeless, too humdrum, and too theoretical truly to appeal to the popular imagination. We believe that it is enough to condense socialist and anarchist ideas into more or less precise strategies and known effects, and we believe that we can save time and effort by presenting *those results* to the masses. We ourselves, at least the oldest and best part, have perhaps gone through a utopian period and wish to save people from what appears to be a roundabout route and show them a direct path to revolutionary action. Is this truly possible? That's the question. We must not underrate the imagination, the dream—all of the world needs them more or less, and the man who lives without them very often possesses a marked authoritarian spirit, one that is impregnated with a feeling of superiority, a sense that he knows he has elevated himself above human weaknesses.

I believe, then, that socialism and anarchy need to reverberate in the imagination, in the dream, in the tangible perceptions of fantasy, for these are powerful agents that work on a larger number of men than statistics, logical conclusions, and even learning do. Knowledge, in an educational system monopolized by the privileged, appears to the people as nothing more than another instrument of domination since every scientific discovery serves only the monopolists and never the wage earners. For the people, there is nothing more than imagination, impulse, and instinct. Socialism, in its modern form, understood this a century ago, but does not understand it well enough today. It believes it's enough to be practical, but by discarding the imagination it has become pinched, anemic, isolated. By giving much more room to imagination, to utopia, we can renew the attractiveness of our ideas. It is essential that we do so.

We must not forget that *anarchism* in a strict sense is a form of socialism, for the true anarchist is impregnated with the need for liberty—personal liberty and liberty for everything around him. This liberty is not yet widely diffused, but it is our conviction that it exists in a latent form and is capable of being developed in every individual. Without doubt, all around us, there will be many forms of socialism that are less liberating or not liberating at all, old-fashioned, even authoritarian. This will be the case for one of two reasons: either this imperfect socialism will be fully achieved *before* anarchism can appear (and here the example of Russia since 1917 shows us the shameful situations that can result), or *anarchism* will be realized first but will find itself faced with grave problems caused by the backward state of large sections of the population. In any case, it is crucial that our ideal is, if not accepted, at least *understood* by the largest possible number of men, and that this ideal is not overwhelmed by theory. If it is overwhelmed, those who are indifferent will not give any thought to it, and the thousand organs of reactionary propaganda will perpetuate their ignorance and prejudice. Perhaps the only possible way forward is to appeal to the imagination, and for that our ideas must be presented in a more tangible, more palpable way than they have been in even the most popular pamphlets. It is no longer the descriptions of misery, of the suffering of the people, of the victims martyred for our ideas that affect the hearts of the indifferent, for even the most slow-witted among the indifferent feel the limits of such descriptions. Instead, they stuff their minds to escape the banality of everyday life. It's as if they have taken opium. It's essential that the true utopia—of future liberty, of revolution, of solidarity—be presented in ways that grab the imagination. The people would not need works of art because they know too little of true art, they feel removed from it, forcibly excluded, and without hope.

In a word, it seems sad to me to see the years go by with the masses—as in earlier times when churches, processions, and drink were almost their only distractions—once again, but ever more intensely, absorbed in the diversions I've already mentioned, diversions that are *all* at the service of the bourgeoisie. The organization and the cause [of anarchism] constitute happiness for many of us, but they do not exert an overwhelming power of attraction for all; if they did, our ranks would be infinitely more vast. The struggle, the mutiny, the strike, and so on do not happen every day and most often include too few people. The experience, the story of the events themselves, an understanding of them, only moves a few. There remains, as I have tried to show, only the imagination, the effort to revive those dreams of a golden age and to put them this time within human reach, to make them accessible to those who unite with us to achieve the dream through common effort. *Utopia* must not be scorned. It must not be commanded. It should be the result of a true need that someone feels to create it just so—that is the origin of any product of intrinsic worth. Utopia would certainly have come into being by now were we not disheartened again and again. Up till now, the tendency has been to get discouraged, to consider utopia as relevant only to a past age because we ourselves know more or less everything and do not need the help of the imagination. Let us not discourage utopia anymore, then, and be content if someone grabs the popular imagination, which is not easy at all. There are two kinds of utopia. There is the boring utopia that attracts no one, and there is the enchanting utopia that cannot help but explore new terrain, finger untouched strings and make them resonate.

It is to those who are not completely in disagreement with these reflections that I wish to speak a little about utopias of social reform and their history.

Chapter 2
THE CLASSICAL AND MEDIEVAL AGES

From now on when discussing utopias, I have to include authoritarian utopias, for they make up the great majority of texts in the genre. The oldest expressions of libertarian feeling are, one knows, very rare. Rebels at that time primarily acted directly or succumbed to persecution so that even the memory of them has been lost. Their literary works were always quite few and were often lost. In general, one has to be content with the fact that the author of a utopia then almost always had in mind a better state of affairs than existed in his own time, but he could only partly free himself from the thinking of his time, which was most often authoritarian. Utopias in the aggregate, however, present a wide range of viewpoints: from those who accept unrestricted authority, to those who believe it necessary to augment it by regulating everything, to those who try their best to diminish it, to make it disappear, or, at least, to search for what they believe are guarantees against its abuses. Utopias thus present the human spirit grappling with authority, an entity which is considered a panacea by a few and instinctively draped in the cloth of justice by others. How can the people set themselves free, if even the most adventurous spirits who move freely across the terrain created out of their own fantasy almost never know how to bring that freedom about? Now the hour has arrived, but the foremost seekers, after thousands of years, have not arrived there yet.

Utopias arise from thinking about how to govern and to educate, from being aware of social injustice and the monopolizing of land, from the critique of mores, and so on. The Greeks cultivated this genre to a very high degree in myth without their country experiencing any great social convulsions. The Romans didn't write utopias, but there was fighting between plebians and patricians; there was the agrarian war of the Graci, and a fight to the death by the slaves against their masters in the time of Spartacus. They even saw the idealism and the self-denial of the first Christians, but they also experienced the loss of the social ideals of primitive Christianity when superstitions were created and a Christian hierarchy came into being. This hierarchy was as reactionary as those forces that devoured and consumed the Roman people along with their entire social order and caused their civilization to suffer a general eclipse.

The Greeks lived through epochs of local tyranny and feuds and intolerable civil wars, throughout which they preserved the tradition of a better state than popular fantasy allowed. They transformed the hatred of the tyrants in power at the time into the myth of the *golden age*, which was sung of by Hesiod and, some centuries later, by Empedocles too. They saw agrarian reform and a rigid centralized state come into being in Sparta, a system that was idealized much later, and particularly by Ephorus, as the communism of Lycurgus. Athens suffered through some rather subtle constitutional changes whereby democracy was very much submerged beneath a demagoguery that idealized a purer form of the ancient state than that envisioned by Socrates. They debated absolutely every social question—except that of slavery, which was taboo. The anti-socialist comedies of the aristocrat Aristophanes bear witness to the breadth of debate, above all his *Ecclesiazusae* [The Parliament of Women; 391 BC]. These virulent publicly performed polemics could not have appeared if the ideas in them had not had adherents as well as public support in their favor which preserved the texts. It is known that other playwrights, among them Theocritus, described a golden age or some happy isle. The Greeks, who were very active colonizers—that is, founders of new cities in distant countries—had considerable practical experience with the organization of societies and clearly had differences of opinion about how societies should be organized, controversies indeed that fueled the construction of model, ideal cities within the context of fantasy. Philosophers discussed in depth all of the political, social, and moral problems (with the exception, always, of slavery). These discussions led to conceptions of the ideal *State*: the *Politeia* by Phaleas of Chalcedon; the version by Plato (the most famous theory of the state and the only one that has come down to us); and the later ideas of Zeno, which come closest to the idea of liberty. Much later came Euhemerus of Messene, Iambulus, and Aratus of Soli, the last of these thinkers coming closest to Zeno's ideas. If these writers had no fear of professing very advanced social ideas, neither did the arch bourgeois Aristotle at the other extreme. Between the two extremes lie the practical theories in Plato's *Laws*.

These writers were still influenced in a general way by Hellenism, which during much of the time was very nationalistic, very exclusionary, and very patriotically in support of state or city. Hellenism, however, broke apart quickly under pressure first from the Macedonians and then from the Romans until it disappeared and was mixed with Roman ideas on the one hand and with Eastern thought on the other. The Greeks of recent times have sustained their pride in their literary education, knowing themselves to be the indispensable middle-men for less literary people who are their political masters. However, their nationalistic feelings have disappeared; they crumbled before the Romans and any other country that proved more powerful. Thus, their literary life was assimilated by their conquerors: it looked towards the East and bowed down before the Romans in the West. The social theories of the Greeks disappeared in the West, for the Romans killed off the Greeks and the Spartans were certainly not lovers of utopias. In the East, utopian thought blended with the mysterious and the marvelous; wholly fantastic voyages became objects of amusement or repositories of occult ideas. Satire, too, became mixed in with all these ideas. Lucian of Samosata is the type of author whose imaginary trips have no social content. One sees that utopia *alone*, without true change, would be powerless and could do nothing but decay. But the life of the Greeks during their best times has always been considered to be quite complete and harmonious, and one can see that utopia had a well-appointed place in it. By contrast, in our time, which is felt to be so perfect, utopia is missing, for the programs of the various parties include so much real-world thinking that they disdain to look to the future.

The Hellenistic years gone by did produce a genre of literature that, without being utopian, at least developed an imaginary world and undermined or dismantled convictions and wrong-headed ideas. I allude to writings such as the *Dialogues of the Gods* by Lucian of Samosata, parodies and enchanting absurdities about the gods and goddesses of Olympus. The true method of destroying a religion is by laughter, by ridicule. Very few authors have openly laughed through satire at the mythology of Christianity. Some examples, however, are Henri Joseph Du Laurens' *Étrennes aux gens d'église ou la chandelle d'Arras* [New Year's Gifts to the Men of the Church or the Candle of Arras] (1765); Evariste de Parny's memorable *La guerre des dieux* [The War of the Gods, 1799] at the end of the eighteenth century, and Oskar Panizza's play *Das Liebeskonzil* [The Love Council] (1894).

The ancient mythology exhausted the patience of man. For free thinkers, it then took the form that was recaptured in the light operas of Offenbach—*Orpheé* [1858, 1874] or *La Belle Hélène* [The Lovely Helen, 1864]—during the 1860s (which were actually satires directed at Napoleon III and the life of his court); for the common people, the mythology was first replaced with an ostentatious oriental cult, that of Mitra, and then later by Christianity. The affirmations and promises of Christianity, it must be acknowledged, took a strong hold on the sensitive and weak souls of the subjugated masses. When one controlled Christianity, one controlled the development of society, and, at the same time, one could divert the intellectual life that had begun to grow away from the pursuit of learning, a pursuit that was in its infancy. Along with Christianity, faith, submission, and ignorance were guaranteed; at this price, well might the Emperor Constantine choose to make Christianity the religion of the state.

From that fatal moment, a crisis in human thought began that continues to this day. The people, ignorant of the knowledge that was lost or buried, in so much as they dared to emancipate themselves from a blind faith that was enforced at the stake created anew a special world, a refuge of hope, a utopia. These places they created contained the memories of a banned paganism which they still loved despite the Christian priests who put their feet on their necks. At this time, in the dark ages of history, the cult of the numerous small Greek and Roman divinities and semi-divinities, of the nymphs and dryads, and all of the other personifications of the powers and the phenomena of nature was driven into a corner. There were similar divinities in the mythology of the Germanic, Celtic, Slavic, and other peoples; these were Christianized by force, either through wars of conquest or by the will of sovereigns who considered it opportune to side with Christianity, the only way, in the Middle Ages, of avoiding the worst possible form of death—being exterminated as a result of a special crusade. Only the Moslems showed some fight and refused to submit. Where would they have been today if they had behaved differently!

This popular opposition to Christianity was so strong that the Church, powerless to defeat it by force, once again succeeded by deceit, scattering these last rays of hope, as it had done before with the age of gold. Methodically, patiently, the Church substituted its saints for the little pagan divinities, attributing to them the same qualities and others even more fictitious in their professional role as fabricators of miracles. The saints replaced the fauns and nymphs and the satyrs and the dryads, and since the saint answers to the good Lord all is in order. The more miracles attributed to them, the better for the renown of the good Lord. Thus, most of the popular traditions were Christianized, castrated, transformed into a source of magnificent income for the Church, which added trafficking in the official recognition of false saints to its brisk business in wood from the Cross of Christ. To this day, the Church is happy to exploit pagan superstitions.

The people from whom they took everything by disguising it managed to save their utopia in the form of the popular tale, or folk tale, in which the forces of a *just* nature, personified as fairies and goblins (or, in order to give some satisfaction to the church, as brave hermits and as pious old men, as a sort of christianized Philemon and Baucis), know how to procure *justice* for the people when no one else does. For, the people are so deceived, terrified, powerless that revolt is rare, although without doubt it does exist, personified by the people in *William Tell* and in *Robin Hood* of Sherwood Forest in England and in other semi-legendary and completely legendary heroes to whom the acts of many anonymous people are attributed. The folk tale foreshadows the struggle against deception (a form of struggle that is peculiarly oriental) or against fate and the idea of an inescapable justice, itself a relic of the spirit of ancient tragedy. In one way or another, these tales give the people confidence that there is also justice for them. The elements of the ancient social-reform utopia are rediscovered, above all in the promise of future plenty (the land of Cockaigne in its simplest form), in the rights of the poor and their equality with the rich, in the spirit of adventure and discovery, the distant isles, the investigation of the unknown.

This need for an ideal was so great in the Middle Ages that it was felt even among the powerful, among the sated, above all among the men of violence—the nobility. The nobility, after a time, became steeped in the bloody stories of the lives of the Christian saints and demanded something else. So, the professional entertainers, the wandering minstrels, presented them with that which they themselves, poor devils, had taken from the available popular traditions but which the nobility, as official defenders of Christianity, had ignored. They elaborated on the stories of the model knights, of the knights of King Arthur and the Round Table or the comrades of Charlemagne, and created a type of utopia founded on good conduct, on defense of the weak, on equal terms for combat, on a degree of moderation—except when encountering pagans, who were all the better for being dead. In a similar way, they established a definite code of behavior to follow with respect to women, at least to those within their own class. And so, they became a little less barbaric. I think that the secret powers of the Church, from which these brutal men escaped but not without some new intellectual and moral restrictions, and some popular forces (those singers who owed neither love nor respect to the nobility) worked together to impose a code of honor on the nobility in the form of a chivalric utopia. Once the Church had tamed the nobility in this way, it sent them off to the Crusades.

In the following centuries, there were also fictional utopias which became fashionable for some time. There was the *pastoral* genre of the sixteenth century, for example, which harked back to the patriarchal life of the Arcadian shepherds. In art, this genre culminated in the work of Watteau and had its final incarnation in the anarchist Sylvain Maréchal. From there one can draw a direct line to the French Revolution. In France, in the seventeenth century and in the first half of the eighteenth century, when Catholicism was even more powerful than it is now and had outlawed protestantism, before the Encyclopédists gave it the coup de grâce in the arena of public opinion, one took pleasure in seeking refuge in the land of fairies that Perrault had discovered again. Very soon the Count of Gabalis resurrected sylphs and ondines and all kinds of sprites; bewitched forests and fountains made a final reappearance, which no one believed anymore but which many enjoyed seeing presented in the charming fairy tales of Madame d'Aulnoy and many others.

This was a final echo of the utopian paganism in which one could take refuge from the stupid banality of Christianity. As for the rest of the story, this age created a definitive inventory of ancient utopias in the form of collections of popular, absolutely traditional stories that had been put together in Europe since the end of the eighteenth century. These collections were continued under the guise of folklorism (which is concerned with everything traditional around the world). This period, when it was still socialist, also spread learning and free thought. However, it also ruthlessly destroyed the popular ancient utopia. All the more reason, then, that it should have given the people a new, more tangible, utopia, one in keeping with their way of life and one which would be achievable this time if the people truly put their shoulders to the wheel. Either that, or it would be condemned to remain a beautiful dream.

Chapter 3

THE RENAISSANCE AND NEO-CLASSICAL PERIODS

Serious utopian thinking about a better society was only revived eighteen centuries after Plato by Thomas More (1478–1535) with his *Utopia* (1516).

An awareness of a lack of social justice was not missing during the long span of the Middle Ages. The idea of natural right (i.e., a theoretical utopia of abstract forces) and even the notion of a golden age were acknowledged, albeit only in a Platonic sense, by hard-hearted jurists and by Church fathers greedy for temporal as much as spiritual dominion. This natural right established the existence of an aboriginal equality and liberty; it recognized neither the exclusive right of the few to wealth nor the exploitation of the rest. The law and the Church have always provided themselves with loopholes by means of which they could deny that they were defending their positions of power. This strategy did not prevent them from being fierce apologists for every part of the power structure or from taking advantage of that structure in order to threaten natural rights and social Christianity when the people showed themselves to be fed up with being dominated and exploited. In this way, the two (the law and the Church) have acquired absolute political and administrative power and, as far as the Church is concerned, enormous wealth. And at the same time, the ideal utopian element in their theories has appealed to men of great intelligence and heart. Thomas More is the perfect example of a man of this sort, one who understands the idea of natural right and the social criticism directed at the church, and one who understands the Renaissance, Platonic humanism, Plato's *Politeia*, and the best that the Romans and Greeks produced. More is such an expert in justice as well as commerce that, in this age of great discoveries, he conceives vast plans, and sees unknown worlds brought nearer to discovery by every journey. He also sees the suffering of the poor and the machinery of government that crushes them. He says clearly, and these words always have worth, that all modern states seem to be nothing more than a conspiracy of the rich who, under the pretext of a common salvation, look after nothing more than their own fortunes; they pass regulations in the name of all, and therefore in the name of the poor also, and call them laws. What More, who weighed every political and economic factor of the period and constructed his utopia with those materials, could not even begin to understand was the will of the people, who, if they felt wretched and at some point rebelled, they did so as an act of defense, did so from hopelessness or religious exaltation. As a result, More, as an early representative of the bourgeoisie, couldn't see beyond the workings of a bureaucratic government, the regulation of production by wise authorities which would then permit a relatively independent private life for the citizenry.

On the basis of such thinking, Thomas More constructed his *Utopia* as a socially revivified England. Authors of utopias much later on have tried to leave out the conditions of their country and of the times in which they lived; the first utopists, by contrast, maintained contact with the real life of their times, building on the progressive tendencies and eliminating the troubling inclinations. This characteristic of the first utopists has probably added to interest in their writings, which, with respect to More's *Utopia*, has been very great and long lasting: Next to the Bible and the works of Classical authors, utopias are among the most widespread texts through translation. Indeed, More, helped by his talent and knowledge, created a work that is in a class with Plato and that has held onto its position in the first rank of utopias. It would be easy to write a utopia that is more plausible and more marvelous, but not to write one which is more intelligent, more reflective, more connected to the possible. There is one particular reason why this is the case—the vast experience of the author that protects him from exaggerations and leads him to predict where the tendencies of his time will end even when he cannot see their beginnings.

In France in the sixteenth century, the social conflicts were no less acute than in England, Germany, and Italy. Then, aristocrats and peasants, the court and the bourgeoisie were as separate from each other as on the eve of the French Revolution, but the bourgeoisie and the clergy were so comfortable and so wealthy that it diverted attention away from the major questions about international commerce and maritime power which, at that time, were being so hotly debated in Spain, England, Flanders, and Italy. Comfort and luxury were pursued at the expense of the peasants (the beasts of burden), so that the recovery of the riches of ancient times added to the wealth of the gentry, and the bourgeoisie of the Middle Ages ensured for the privileged a magical life. The works of Rabelais show this abundance and luxury in all its many forms, the vulgar delight in the most refined pleasures in the *Abbaye de Thélème* [The Abbey of Thélème], a libertarian phalanstery where "do whatever you please" is the only rule. This is all very well but what it amounts to, socially, is château life, sweet idleness, everything based on the work of the blacks of whom no one speaks, just as in antiquity the free Greek citizen never spoke of the work of the slaves that fed him. Etienne de la Boétie puts his finger on the problem—the voluntary servitude of the people who break their backs satisfying the parasites, but Rabelais, Montaigne, and all of the rest let these things go and did not look too closely.

Among the most famous utopias and utopian writers, I should mention Francesco Doni's *I Mondi celesti, terrestri et infernali de gli Academici Pellegrini* [The Celestial, Earthly, and Infernal Worlds of the Pellegrini Academy] (1562); Francis Bacon's *New Atlantis* (1627); the Calabrian Tommaso Campanella's *Civitas Soli* [The City of the Sun] (1623), written between 1620 and 1623 while he was in prison in Naples; the German Rosicrucian Johann Valentin Andreae's *Reipublicae Christianopolitanae descriptio* [Description of the Republic of Christianopolis] (1619); Bishop Joseph Hall's *Mundus alter et idem* [The World, Different and the Same] (1605?); Francis Godwin's *The Man in the Moone* (1638); Cyrano de Bergerac's *L'autre monde ou histoire comique des états et des empires de la Lune* [The Other World or the Comic History of the States and Empires of the Moon] (1657) (and *Les états et empires du soleil* [The States and Empires of the Sun, 1662]); and, last, James Harrington's *The Commonwealth of Oceana* (1656). Among these, the works of Bacon, Campanella, and Andreae offer the greatest interest. In the general structure of the work, they do not rise above More. However, they offer some remarkable perspectives on learning, inventions, and the organization of labor. One can also see this literature turning to the marvelous, to satire and allegory, and to political rather than social structures, as in Harrington's *Oceana*. This text, scholars have tried to show, had some influence on the authors of the United States' Constitution (see Dwight). One could also consult the writings of Bolesław Limanowski [1873], Karl Kautsky [1854–1938], and Professor [Ernest?] Nys [1851–1920] on More and Campanella. There are well-researched Italian studies on Campanella, and there is Juppont's essay on de Bergerac.

One could say that the utopias of More, Bacon, and Campanella (who spent his last years in Paris and influenced Cyrano de Bergerac) constituted a part of the international literature read by all educated men of the seventeenth century, but that, for a long time, no one was up to the task of writing utopias of comparable difficulty. Were wars and royal absolutism on the Continent the cause? In England, without doubt, very serious voices arguing for social reform were heard after the middle of the century. Gerrard Winstanley proposed taking back the land. In Holland, P. C. Plockhoy, writing in English [under the pseudonym of "Peter Cornelius, van Zürich-Zee, a lover of truth and peace"] (in 1659), and John Bellers (in 1695), proposed organizing agricultural associations in which membership was not voluntary, with start-up money to be advanced by the rich and by men of business, and so on. This is utopian thinking stripped down to a proposal with immediate, practical application. Such ideas, the fruit of thinking that is only remotely utopian, bear some responsibility for reducing the interest in utopias in England.

In France, by contrast, towards the last quarter of the seventeenth century interest in utopia was finally born and grew quite rapidly, helped perhaps by an interest in travels, in the colonization of North America, and so on, that was characteristic of this epoch. A Huguenot from Languedoc and an old soldier, Denis Vairasse [d'Allais] first published in English *The History of the Sevarites or Severambi* (1675). This utopia, which one could say was adapted for form's sake to the political situation in the ultra-monarchist France of Louis XIV, nobly develops its social ideas in complete independence, denounces and rejects private ownership, and carefully studies how production is organized. In a word, it puts before the public a new, modern, and well-developed utopian scheme, devoid of all that fantastic nonsense, and the public must have read it based on the numerous editions and the similar, lesser utopias which began to appear after it. However, with the possible exception of Gabriel de Foigny, no one truly continued on after Vairasse and the genre degenerated once more.

Gabriel de Foigny published [anonymously], in Geneva, *La terre Australe connue* [The Southern Land Discovered] (1676). Here, the author expounds on a life without laws or almost so, but one lived by extra-human creatures, hermaphrodites. The question of liberty, which the author loved and affirmed, is not seriously tackled. Still, the conception of a life not carefully regulated is so rare in utopias that Foigny's utopia is as memorable on this point as is Rabelais' Thélème. Also, Fénelon, in a section of his *Télémaque* [Telemachus] (the peasants of la Bétique, Book VII), describes small, rare groups in isolated valleys, living in supreme harmony and happiness, without property and without bosses. This was a utopian ideal that was much loved but was believed to be so distant that no entire books were devoted to it. The German Republican [Andreas Georg Friedrich] Rebmann a century later wrote in similar terms to Fénelon's of "Abenazar's kleine Republik" [Abenazar's little republic] in a book of travels (1794), and occasionally there were small enclaves in French travel novels and other texts published in France in the eighteenth century.

Among the lesser utopias, satire blended with the genre of the fantastic voyage powerfully began with Swift's *Gulliver* (1727), and, along with the creation of miniature communities inspired by Defoe's *Robinson Crusoe* (1719), the following texts are worth mentioning: *Histoire de Calejava; ou De l'isle des hommes raisonnables* [The History of Calejava, or the Island of Rational Men] (1700). It's called the rarest of utopias, and I am not familiar with it. Then there are Pierre Lesconvel's *Idée d'un règne doux et heureux, ou relation du voyage du Prince de Montberaud dans l'île de Naudely* [The Idea of a Sweet and Happy Reign, or the Account of the Prince of Montberaud's Voyage to the Isle of Naudely] (1703); and Simon Tyssot de Patot's *Voyages et avantures de Jacques Massé* [The Travels and Adventures of Jacques Massé] (which was translated into German by J. F. Bachstrom in 1737 and into English in 1743). Bachstrom was himself the author of a utopia about the land of the Inquiraner (1736–1737) (see Ulrich 1909). *Relation du voyage de l'isle d'Eutopie* [Account of a Voyage to the Island of Eutopia] (1711) is a religious allegory [written by someone with the initials E. R. V. F. L]. It has no social value. The same goes for *La Monarchie des Solipses* [The Monarchy of Solipses] (1721) (by Melchior Inchofer or Giulio Clemente Scotti, and "Lucius Cornelius Europaeus"). It is a satire against the Jesuits. The content of the Danish writer Ludvig Holberg's *Nicolai Klimii iter subterraneum* [Nicolas Klim's Subterranean Voyage] (1745) is very different: a mixture of political and social satire along with utopian fantasy. This work, translated into all major languages in the eighteenth century, was the model for Bulwer-Lytton's *The Coming Race* (1871). Also worth mentioning are Samuel Brunt's pseudonymous *A Voyage to Cacklogallinia* (1727); l'Abbé Desfontaines' *Le nouveau Gulliver* [The New Gulliver] (1730); de Varennes de Mondasse's *La découverte de l'empire de Cantahar* [The Discovery of the Empire of Cantahar] (1730); and Charles de Fieux Mouhy's *Lamekis ou les voyages extraordinaires d'un Égyptien dans la Terre intérieure* [Lamekis, or the Extraordinary Voyages of an Egyptian beneath the Earth] (1735). The last of the four listed was reprinted as volumes 20–21 in Charles Garnier's great collection *Voyages imaginaires, songes, visions, et romans cabalistiques* [Imaginary Travels, Dreams, Visions, and Mystical Novels] (1787–1789). In that same collection is the Chevalier de Béthune's *Relation du monde de Mercure* [Account of Mercury's World] (1750) as Volume 16. *Le nouveau Gulliver* is also found there in Volumes 15 and 16.

Of more importance than some of the last texts I mentioned is one of the few English utopias of the eighteenth century, Simon Berington's *The Memoirs of Sigr Gaudentio di Lucca* (1737). This was published in French as *Memoires de Gaudence de Lucques* (1753) and in German in 1792. It was also published as Volume 6 in the great collection, *Voyages imaginaires, songes, visions, et romans cabalistiques*. I do not know the content of Zaccaria Seriman's *Viaggi di Enrico Wanton alle terre incognite ed al paese delle scimi tradotti da un manoscritto inglese* [The Voyage of Henry Wanton to the Unknown Southern Land and the Country of the Monkeys, Translated from an English Manuscript] (1749).

We should add to this rather incomplete list that genre of educational novels of a utopian tendency that have as a framework the life of an ancient or thoroughly fictitious sovereign, his education, and his idealized acts. He serves as a complete contrast to the kings of the epoch, who have none of the noble qualities that are stored up in kings of utopia. The contemporary public must have understood the purpose behind this idealization of another king rather than the present one because there are numerous editions of these books. The best-known example of this genre, *Télémaque* by Fénelon, is one of the most widely published. The same goes for Chevalier de Ramsay's *Travels of Cyrus* (translated as *Voyages de Cyrus*) (1727). There is *Sethos*, by l'Abbé Terrasson, a work of Masonic tendencies in three volumes (1731–1732) with a German translation, *Geschichte Sethos Königs in Aegypten* [The History of Sethos, King of Egypt] (1794). This book served as the basis for the text of Mozart's *Zauberflöte* [The Magic Flute]. Much later there appeared educational utopias with very reactionary tendencies, such as those of the Baron of Haller's *Usong* (1771), *Alfred König der Angel-Sachsen* [Alfred, King of the Anglo-Saxons] (1773), and others. There are also, for example, *Le vieillard Abyssin* [The Old Abyssinian Man] (1779) [written pseudonymously by "Amlac, empereur d'Ethiopie" (Amlac, Emperor of Ethiopia)] and Antoine Esprit Gibelin's *Tulikan, fils de Gengiskan* [Tulikan, son of Genghis Khan] (1803). This genre died out, as it were, with M. de Florian's *Numa Pompilius* (1786).

Another utopian narrative framework brings an honest, ingenuous, noble, uncorrupted savage to Paris and has him speak his thoughts regarding the effects of its artificial and corrupt civilization. Nicolas Gueudeville's *Dialogues ou entretiens entre un sauvage et le baron de Lahontan* [Dialogues or Interviews between a Savage and Baron Lahontan] (1704) introduced the noble Huron; later, a Tahitian replaced the Huron, hence Nicolas Bricaire de la Dixmerie's *Le sauvage de Taïti aux Français avec un envoi au philosophe ami des sauvages* [The Tahitian Savage to the French with a Dispatch to the Philosopher Friend of the Savages] (1770). Related to this genre are a great many series of letters supposedly written by distant foreigners that examine the things of Europe from a more just perspective. The cosmopolitanism of this epoch led to this textual form being chosen, and such a framework reinforced cosmopolitanism. On principle during this epoch, no one ridiculed any foreigners; sometimes, indeed, they were well respected. So there were the famous *Lettres persannes* [Persian Letters] (1761) by Montesquieu; Joubert de la Rue's *Lettres d'un sauvage dépaysé* [Letters of an Exiled Savage] (1738); Jacob Wetstein's *Lettres égyptiennes et angloises* [Egyptian and English Letters] (1742); Jean-Baptiste de Boyer, Marquis d'Argens' *Lettres juives* [Jewish Letters] (1739); Jean-Henri Maubert de Gouvest's *Lettres iroquoises* [Iroquois Letters] (1752); and Philip-Auguste de Sainte-Foy's *Lettres d'osman* [Ottoman Letters] (1753), and others.

There was, furthermore, the genre of various isles being described, often seen in the theatre: Pierre de Marivaux's *L'île des Esclaves* [Slave Island] (1725); Catalde's *Le paysan gentilhomme, ou Avantures de M. Ransav, avec son voyage aux Isles Jumelles* [The Peasant Gentleman, or the Adventures of Mr. Ransau, with His Voyage to the Twin Islands] (1737) and others. And there are innumerable allegorical or satirical isles, the taciturn isle, the festive isle, the isle of love: Guillaume-Hyacinth Bougeant's *Voyage merveilleux de Prince Fan-Férédan dans la romancie* [Prince Fan-Férédan's Marvellous Voyage in the World of Romance] (1788), l'Abbe Maillot's *Voyage mystérieux à l'isle de la vertu* [The Mysterious Voyage to the Island of Virtue] (1788), the island of the Hermaphrodites, and others. All of these genres and others like them are inexhaustible because very often in novels with utopian episodes, some island or other or the foundation of some distant republic is inserted into the text without the title indicating it is even there. I've found a great variety of volumes from this period, and numerous utopian oases are found scattered throughout.

In general, in the first half of the eighteenth century in France, the impulse towards communism provided by Denis Vairasse (with his *History of the Sevarambes*, 1675) and the impulse towards libertarianism provided by Gabriel de Foigny (with his *La Terre Australe connue*, 1676) became continually weaker and almost disappeared. However, despite this decline the utopian genre was well respected and formed one of the ways in which one could speak freely. It was similar to other methods in fashion at the time, such as the printing of uncensored books in Holland, London, Geneva, or—most often—clandestinely in France with a foreign or fictitious place of publication on the title page. All of this, the criticism in every line, was done with the active or tacit concurrence of the whole of society until all of the coercive methods of the government were rendered powerless. Utopia, the use of a pseudonym, clandestine printing, and the importation of pirated books all belong to a good war that prepared the people's spirits for the great Revolution. If I stress all these very different methods, it is because the same mission is incumbent upon us now: to prepare the spirit for a great revolution. And it would be strange if human nature had changed so much that this abundant diversity of methods was not as useful today as it was then.

Time passed, and at last socialist criticism saw the light of day in the form of a new, very familiar utopia that raises the tone above that of the *Sevarambes* of 1675. This new utopia was Étienne Gabriel Morelly's *Naufrage des isles flottantes ou basiliade du célèbre Pilpai* [Shipwreck of the Floating Islands or the Celebrated Pilpai's Basiliade] (1753), a book by an author who spoke even more clearly in the famous *Code de la nature, ou le véritable esprit de ses lois, de tout temps négligé ou méconnu* [Nature's Code, or the True Spirit of Her Laws, Which Are Always Neglected or Misunderstood] (1755) Morelly has not been forgotten; and one remembers, too, Gabriel Bonnot de Mably, a little of Jean Meslier, and Denis Diderot. From these, the socialists of the French Revolution were formed: François-Noël Babeuf, Philippe Buonarroti, and others.

I still remain fond of the *Floating Isles* in that very rare book, Mr. de Fontenelle's *La République des Philosophes, ou histoire des Ajaoiens. Ouvrage posthume de M. Fontenelle on y a joint une lettre sur la nudité des sauvages* [The Philosophers' Republic, or the History of the Ajaoiens. A Posthumous Work by Mr. Fontenelle, to Which Is Attached a Letter on the Nudity of Savages] (1768). The book is said to relate the travels of S. van Doelvelt in 1676 as translated from the original Flemish. About the Flemish author, nothing is known. This utopia has some truly libertarian sections and some defective parts as well, but, taken as a whole, it is perhaps the finest flower of the French utopian literature of the eighteenth century.

There are other utopias. There is *Entretien d'un Européen avec un insulaire du royaume de Dumocala* [Interview between a European and an Aboriginal Islander of the Kingdom of Dumocala] (1752). Its author was Stanislas Leszczyński, the king of Poland and the father-in-law of the king of France, Louis XV. It is, of course, not a revolutionary utopia. There are Daniel Jost de Villeneuve's *La voyageur philosophe dans un pays inconnu aux habitants de la terre* [The Philosopher-Voyager in a Land Unknown to Earth's Inhabitants] (1761), and de Puisieux's *Les hommes volants, ou les aventures de Pierre Wilkins* [The Flying Men, or the Adventures of Peter Wilkins] (1763), and James Burgh's *Account of the First Settlement, Laws, Form of Government, and Police of the Cessares, a People of South America* (1764). It's a book that I have never examined. There's also Charles-François Tiphaigne de la Roche's *Histoire naturelle, civile et politique des Galligenes antipodes de la nation française, dont ils tirent leur origine* [The Natural, Civic, and Political History of the Galligenes, Diametrically Opposite to That of the Nation of France, since Their Origins] (1770), and Louis-Sébastien Mercier's *L'an de mille quatre cent quarante: rêve s'il en fût jamais* [The Year 2440: A Dream If Ever There Was One] (1771). Its author was well-known for his role among the moderates in the French Revolution. It's a utopia of general progress and not a socialist one. Retif de la Bretonne was a thinker alive with utopian concepts and reunited the extreme utopia with that which emphasizes an immediately achievable project, as did Peter Cornelius Plockhoy and John Bellers in seventeenth-century England (with their idea of an "agricultural college"). Retif de la Bretonne wrote the *Statuts du bourg d'Oudun, composé de la famille R**, vivant en commun* [Statutes of the Town of Oudun, Drawn up by the R** Family, Who Lived in the Commune] which came at the end of his *Le paysan perverti* [The Peasant Perverti] (1776), and wrote in a more practical vein, *Le thesmographe, ou idées d'un honnête-homme, sur un projet de règlement, proposé à toutes les nations de l'Europe pour opérer une réforme générale des loix* [The Thesmographe, or the Ideas of an Honest Man about a System of Rules Proposed to All the Nations of Europe to Create a General Reform of the Laws] (1789). This book includes (on pages 515–556) a small theatrical work, *L'an 2000* [The Year 2000]. He expands more on socialism in his *Andrographe* (1782), which was first titled *Anthropographe*, and he is completely socialist in his thinking with his utopia *La découverte australe par un homme volant ou le Dédale français* [The Southern Discovery by a Flying Man or the French Daedalus] (1781). I observe in passing that the texts which make some proposition achievable through some voluntary initiative are much less common than the utopias that make general demands. One of this rare sort of utopia, which I have not seen, must be the work, published anonymously, titled *Maison de réunion pour la communauté philosophique dans la terre de l'auteur de ce projet* [A Meeting House for a Philosophical Community in the Land of the Author of This Project] (1779). Its author was J. A. V. d'Hupay de Fuvéa, a "prophet of the communal life." However, he was very much ignored by the rest. The *Télèphe* (1784) is a utopian poem by Pechméja, one of the encyclopédists. See also Lichtenberger (1893).

During this epoch, the first and one of the very few utopias in the Russian language appeared, Prince M. M. Shcherbatov's [unfinished work] *Cesta do Ofírské země* [A Journey to the Land of Ophyr]. It can be found in the complete edition of his works. It is heavy-going and moderate in its views, but it is a genuine utopia. In Tchetschouline's study (1900), which is dedicated to him, I have been able to see that many other utopias were translated into Russian in the eighteenth century, noteworthy given the small number of books that were printed at the time in Russia not only because of censorship but also because almost everyone who was at all literate knew French well and often German, too. Utopias were undoubtedly also written in Russia in the eighteenth century although they are certainly rarities today, but I myself found one day, to my great surprise, Montesquieu's *Lettres persanes* [*Persidskija pišma*] in Russian and published in St. Petersburg in 1789.

The famous Casanova also wrote a utopia: *Icosaméron, ou histoire d'Edourd et d'Elisabeth qui passérant 81 ans chez les Mégamicres, habitants aborigènes du Protocosme dans l'intérieur de notre globe* [Icosameron, or the Story of Edward and Elisabeth, Who Lived for 81 Years among the Megamicros, the Original Inhabitants of Protocosme in the Interior of Our Globe] (1788), a very rare book that I have never seen. It is said that it is more given to fantasies in the fields of natural history, cosmogony, and the rest than in social matters, but I cannot guarantee the accuracy of this judgment.

It is also worth mentioning Guillaume Resnier's *Republique universelle, ou l'humanité ailée, réunie sous l'empire de la raison* [The Universal Republic, or Winged Humanity Reunited under the Empire of Reason] (1788). Its flag is still fluttering these days, but the empire of reason gets talked of less than ever! It is a rather curious book. Even more curious and enigmatic for me after examining it again is a book in two small volumes *Zilia et Agathide, ou la volupté et le bonheur* [Zilia and Agathide, or the Ecstatic and the Good] (1787), a book that appears to foresee the events that were drawing near. The author is unknown but went under the pseudonym of M. ****.

In 1787–1789, the great collection titled *Voyages imaginaires, songes, visions, et romans cabalistiques* was put together by Charles Georges Thomas Garnier in 39 large volumes. It begins with serious utopias but proceeds to give samples of every type: allegories, dreams of occult fantasy, and so on with the last three volumes being filled with actual shipwrecks. Overall, it is a very varied collection and was ideally placed, on the eve of the French Revolution, to summarize this sort of literature in its most entertaining productions.

It is worth paying some attention to the educational utopia: After all, is Jean-Jacques Rousseau's *Emile* (1762) anything else? Education was one of the rare fields where–apart from the poor, who were very often deprived of education–people had enough elbow room, at least in some countries, to emancipate themselves from the obstacles of the past. It came into its own in the age of Pestalozzi, Rousseau, Basedow, Campe, Bell and Lancaster, and it did so without official support. *Robinson Jeune* [Young Robinson], as told by Campe, a book that was widely known throughout Germany for a century, is one of these practical, educative utopias, but the tradition of the educational utopia was interrupted by the genre of the educational novel, as in Goethe's *Wilhelm Meister's Lehrjahre* [Wilhelm Meister's Apprenticeship] and *Wanderjahre* [Journeyman Years], and Christoph Martin Wieland's novels of princely education, such as *Der goldne Spiegel oder die Könige von Scheschian* [The Golden Mirror, or the Kings of Scheschia] (1772). Wieland used the utopian form a lot even without mentioning his unfinished projects. It would be useful to consult Dr. Oskar Vogt's "Der goldne Spiegel und Wielands politische Ansichten" [The Golden Mirror and Wieland's Political Views] and "Louis-Sébastien Merciers Beziehungen zur deutschen Literatur" [Louis-Sébastien Mercier's Connections to German Literature] by Oskar Zollinger. Of the French texts that particularly call for a return to nature, I remember Henri-Joseph Du Laurens' two-volume *Imirce, ou la fille de la nature* [Imirce, or the Daughter of Nature] (1765) (published under the pseudonym of Modeste Tranquille Xan-Xung), and Gaspard Guillard de Beaurieu's two-part *Elève de la nature* [Student of Nature] (1764), a book that has been occasionally reprinted.

It is worth noting, too, the influence of the allegorical, spiritual story that is still a type of utopia, such as Voltaire's famous *Candide* (1759), his *Zadig* (1747), and his *Micromegas* (1752). These works created an entire subgenre of imitations. Pierre-Sylvain Maréchal created the utopian country of the Arcadian shepherds who were patriarchs and anarchists at the same time. His *L'age d'or* [The Golden Age] (1782) written under the pseudonym of Sylvain the Shepherd includes the sweetest pastoral utopian anarchism.

His *Premières Leçons du fils aîne d'un roi* [First Lessons for the Eldest Son of a King] (1789) presents an entire educative utopia through anecdotes, one of which even contains a serious lesson about a general strike, perhaps the first evocation of this idea after *Servitude Volontaire* [Voluntary Servitude] by Etienne de La Boétie in the sixteenth century (1576). And a few years later, in the year II, on October 18, 1793, Maréchal's theatrical work *La Jugement dernier des rois. Prophétie en un acte* [The Last Judgement against the Kings. A Prophecy in One Act] was performed—a piece in which the kings of the era and the empress Catherine II are forced to disembark on a deserted island where truths are told, where they argue, and where, finally, a volcano blows up and devours everything.

When one considers the period leading up to 1789–1793, which has been reached in this discussion by a very quick look at some utopias, we see periods of energy and periods of decline, and also how a work that emphasizes freedom sits next to one which stresses authority. So, we have Plato and Zeno, followed by More and Rabelais, followed by Vairasse and de Foigny, followed by Morelly and [Fontenelle], the author of *Ajaoiens*, and even later, next to authoritarians such as Rousseau and even Voltaire, there are Diderot and Sylvain Maréchal. The voice calling for freedom is weaker, less frequent, it should be noted, given the frightening degree to which the authoritarian infection has spread throughout humanity. Yet, freedom has always been there when it has been needed, and it always will be.

In order to judge the effect of the great utopias, it would be worthwhile, first of all, to examine if other socialist literature, either theoretical or propagandistic, was available to the public at the same time as utopias were. One would probably find that there were very, very few such texts, and if socialism is disseminated in some books, those books are only lightly colored with it. There were very few, often nearly no, specialized publications that were readily available. There were no socialist newspapers, almost no books, leaflets, or manifestos (published at great risk in times of crisis) while utopias circulated quite freely. At least, I don't remember reading of memorable persecutions of utopians. And so, these utopias were a vehicle for ideas that did the best that they could do at the time, and one gets the impression that it was not for want of public interest that there was little socialist literature, but that there were too few authors capable of writing such texts. In fact, there were More, Bacon, Campanella, Harrington, Vairasse, de Foigny, Morelly [Fontenelle], the author of *Ajaoiens*, Retif, but few others. In England, the literature of social reform stops for a period after Winstanley. Then, there are Hobbes, Locke, Hume (one of whose discourses is titled, "The Idea of a Perfect Government" [1752]), and a group of classical and pre-classical economists and very good socialist authors and socialist pamphleteers in the eighteenth century. In France, there is enough economic literature but little social-reform literature during this time; indeed, social criticism is found most often in books of moral criticism and free thought.

In short, I think that utopia fulfilled its mission in previous centuries. It was a beacon that, for the most part brilliantly, illuminated humanity and showed it the way to the future. Without it where would poor humanity have strayed since humanity is so insecure about the route to follow and runs in place when it doesn't retreat?!

Chapter 4

THE NINETEENTH CENTURY (TO 1888)

What produced a lengthy eclipse in utopian writing was the fact that public life after the end of the eighteenth century was largely open. This openness offered a more direct means of propagating ideas than the literary platform offered by utopian thinking. In England, at least at first sight, there was an intense political life: pamphlets and newspapers, discourses and associations. In France, the year 1789 saw the entire bourgeoisie and large sections of the citizenry enter into public life, which until that time had been reserved for an elite. Assemblies, clubs, newspapers, pamphlets provided a direct means by which thousands of diverse ideas could be heard. Things changed from day to day so there was no time [for utopian thinking], even though much time was wasted in high-sounding discussions, in allegorical phraseology, in imitation of the ancients. However, these were novelties, and the public was avid for them; they had had enough of a century of a literature of allusions, of cleverly hidden satire. And then, too, there was this: the public was fascinated by constitutions and legislation, and were distrustful of social questions since there was still a lack of material goods. There was poverty, hunger, famine, speculation, and hoarding, and in this situation and with a strengthened, better-off bourgeoisie, nothing less than true social reform was looked for. The State used violence—in the form of the Draconian dictatorship of the committees—to intervene, but the State was as horrified by the speculators as by the hungry, by the hoarders as by the agrarian law. And if they cut the heads off the entire class of traditional farmers, they would also have to cut off the head of Babeuf, the only socialist who remained standing and did not hide his opinions behind a vague idea of an ultra-patriotism for everyone, what could be called "howling with the wolves."

The tender flower of utopia could not flourish under these conditions; there was only a cynical utopianism that confirmed the triumph of the strictly antisocial bourgeoisie. That sort of utopianism is seen in that massive two-volume work by Pierre-Paul Le Mercier de la Rivière, *L'heureuse nation, ou relations de gouvernement des Féliciens; peuple souverainement libre sous l'empire absolu de seês loix* [The Happy Nation, or Governmental Relations under the Feliciens—A People Free and Sovereign under the Absolute Rule of Law] (1792). The utopian form also was used by the reactionaries and the moderates to cloak their polemics: this is the origin of what I would call the *anti-utopia*, which was meant to make the reader start in horror at specious conclusions and supposedly advanced ideas. This reaction to advanced ideas continually served its purpose. For example, the royalist François Louis Suleau published his *Voyages en l'air* [Travels through the Air] (1791), and Cousin Jacques (L.-A. Beffroy de Reigny) published his *La constitution de la Lune; rêve politique et moral* [The Constitution of the Moon, a Political and Moral Dream] (1793). The latter's play *Nicodème dans la Lune* [Nicodemus on the Moon] was performed hundreds of times between 1790 and 1796. Much later, moderates such as J. de Sales (*Ma république* [My Republic,1800]) and even the archbourgeois economist Jean Baptiste Say (*Olbie, ou essai sur les moyens de rèformer les moeurs d'une nation* [Olbie, or an Essay on How to Reform the Mores of a Nation, 1800]) made utopias seem colorless.

In order to move away from the present, refuge was once again sought in the past. Sylvain Maréchal, the pastoral anarchist and the comrade of Babeuf, began to compile the many volumes of his *Viaggi di Pitagora* [The Voyages of Pythagoras] (1827). These showed the intellectual aspirations of the ancients, and Maréchal reunited free-thinking men in his great *Dictionnaire des athées* [The Atheists' Dictionary] (1799).

The Empire of Napoleon I had no love for authors. It knew that it was despised by intellectuals (what it termed *ideologues*), and it sniffed out satire everywhere. Utopias from this time are, indeed, very rare and not widely disseminated. The regime seized nearly every copy of a book undoubtedly written in honor of Napoleon, in which the authors, Jaunez-Sponville and Bugnet, wished to attribute to him a triumphant social mission much greater than his triumphant military mission: *La philosophie du Ruvarebohni* [Ruvarebohni's Philosophy] (1809); reprinted in 1881 as *La Ruvarebohni (le vrai bonheur), réédité d'après un exemplaire èchappé pilon de la haute police imperial* [The Ruvarebohni (The Truly Happy), Reissued after a Classic Escape from the Imperial Police]. Only 25–50 copies exist of the first volume of Charles-Hélion Barbançois-Villegongis's *Le rêve singulier ou la nation comme il n'y en a point* [The Remarkable Dream or the Nation as It Has Never Been] (1808). *Les voyages de Kang-Hi ou nouvelles lettres chinoises* [The Travels of Kang-Hi or New Chinese Letters], by M. de Lévis, 1810—which describes Paris in 1910— is a reactionary book. I do not know what *Le vallon aérion ou relation du voyage d'un aéronaute dans un pays inconnu jusqu'à present, suivi de l'histoire de ses habitants et de la description de leurs moeurs* [The Valley in the Sky, or an Account of the Travels of an Aeronaut in a Country Unknown Until Now, Followed by the History of Its Inhabitants and a Description of Their Customs] by

[J.] Mosneron (1810) could be, except that it is—I know—a utopia set wholly in the time of Napoleon I, an era that, it is true, saw the first theoretical works of Saint-Simon and of Fourier, *Lettres d'un habitant de Genève [a ses contemporains]* [Letters of a Resident of Geneva to His Contemporaries] (1802) and *La théorie des quatre mouvements* [The Theory of Four Movements] (1808).

Over the rest of the continent of Europe, the hard times worked to kill off utopia and satire. These genres were mined quite a lot at times when there was some trust in reforms through the good will of monarchs who followed the example of the [Holy Roman] emperor Joseph II. He carried on a policy of religious tolerance, of anti-clericalism, and of reforms in the condition of the peasantry. He also minimized the system of censorship. For example, at that time, Sonnenfels often expressed himself in utopian form; later there would be Pezzl, Fessler, and others. The French example created a German republican movement, and when these German republicans saw the other countries unified in the same way that France was, the division of Germany into hundreds of small states and cities, each one imitating from top to bottom the way in which a great authoritarian state was organized, was seen as unbearable. This movement produced a great deal of satirical literature in diverse utopian forms by the likes of Rebmann, J. F. E. Albrecht, and many others who remain unknown or forgotten. These writings have not yet been examined for their possible social content. Examples are Carl I. Geiger's *Reise eines Erdbewohners in den Mars* [Journey of an Earthling to Mars] (1790), and the novelist Julius von Voss's *Ini: Roman aus dem 21 Jahrhundert* [Ini: A Novel of the Twenty-first Century] (1810). This satire includes the description of fictitious states or populated places which are notable for being ruled by very silly magistrates, similar, of course, to those who really existed and who were, thus, ridiculed. The Greeks had already created this form, focusing their satire on a place called Abdera. Wieland, who knew close up the life of his locality, Biberach, a small autonomous city that formed a small state in the south of Germany, took Biberach as a model for his *Geschichte der Abderiten* [History of the Abderites] (1781). The Schildbürgers and the inhabitants of Krähwinkel (both symbolizing the absurd) were also the object of continual laughter, which, in reality, expressed a disgust at the work of contemporary governments.

Another literary form which masked criticism was the animal fable, based principally on the kingdom of the animals as already established in the Middle Ages by authors who recorded the ancient fables of Aesop and others. This was a form in which governments and mores could be criticized indirectly, and it was based on the very old popular traditions about animals and nature, traditions dating from prehistoric times. At that time, humanity did not yet feel itself so separated from and above nature as it has felt since the priests carefully separated humanity from nature. This separation asserted humanity's superiority but weakened humanity through isolation and by a submission so much more complete to an autocratic god. The kingdom of the animals, was, then, established by the satire of the Middle Ages. In this sort of satire, the rebel element was represented by the fox, Reinecke der Fuchs [Reynard the Fox], who was beaten in the end (these authors were good little authoritarians after all) just as the devil is always outwitted in the end. Without a doubt, this kingdom of the animals offers a refuge for utopia and satire. On the margin of this genre are the animals that are purely invented, such as the later inventions of Jonathan Swift in *Gulliver's Travels.*

Criticism in the form of utopias attacks war and the monarchs who make a game of it amongst themselves. There is some vehement criticism in [Ange Goudar's] *Le procès de tres rois: Louis XVI de France-Bourbon, Charles III d'Espagne-Bourbon et Georges II d'Hanovre ...plaidé au tribunal des puissances européennes* [The Trial of the Three Kings: Louis XVI of France, Charles II of Spain, and the Hanoverian George II ... Conducted before a Tribunal of European Powers] (1780). The author is unknown, but it is believed that he was among the French authors who took refuge in London at the time of the French Revolution. We have seen Sylvain Maréchal in his *Jugement dernier des rois* [Last Judgment against Kings] (1793), where he finishes the kings off by putting them on a desert island where a volcano explodes. The novelist C. F. Van der Velde proceeds more gently in his short educational novel, *Die Heilung der Eroberungssucht* [Healing of the Wish for Conquest (1827). There are also N. J. Sarrazin's *Le retour du siècle d'or* [The Return of the Golden Century] (1816) and [James Fazy's] *Voyage d'Ertelib* [The Voyage of Ertelib (i.e., Liberty)] (1822).

A novel set in the time of the Renaissance, *Ardinghello* (1787) by the German poet Heinse, ends with a small utopia made up of a group of free pirates in the Greek islands. Another widely read novel, W. Fr. Meyern's *Dya-Na-Sore* (1789–1791), joins the subgenre of stories of symbolic Asian monarchies developed by Wieland. In 1800, the philosopher Fichte wrote *Der geschlossene Handelsstaat* [The State Closed to Trade]. This work does not have any utopian framework, but it does include the construction of a state. An Austrian philosopher, little known in his own time but later studied, Bernard Bolzano, wrote *Vom besten Staat* [On the Best State]. (See the study by Horacek in 1911).

The poet Klopstock chose the utopian form for *Die deutsche Gelehrtenrepublik. Ihre Einrichtung, ihre Gesetze* [The German Learnéd Republic. Its Construction, Its Laws] (1774). I don't know the tenor of *Le monde des Émiles* (the same *Émile* as Rousseau's) *ou l'education sociale* [Émile's World or Social Education] (1820). Among a good number of fantastic and satirical works, it's worth mentioning H. Bowman's *The Travels of Hildebrand Bowman, Esquire, into Carnovirria, Taupiniera,*

Olfactaria and Auditante in New-Zealand (1811). Then there is James Lawrence's utopian novel *The Empire of the Nairs* (about the Jews and the rights of women) (1811), a work which was read by Percy Bysshe Shelley. William Thomson's *The Man in the Moon* (1783) is a satire. Thomson is also the author of the curious *Mammuth* (1789). There is Lord Erskine's *Armata*, in two parts (1817), with Erskine being once a famous lawyer, and also John Trotter's *Travels in Phrenologasto* (1825). Among the many works I have not been able to see are Daniel A. Benda's *Die Felicier* [The Lucky One] (1827) and J. K. Friederich's *Dämonische Reisen in alle Welt* [Demonic Journeys throughout the World] (1847). (See the December 1895 issue of *Zeitschrift für Bücherfreunde* [Magazine for Friends of the Book].) In short, this subgenre was not stamped out, but played a minor role overshadowed by the huge amount of criticism that argued for *direct* action and for political and social renewal.

In essence, the methods that argue for more direct, sweeping action are those that render useless the roundabout routes characteristic of utopian teaching. In England above all, since the time of John Wilkes and Junius, of Thomas Paine and Godwin, of Byron and Shelley, men really used frank language, and popular propaganda was born on a large scale. There were books like *The Rights of Man* and *The Age of Reason*, by Thomas Paine, which, in the years of the French Revolution, were an indication of and a response to the growing interest that this great change promoted in England. A great many democratic and free-thinking works were widely disseminated at the time in spite of the persecutions, disseminated by tenacious and brave editors, by associations, and by those irrepressible propagandists who worked on their own. This dissemination really led to these ideas making their way into the ranks of the artisans and the petites bourgeois in the cities, and created a radicalism which was much later steered towards Chartism.

Also, at this time, Thomas Spence, the first socialist propagandist, appeared. Before him, a very intelligent socialist, Robert Wallace, author of a remarkably thoughtful socialist work published in 1761 [*Various Prospects of Mankind, Nature, Providence*], made his appearance, but he has to date attracted little notice. Spence had the true spirit of the propagandist; he was one who was inspired, perhaps by his consciousness of man's freedom, perhaps by the example of religious propaganda. Since the founding of unofficial churches during the seventeenth century, this propaganda had made its way directly to the people by means of a great many private preachers working in any local building or even outdoors. Spence adopted similar methods for his socialist propaganda: haranguing the people; selling his pamphlets or copies of his small newspaper full of the most advanced writings; publishing little utopias; holding conferences. He also struck copper coins, similar in size to a large sou, displaying pithy phrases summarizing ideas of his and embellished with an emblem or two. He also organized a group of Spencean propagandists who continued his work after his death. The utopian description of his future republic exists: "The Marine Republic" (1794) (a description of Spensonia) and *The Constitution of Spensonia* (1801), but these utopias are no more than ancillary to the propaganda, one method among several, and this is the position that utopias occupied for a long time to come in socialist propaganda.

The French Revolution and the earlier American Revolution exemplified change, and great changes occurred too as a result of the wars of 1792 and 1815. Social life was radically altered by the modern industrial system, with machinery everywhere, and by the birth of world trade. This alteration happened without hindrance in the years of peace after 1815, years that saw the collapse of the absolute secular power of Spain in foreign affairs from Mexico to Argentina, and saw Australia—that was still terre austral [the southern land] in eighteenth-century utopias—rapidly populated, even though it was only populated by criminals deported from England. As a result, during this time, too, a faith was born in the possibility that socialism could be directly achieved by coming down to earth from the clouds of utopia. What this [descent] meant was winning over opinion through economic study, through directing a rallying cry at the hearts of man, through the patient organization of the masses, through energetic groups engaged in popular agitation, and through conspiracy and rebellion. None of these were common then in England or France. In this great flowering, the direct utopia disappeared; its socialism was advocated for more straightforwardly. However, the utopia that I would call indirect or artificial, the sort of utopia which described an already established social system, this sort of utopia was coming back to life though it was not doing so on a grand scale, for there was too much to do already in terms of direct propaganda.

Thus, in essence, the desire for experiment replaced utopia, people burned with impatience, burned to have their ideas realized in the flesh and at once. Hundreds of times, Robert Owen explained his ideas in great detail and did as much as possible to prove their efficacy at New Lanark and, later, at New Harmony. He devoted a great deal of effort to those ideas, but never took the trouble as far as I know to write a single line of a utopia. Saint-Simon and Pierre Leroux were the same, as was Fourier, even though the last of these lived in a theoretical utopia to which his fantasy gave the plasticity of a real utopia. He glimpsed future developments in the several stages of perfecting society, developments which belong to the purest utopia. These founders of modern socialism, then, did not have the slightest inclination to write utopias: their ideas deserved and needed a much more practical application. For them, this characteristic meant not imposition by force (a dictatorship) but, on the contrary, practice suitably balanced by experiment.

It is truly strange and the height of ridiculousness that, later on, members of the school of Marx and Engels as well as Marx and Engels themselves—people who dreamed only of imposing *their* systems by a dictatorship—dared to call their own brutal method *scientific* socialism, a phrase which runs totally counter to what science is. Even as they did so, they called these founders of socialism whom I have mentioned, these *experimenters* who conformed to the scientific method, utopists (meaning fantasists), men without the least idea about science! Utopia and intentional community (phalanstery, colony, and so on) bear the same relationship with each other as hypothesis and experiment, and both are in the purview of science. Dictatorship is nothing; it means imposition by brute force whether by a czar or a Marx or a Lenin or a Mussolini—whoever the bludgeon. The social revolution, unleashing incalculable forces both visible and latent, will probably see both attempts at dictatorship and attempts at experiment as the two tendencies—and how many others within each tendency!—representing living forces, the power of which no one can calculate in a moment of great crisis at some unknown time in the future. Society will be dragged down towards ruin by dictatorship, but then it will be saved by the spirit that watches over experimentation, the spirit of science. We hope that this happens, thanks to the effort to create a state of mind which allows society to get beyond atavistic dictatorship.

Moving on to the more noteworthy examples of the socialism that has come into being since Thomas Spence's "Marine Republic" and *The Constitution of Spensonia*, America, which followed the pattern of English radicalism closely, produced in 1801–1802 a quite remarkable socialist utopia. It appeared in *The Temple of Reason*, a periodical published in Philadelphia. It appeared in book form in America as *Equality, or a History of Lithconia* (1837) and was written by James Reynolds. It was known in Europe in 1838 only through several extracts in the *New Moral World*, that great Owenite journal. It was perhaps the last of the great old-fashioned utopias, or, perhaps, it was the beginning of modern utopias. It has been too little studied. Another independent American product is J. A. Etzler's *The Paradise within the Reach of All Men, without Work, through the Power of Nature and Machinery* (1833). It doesn't have a utopian framework (dream or imaginary travel), but it does describe a new utopian America, one which has been transformed into a human paradise by the decentralized use of machines and by the power of nature in the hands of groups of free men. Later, I believe, there were many small intentional communities in North America because at that time people more often decided to found a community themselves than to write a book. Especially in the 1840s, there was a great number of experimental groups derived from eighteenth-century communities. They were the product of religious communism (Shakers, Rappites, and so on), or they were driven by the ideas of

Robert Owen and his New Harmony in the 1820s, by the Fourierists primarily in the 1840s, by the communism of Cabet and Weitling in the 1850s, and later by individualist anarchists such as Joseph Warren and others.

Many of these colonies have left some written accounts in newspapers and other small publications, which are unlocatable today. Some wrote accounts in well-established newspapers that have survived, especially the famous newspapers associated with New England intellectuals who joined Fourierist ideas to transcendentalist aesthetics, that is the men and women of Brook Farm. Their life has been symbolically described in the novel *The Blithedale Romance* (1852) by that famous author Nathaniel Hawthorne as well as in those journals with which David Henry Thoreau was associated. Thoreau's *Walden* (1854), about his life in the wilderness, is one of those utopias of genuine individualism by a man who lived his own life. Other notable utopian newspapers were Weitling's *Die Republic der Arbeiter* [The Worker's Republic], in which the efforts of the German experimental communists in the 1850s are described. Then there are the newspapers of the Icarians, which lasted almost 30 years. Finally, an old American who spent his life in communities, Alcander Longley, published *The Altruist* in Saint Louis from 1880 to about 1910, and another American, John Humphrey Noyes, in 1870, wrote the history of American socialism. In this work, Noyes gave a historical account of a large number of groups and made use of the notes of a Scot who had had the idea for a number of years of living life among these groups, one after another, and of relating their history in his personal anecdotes. Noyes himself belonged to the Oneida Community. *Lived* utopia was, indeed, so accessible—for example at Modern Times, which was no great distance from New York City itself— that until the time of Bellamy—1888—the written utopia was, I think, never really in vogue in the United States.

There is one memorable exception to this generalization: Joseph Déjacque's *Humanisphere*. This is a brilliant communist, anarchist utopia. It appeared in *Le libertaire* of New York in 1858–1859, and most of it was reprinted in Brussels in 1899. Déjacque had founded the newspaper in order to make publishing this text possible. It was the work of a recluse who was separated by language from English culture, was interested in the European revolution, and knew nothing more of America than the environment of a slave-owning New Orleans (at that time very corrupt) and the milieu of the French exiles in New York. In writing this first "anarchist utopia," Déjacque could not have been influenced by what he saw in America. He says the following: "My plan is to sketch a future society just as it appears to me," he says, "with individual liberty filtering anarchically into the community and producing harmony." He continues:

> I yearn for happiness and evoke the ideal. If this ideal makes you smile, do as I do: love it. If you find imperfections, correct them. If you are

displeased with it, create another. I do not exclude, and I will willingly abandon my vision for yours if yours seems more perfect to me. It's just that I see only two great images possible ... that is, absolute liberty or absolute authority. For myself, I have chosen liberty. As for authority, I have seen it in action, and I condemn its acts. It is an old prostitute who teaches only depravation and engenders only death. Liberty has not yet become known by more than its timid smile. It is a virgin whom the kiss of humanity has not yet made fertile; but if man lets himself be seduced by her charms, he will give her all his love, and very soon she will give birth to generations worthy of the great name she bears.

Here is the spirit in which to write and to read utopias, and, more than that, to have a hand in their realization.

I know very little about the vast literature on the ideas of Robert Owen and William Thompson. In this case, too, direct means were available for the cooperative associations and the communities founded here and there in England, Scotland, and Ireland, but there were no very well-known utopias. I hardly know if Joseph Marriott's play *Community* (1838) is one of them. In the small English communist groups, of which Goodwyn Barmby was the literary guiding spirit, a series from the Communitarian Library (which was created to gather together utopian texts) began with Greek fragments in 1842. Barmby wanted to bring out *The Book of Platonopolis*. Was it really published? In short, one could say that with propagandists of the intensity of Robert Owen, with Chartism and its modern revolutionary tendencies, with the birth of trade unionism and the projected founding of various communities in England—with all this going on, there were so many lively movements in the 1830s and 1840s that few men still felt the need to write utopias.

The first German socialists of the time dedicated all of their efforts to books, pamphlets, and propaganda newspapers so that the publication, in 1842, of a book as great as Weitling's *Garantien der Harmonie und Freiheit* [Guarantees of Harmony and Liberty] (1842) was as great an effort as the labor of hundreds of poor workers. Who among them would have had the leisure for utopias? There are utopias, perhaps, in their newspapers, such as *Europe en 2000* [Europe in 2000], which appeared in a magazine published by Weitling, but I have not made a complete investigation. When such an investigation is done, when we take a look at the literature— ephemeral, persecuted, the suppressed militant propaganda of a country— we will discover some utopias of which we know nothing more than the first few chapters or merely the intent to publish, for the newspapers and series produced by militant groups enjoyed only short duration. So, did the French communist [Jean-Jacques] Pillot, the one who was a member of the Paris Commune in 1781 and died in prison, did he publish his utopia *Félicie* [*Lucky*] in 1840, a text which deserves to be paired with his *Histoire des egaux* [History of Equals]? Probably not, and he is only one among many. One of the German communists of 1848, Johann Petzler, had never managed more than to publish his theoretical and utopian writings in his old age, works which were then like an echo of the old time. After a pamphlet of 1870 and the book *Social Architecture*, in English in 1876, he produced a German translation of the latter work, *Die soziale Baukunst* (1879–1880), in two large volumes. This text is, it should be noted in passing, the first communist book which, in 1881, fell into my hands in scattered installments. Petzler finally published his *Life in Utopia* in 1890, and another German utopia in 1897.

The Fourierists and Fourier himself continually gave descriptions of life in the phalanstery without, however, providing a utopian framework for them. One work with such a framework is Math Briancourt's *Visite au phalanstère* [Visit to a Phalanstery] (1848), and Antoine-Rose-Marius Sardat's *Loi d'union* [The Law of Union] (1847) is marginally utopian. From an old man of the Fourierist movements, J. Terson, there's *Idéalie* [The Ideal] (1882). I have not seen Vuilmet's *La cosmopolie ou la republique universelle* [Cosmopolis or the Universal Republic] (1869). I have been told it is by an old socialist, perhaps a Fourierist. The doctor Tony Moilin, martyr of the Commune of Paris, who was executed by firing squad in the Luxemburg Gardens, wrote *Paris en l'an 2000* [Paris in the Year 2000] (1867). Léonie Rouzade, a socialist, wrote *Voyage de Theodosie à l'ile de l'utopie* [Theodosie's Voyage to the Island of Utopia] (1872).

Everyone knows the most famous utopia of the first half of the nineteenth century: Etienne Cabet's *Icarie* [Icaria] (1849). The first edition bears this title: *Voyage et aventures de Lord Villiam Carisdall en Icarie, traduits de l'anglais de Francis Adams par Th. Dufruit, maître de langues* [The Voyage and Adventures of Lord William Carisdall in Icaria, Translated from the English of Francis Adams by Th. Dufruit, Master of Languages] (1840). This was an edition printed in 1838 but put into circulation in January 1840. The second edition (February 1842) is called *Voyage en Icarie* [Travels in Icaria]. There are several editions before 1848; a German translation (1847); and a great deal of literature that refers to the novel, for this work was one of those rare utopias which people tried to achieve through patience and self-denial but, nevertheless, met with many disappointments.

At the time of Herschel's discoveries in astronomy, in 1836, a lively pamphlet celebrating the occasion described the life of the men in the moon and other heavenly bodies [*Publication complète des nouvelles découvertes de Sir John Herschel dans le ciel austral et dans la Lune tr. de l'anglais* (Complete Report of the New Discoveries by Sir John Herschel in the Southern Sky and on the Moon tr. from English)]. This pamphlet, which also exists in German (1836), is by Victor Considerant and so will bear the stamp of the best-argued Fourierism of this epoch. I am not familiar with it. It is known what efforts Considerant took with the Fourierist colony in Texas. There were the four issues by him of *Au Texas* [To Texas] (1854–1855), and the report *Du Texas* [On Texas] (1857). There is also a pamphlet from June 1856 where this colonization effort is criticized in a lively fashion by men of anti-authoritarian tendencies.

A new utopian genre is represented by *Uchronie*, which first appeared in the *Revue philosophique et religieuse* [Philosophical and Religious Review], the organ of the old men of the pre-1848 socialist school. It ran as a serial beginning in May 1857, but it probably is not a complete text in the *Revue*. The text appears in a book form as *Uchronie (l'utopie dans l'histoire). Esquisse historique apocryphe du developpément de la cvilisation européenne tel qu'il n'a pas été, tel qu'il aurait pu étre* [Uchronie (utopia in history). An Apocryphal Historical Outline of European Civilization—What It Never Was, What It Could Have Been] (1876; second ed., 1901). Its author is the well-known philosopher, Charles Renouvier. He takes the date of a particular battle in which, if I am not mistaken, the Romans triumphed definitively over the Gauls (or was it a battle between the Francs and the Gallo Romans?). At the end, it describes how, without the use of force, a free and happy Europe could have developed over time from the elements that make it up. This narrative frame is reminiscent of Retif de La Bretonne's *Les rêvies: suivi de "Les converseuses"* [The Reborn; Sequel to "The Conversationalists," 1798–1799].

The utopias which are clearly socialist and date from before 1888—I will take the massive push given to the utopian genre by Bellamy's book as a point of departure for the next chapter in this work—are few in number since propaganda and direct organization absorbed the efforts of socialists. Also, little by little these [utopian writers] came, in my opinion, to be a little too certain of their facts, believing themselves to possess the definitive program to be achieved in the future—a *ne varietur* [not to be varied] idea of the future. So, no more need for utopia! I think that this was a mistake. The authoritarians were clearly the first to abandon utopia by putting dogma in its place. The anti-authoritarians wasted themselves on propaganda and action but did, nevertheless, express their utopian ideas a few times. Coeurderoy asked for nothing less than utopia, and in the second volume of his *Jours d'exil* [Days of Exile] (1854–1855), he gave some extracts from *constructive* parts of his assemblage of ideas that he planned to write after he had written the *destructive* parts. The celebration of regenerated humanity in Lisbon forms part of this text. James Guillaume composed an outline, *Une commune sociale in der Almanach jurassien* [A Social Community in the Almanach Region] in 1871, and he elaborated on his ideas in the pamphlet of the same title in 1876.

The discussions about public service in the society of the future within the anti-authoritarian Internationale are very well known. They lack a utopian framework, of course, but everyone has their own opinion about the society of the future. Kropotkin added a conclusion on the social revolution and the society of the future to a Russian pamphlet written for the peasants in 1872 or 1873. This was, perhaps, his first expression of opinion on the subject which he treated so intensely in the constructive volume, *La conquête du pain* [The Conquest of Bread] (1892), which followed on from his destructive volume, *Paroles d'un révolté* [Words of a Rebel] (1885). He wrote in the *Le révolté* [Revolt], from November 30–December 28, 1889, a series titled "Le vingtième siècle" [The Twentieth Century] to mark the publication of Bellamy's book [*Looking Backward*]. Andrea Costa, already won over to socialism by that time, wrote in an Italian almanac for 1882 a short utopia, *Un sogno* [A Dream] reprinted many times in pamphlet form (1900; 1910). Dr. Giovanni Rossi is the author of *Un comune socialista* [A Socialist Community], published in 1878 under the pseudonym of Cardias. A later edition published in Liorna in 1891 also contains *La colonia Cecilia* [The Cecilia Colony]. This is a utopia that he intended to bring into being, and I will speak of it later.

Let us mention the following. *La liquidation sociale. Prophetie* [The Disintegration of Society. A Prophecy] (1872) is collectivist anarchistic in its point of view, but its author, V. Cyrille, later came to a bad end. *Etymonia* (1875) is socialist. There is Henry Wright's *Mental Travels in Imagined Lands* (1878); and *Lumène ou la fille des grands martyrs* [Lumène or the Daughter of the Great Martyrs] (1881) by the ex-abbot François Junqua, which was dramatized in 1895. An Austrian, Ferdinand Amersin, expressed independent socialist ideas in books published in Graz and Trieste in 1871 [*Weisheit und Tugend des reinen Menschenthums* (The Wisdom and Virtue of Pure Humanity)], 1874, and 1881; and *Gemeinverständliche weisheitslehre (wahrheits- klugheits- und geschmackslehre)* [The Easy to Understand Doctrine of Wisdom (Truth, Sagacity, and Taste)]. One of these, *Das Land der Freiheit* [The Land of Freedom] (1874), is a utopia while the other two contain theoretical explications. There are still more writings of a socialist tendency from this epoch, but I will stop here.

I move on to the descriptions of a glimpsed future which are not socialist. I have chosen the most characteristic, and there are many of these. So, there is *Le monde nouveau* [The New World] (1831) by Rey-Dussueil, author of *La fin du monde* [The End of the World] (1831); *Le roman de l'avenir* [The Novel of the Future] (1834) by Felix Bodin, a deputy; Lous Desnoyers' "Paris révolutionné" [Paris under Revolution], in the great collection *Paris révolutionaire* [Revolutionary Paris] (1834; vol. 4: 419–475); Theophile Gautier's "Paris futur "[Paris of the Future], in the collection *Le diable à Paris* [The Devil in Paris] (1845); Victor Hugo's chapter titled "L'avenir" [The Future], which constitutes five pages (I–V) of his introduction to the *Paris guide* (May 1867); the Comte de Villedeuil's *Paris à l'envers* [Paris Upside Down] (1853), which is a criticism of civilization by a fictional Australian traveler; Henri Le Hon's "L'an 7860 de l'ère chrétienne" [The Year 7860 of the Christian Era], which appeared in the *Revue trimestrielle* [The Quarterly Review] in July 1860; Edouard Laboulaye's *Paris en Amerique* [Paris in America] (1863), which appeared in a German translation in 1868 [*Paris in Amerika*]; Jacques Fabien's *Paris en songe* [Paris in Dreams] (1863); G. Descottes' *Voyage dans les Planètes* [Voyage among the Planets] (1864); Alexandre Cathelineau's *Voyage à la Lune d'apres un manuscrit authentique projeté d'un volcan lunaire* [Voyage to the Moon Based on an Authentic Manuscript Hurled into Space by a Lunar Volcano] (1865); Dr. Hippolyte Mettais' *L'an 5865, ou Paris dans quatre mille ans* [The Year 5865, or Paris in Four Thousand Years' Time] (1865); Alfred Franklin's *Les ruines de Paris en 4875* [The Ruins of Paris in 4875] (1875); Antonin Rondelet's *Mon voyage au pays des Chimères* [My Voyage to the Land of the Chimeras] (1875); J. G. Prat's *Voyages et aventures d'Almanarre* [The Voyages and Adventures of Almanarre] (1876); Pierre Véron's *En 1900* [In 1900] (1878); and Georges Pellerin's *Le Monde dans deux mille ans* [The World in Two Thousand Years] (1878).

We note that Charles Dickens—according to a letter to his friend John Forster in 1839—conceived at that time a plan of writing *The Relaxations of Gog and Magog* about the London of the past and the future, a plan he never executed. He also proposed to write satirical articles supposedly taken from the chronicles of a savage people on the administration of justice in an imaginary country. J. Silk Buckingham, a very thoughtful man, proposed in 1848 a regeneration of the cities by means of associations, ideas half utopian and half practical, which town planning (thoughtful projects for the construction of urban spaces) of Garden Cities has since partly realized. Buckingham's ideas were published as *National Evils and Practical Remedies with the Plan for a Model City* (1849). Robert Pemberton's *The Happy Colony* (1854) seems also to have been written with a practical application in mind while we soar to a perfect utopia with Sydney Whiting's *Helionde: or, Adventures in the Sun* (1855), a utopia which loves beauty. There is H. J. Forrest's *A Dream of Reform* (1848) and a very well-known utopia by the famous novelist Bulwer-Lytton, *The Coming Race*, which was first published anonymously in 1871 and has been often reprinted. *Erewhon or Over the Range* (1872) (*Erewhon* being almost *Nowhere* or on the other side of the mountains) is by the English satirist Samuel Butler.

It was translated into German as *Ergindwon* (1879). There is a continuation of the story, *Erewhon Revisited: Twenty Years Later* (1901).

Kurd Lasswitz has written very elaborate German utopian novels situated on other planets (most famously *Auf zwei Planeten* [On Two Planets] in 1897). The Hungarian novelist Mór Jókai published *Der Roman des kunftigen Jahrhunderts* [The Story of the Coming Century] (1879). Berthold Auerbach proposed to write about an "Ideal Colony," an old project he said (letter dated June 3, 1875), but it was never done. Nearly every writer thinks about such a project at one time or another. We still have to mention *A Journey to the Sun* (1866) by "Heliomanes"; *Anno 2066: Ein Blick in die Zukunft* [The Year 2066: A Look into the Future] (1866) from Dr. Dioscorides (pseud. of Pieter Harting), a work which was translated from the Dutch; Thomas Lee's *Falsivir's Travels* (1886); and William Westall's *The Phantom City: A Volcanic Romance* (1886).

A reactionary text (as cited in many works) is Francesco Vigano's *Viaggio nell'universo. Visioni del tempo e dello spazio* [A Trip around the Universe. Visions of Time and Space] (1838; new ed., 1885). The Italians, absorbed in their national struggles, have not paid attention to the utopian genre. At least, apart from some satirical works I have found no indication of true utopias from the era in question. For Spanish-language countries, I refrain from giving an opinion because I have had very little opportunity to do research. This caveat also applies to many other countries—North America and the Scandinavian countries above all. I remember now that a Danish professor, Sibbern, a Hegelian and a moderate socialist, wrote in the 1850s a socialist utopia with some philosophy mixed in. I have not had the courage to read it, but if one were trying to find utopias of a slightly boring type, it would be on the list. The pages of the copy in the British Museum have not been cut, and as I have avoided opening it, it still awaits a reader. If I have wronged this worthy man, I beg his pardon.

We still have the specialized utopias, for example, works about women within imaginary frameworks, such as A. A. Henlau's *Ambisexia, das land der entjochten Frauen* [Ambisexia, the Land of Unyoked Women] (1848); Mme. Hermance Lesguillon's *Les Femmes dans cent ans* [Women in One Hundred Years] (1859); and Léonie Rouzade's *Le monde renversé* [The World Reversed] (1872).

Works of a satirical sort include the Austrian author Eduard von Bauernfeld's *Die Republik des Thiere* [The Republic of Beasts] (1848) and Louis Veuillot's *Le lendemain de la victoire: vision* [The Day after the Victory: A Vision] (1850). Veuillot was a reputed cleric who, in *L'esclave Vindex* [Vindex the Slave] (1849), told many truths that were hard for the bourgeoisie to stomach. Many extracts from this work were published in the literary supplement *La révolte* [Revolt]. Then there is Paschal Grousset's *La rêve d'un irréconciliable* [The Discordant Dream] (1869), which first appeared in *Diable-à-quatre* [The Devil to Pay] from August 20, 1869; Léon Bienvenu's *Histoire de la France tintamarresque: De 1887 à ... la fin du monde* [A Tintamarresque History of France from 1887 to the End of the World] (1868, 1886) with the satirical mode of *tintamarre* [lit., "uproar"] denoting Bienvenu's particular style when writing as "Touchatout." This book is a continuation of Bienvenu's history of France from the most remote times. It is in the same inimitable style, full of verve, a style which also infuses his *Trombinoscope* (1871) and the rest of his writings. They are perfect in their irreverence towards constitutional authority.

There has also been a literature produced under the guise of utopia or a vision of the future. This literature prepared popular opinion for future wars. The subgenre begins with [George Chesney's] *The Battle of Dorking* (*Blackwood's Magazine* May 1871). It includes cries of anti-socialist alarm such as [Bracebridge Hemyng's] *The Commune in London, or in Thirty Years* (1871) as well as the extraordinary profusion of such works in Paris from 1848 to 1851. Modern science was fought over, too, in a Dutch work *Darwinia* (1878) [by "Jan Holland"] as was free trade in other books. Some writings in this subgenre are issued so as to anticipate reactions, such as André Léo's *La commune de Malenpis. Conte* [Malenpis Colony. A Tale] (1874). This subgenre also includes many didactic short stories written 40 years earlier in London by Harriet Martineau as well as *Das Goldmacher-Dorf* [The Goldmaker's Village] (1819) and similar writings by the German, later Swiss, writer Heinrich Zschokke. These were published over a long period. Last, there is *The True History of Joshua Davidson, Christian and Communist* (1872). This novel was written by Elizabeth Lynn Linton. It is a book of humanitarian sentiments and was thought very provocative for its time.

It is useless to record the scurrilities of anti-utopias that were phobic towards socialism.

There is a small book printed as a real jewel under the imprint of the Chiswick Press, London: *The Island of Anarchy: A Fragment of History in the Twentieth Century* (1887) by Elizabeth Waterhouse. She is the same sweet author who published *The Brotherhood of Rest* (1889), the contents of which I no longer remember. *The Island of Anarchy* describes the deportation in 1887 of anarchists to an island where they kill each other and where Kropotkin alone survives. He languishes there down the ages—a crueler fate than that reserved by Sylvain Maréchal for royalty in his *Jugement dernier des rois*!

Utopia in all its numerous varieties was not extinguished in any way in the nineteenth century although the many new forms of publicity and propaganda as well as the scientific approach and the emphasis on direct and intensive research that characterized the century did markedly decrease the interest shown in the genre in [comparison to] earlier centuries. Then it was nearly the only means—apart from scientific works inaccessible to the outsider—of dealing with advanced questions. We have already seen the genre suffers from flux and reflux: a new soaring was to come to pass in 1888 with Bellamy's utopia, *Looking Backward*.

Chapter 5

1888 TO THE TWENTIETH CENTURY

At the beginning of 1888, utopian literature received an abrupt and extraordinary renewal from the publication of the book *Looking Backward 2000–1887* by the American writer Edward Bellamy. An edition published in Boston and New York (Riverside Paper Series, September 21, 1889) is called the 220 thousandth. By the beginning of 1890, cheap English reprintings were everywhere: there were four editions at one time. In 1896, a penny edition was produced by Manchester Labour Press; in Germany, the book was published in the most popular and cheap book series at that time, and it has been very widely available ever since then. There have been numerous other translations, and in 1897 there was another book by Bellamy, a sequel, which offers further explanations: *Equality*. It is a better novel than *Looking Backward* as far as theory is concerned, but it has neither the verve nor the narrative drive of the earlier work. It did not seize the imagination of the general public as intensely.

However, the immense success of the book by 1889 shows that a well-constructed utopia knows how to reach the public by the hundreds of thousands in a way that theoretical books and pamphlets do not. There are scarcely two or three socialist books that rise above the level of propaganda: There is August Bebel's *Die Frau und der Sozialismus: Die Frau in der Vergangenheit, Gegenwart, und Zukunft* [Woman and Socialism: Woman in the Past, Present, and Future] (1891) and Robert Blatchford's *Merrie England* (1894). I won't undertake to name others, save the contemporary works of Bertrand Russell; but, what has the circulation been of books by Octave Mirbeau, by Anatole France, by Upton Sinclair, by Tolstoy, and so on?! Educational or didactic literature can't do everything; ideas demand to be adorned by art and imagination. The public is not only avid for sensations and rather uninterested in quality, but also curiosity about and desire for a better future have not died out. The public follow those books which have an air of improving the human character. What interest did Camille Flammarion find when, in popularizing astronomy, he cast all of the problems—those concerned with the habitability of the other planets—in a mystical light that excited curiosity?

His book *Les mondes imaginaries et les mondes réels. Voyage pittoresque dans le ciel* [Imaginary Worlds and Real Worlds. A Picturesque Journey in the Heavens] (1865, 1905) also summarizes utopian fantasies about other worlds. The wise Swiss Svante Arrhenius has revived this interest through hypotheses which stimulated the imagination of utopians such as Kurd Lasswitz in his *Sternentau: Die Pflanze vom Neptunsmond* [The Dew of the Stars: Plants from the World of Neptune] (1909) or even [Jean-Henri] Fabre when he uncovered the life of insects while others specialized in bees and ants. Wilhelm Bölsche introduced us to the love life of animals. Others such as Andrew Lang popularized folklore and the mysteries of narrative, those perpetual enigmas that have always excited interest. This ample curiosity and vague desire to advance towards the unknown are well illustrated by the very great interest shown for a quarter century in the writings of Jules Verne, who was a virtuoso far more than a professional, not a man of ideas but a conservative who was always meddling with the most advanced problems—above all those of the entire structure of utopia and its component parts (both scientific and mechanical) and new worlds. He even touched lightly on social questions.

In North America, the great development of capitalism has made the public alert and curious. They did not listen to what the socialists and anarchists had to say, and the movement—from the first of May 1, 1886 to the martyrdom of the Chicago anarchists on November 11, 1887—could not make itself understood by the public, which remains under the instruction of its newspapers and capitalist politicians. By contrast, however, some people knew how to capture the public's interest by presenting their ideas in a form which, in one way or another, rose above the level of didactic or one-sided propaganda. There was, in the 1880s, above all Henry George and his assertion of a unique remedy, the single tax, the tax on the land, a panacea. For some time, there was Terence Powderley and the Knights of Labor, and there was, in 1888, Bellamy's *Looking Backward* and the question of the applicability of its ideas. In many ways, these people and their ideas for change, which were not very advanced at all, struck a chord which the advanced ideas thoroughly and honestly presented by the Chicago anarchists and by Johann Most were not able to strike. I come to this conclusion—it is not because the ideas, the intellectual calibre, the prejudices of the public must be respected, but because there are ways of presenting a cause to the public that people other than ourselves know how to find easily and which we do not know how to find. If we did, our cause would be better known around the world.

Bellamy, who was not a socialist but a disinterested observer of social life, saw two things: the immense and continuous mechanical progress due to cooperation, which was technically so well organized by the forces of labor guided by experts; and the inevitable economic evolution, if it is not stopped, by means of which all the wealth of the United States will fall into the hands of either individual capitalists or consolidated powers (i.e., trusts). Bellamy concluded that nationalization (i.e., socialization) of the instruments of labor and of natural, social wealth would be imposed and that then, thanks to perfected cooperation, everyone would enjoy a level of well-being accessible today only to those who are privileged. He did not concern himself with the question of freedom and was satisfied that in such a society the political powers would have nothing to do and that the industrial powers, guided by science and experience, would know how to do what was right.

These very simple ideas really struck home with the public and their achievement was called for by them. Bellamy began these efforts and created a movement called Nationalism which would return to the nation that which the privileged cornered for themselves. See, for example, Bellamy's article, "What 'Nationalism' Means" in the *Contemporary Review* (July 1890: 1–18), and also his monthly magazine *The Nationalist* as well as a number of other propaganda newspapers in Washington DC, Chicago, Denver, Los Angeles, San Francisco, and so on. Then there is Bellamy's mature and thoughtful explanations of his ideas in *Equality* (1897). Since then, the enthusiasm has ebbed and the propaganda in support of nationalism has died out.

In those first years, there was a lively discussion of Bellamy's ideas in pamphlets and scurrilous anti-utopias. There were utopias rapidly produced to take advantage of the opportunity, and there was socialist and anarchist critique. As far as I can remember those times, assessing them solely from my point of view today, they achieved almost the opposite of what they might perhaps have done. For the first time, the [socialist] movement was faced with widespread interest in questioning monopoly capitalism; it would have been necessary to find a means of reinforcing—of intensifying— this interest, but it was said quickly to Bellamy and his followers everywhere: "We, socialists, have been saying all this for a long time, you have only to join our party." Or other objections were made, with each person staying where he was, in his own party, and inviting everyone to join that party. That never happened. The anarchists of the time were too indignant about the judicial assassinations in Chicago, and they found Bellamy's statism repugnant. It would be worthwhile to reread the impressions of Kropotkin in "Le vingtiéme siècle" [The Twentieth Century] (*La révolte* [November 30 to December 28, 1889]). I know that Kropotkin later read *Equality* (1897) with great interest, and he spoke very highly of it. So, traditional socialism held on above all to its dignity and did not trouble itself with Bellamy nor Bellamy with it, so it was then necessary, in representing Marxist theory, to scorn utopia totally. Bebel just tolerated it. In his *Die Frau und der Sozialsmus* [Woman and Socialism] and in his *Charles Fourier: sein Leben und seine Theorien*

[Charles Fourier: His Life and His Theories] (1883), Bebel showed an interest in utopia that was considered less than scientific by the guardians of theory.

No doubt, the impetus caused by Bellamy brought other good utopias to life which, without it, would never have seen the light of day or would not have been paid attention to as they were. The most notable of these utopias is William Morris's *News from Nowhere*. At that time [when he wrote the novel], Morris belonged to the Socialist League in London. The novel first appeared in *The Commonweal* (January 11– October 4, 1890), the organ of that revolutionary socialist group, to which many anarchists belonged. *News from Nowhere or an Epoch of Rest, Being Some Chapters from a Utopian Romance* was published as a book in 1891. There were other editions, too, one of them published in a famously artistic way by the Kelmscott Press. In that edition, every letter and every ornament were designed by Morris. There were also many translations of *News from Nowhere*. It is one of the most gracious of all utopias combining, as it does, Morris's artistic ideas with his largely libertarian socialism, for he never espoused anarchism. He knew, as an artist and an artisan, to what degree work and individual and collective thought intertwined to achieve productions of a high standard that mattered greatly to him. Then there's also this thoroughly amorphous anarchism of which he is sometimes understood to have been the precursor but which did not satisfy him. However, this labeling is just a question of semantics. His utopia is honestly libertarian and one of the most beautiful in existence.

He had already described a small scene from the day after the Revolution in a satirical piece, *The Tables Turned; or, Nupkins Awakened: A Socialist Interlude*, which was performed by him and his comrades on October 15, 1887 and repeated several times after that, and he brought back to life some scenes of rebellion from the Middle Ages in *A Dream of John Ball* (1888). Unfortunately, in the autumn of the same year as the first publication of his utopia, 1890, the disintegration of the Socialist League constrained Morris's actions so much that he soon almost completely withdrew into his beautiful poetry and left the Kelmscott Press. He died in 1896. So, this utopia, *News from Nowhere*, was almost his swan song for the vast socialist movement to which he had single-mindedly devoted himself for eight or nine years.

Another utopia of the same year, 1890, is very curiously libertarian, even though the author was a bourgeois economist of some renown, Dr. Theodor Hertzka (who died in 1924): *Freiland, ein soziales Zukunftsbild* [Freeland, the Picture of a Socialist Future] (1890). The preface is dated 1889. Subsequent editions were abridged, and the 10th edition is dated 1896. He also wrote [a sequel to *Freiland*] *Eine Reise nach Freiland* [A Visit to Freeland] (1893) and *Entrückt in die Zukunft. Sozialisticher Roman* [Exiled in the Future. A Socialistic Novel] (1887). Various periodicals in Vienna, Amsterdam,

Copenhagen, London, and New York tell the story of all the phases in Hertzka's movement, a movement which united a great many enthusiasts over several years. Hertzka's idea was to found an associationist colony on new terrain, fertile and isolated, a colony with sufficient means to begin work on a grand scale. Hertzka wanted to achieve the maximum of freedom compatible with the greatest well-being of each member by free access to all of the proposed association colonies. He reasoned that the diminished benefits of associations which were full of members would be balanced by the attractions offered at each colony. So, he proposed complete and, as it were, automatic liberty, guaranteed by institutions and independent of personality. This system, called "Sozialliberalismus" [social liberalism], is definitely one way to achieve a maximum amount of personal freedom with a minimum amount of friction, all within associations where technical experience would maintain a high level of efficiency. It is, if you like, both socialism and anarchy together, but only a businessman would try to achieve it. This colony would have been created on the Kenya plateau, which because of its height provides a temperate climate in eastern Africa. The land was under English control, and the English government, which was asked to allow this colonization, prohibited it. No other location was found. So, the hundreds of men brought together for this purpose dispersed. No other modern European colonization movement was so ready to act as this one.

As a consequence of Hertzka's movement, there was much discussion in Germany of the *Siedlungsgenossenschaften* (cooperative colonies). Notably, Dr. Franz Oppenheimer sought to develop this idea while rejecting Marxism because he sensed the need for freedom. He first wrote *Freiland in Deutschland* [Freeland in Germany] (1895). This work encouraged Hertzka's followers to found their freeland community on Germany soil itself, and he published tomes in which he studied in depth these questions posed by agrarian associations.

An old German manufacturer, Michael Flürscheim, at the same time predicted the agrarian colony in books and pamphlets and in the utopia *Deutschland in 100 Jahren oder die Galoschen des Glücks: ein soziales Märchen* [Germany in 100 Years or the Lucky Galoshes: A Social Fairy Tale] (1887). Flürscheim later devoted himself entirely to this idea and made long trips to Mexico and New Zealand to look at existing colonies. He also always recognized the need for freedom in these enterprises. These men, Hertzka, Oppenheimer, Flürscheim, were all searching for a synthesis of liberty and efficiency which would work best to ensure the practical progress of associations.

In the end, all the associationist colonies have still not produced anything concrete, but one man who focused on them reached a definite utopian end outside of a narrative frame: Ebenezer Howard. He was the author of *Tomorrow: A Peaceful Path to Real Reform* (1898). This was the book that inspired the Garden City movement. This movement led to the construction of the city of Letchworth, north of London, which actually exists, and of numerous neighborhoods consisting of cottages and gardens in the outskirts of great cities—mainly in England, Germany, and the United States. One of our comrades, Bernhard Kampffmeyer, initiated this movement in Germany, and another of our comrades, Harry Kelly, is right now, in the area around New York, the prime mover in the creation of free villages with modern schools and the maximum amount of land given over to gardens and social institutions held in common.

On the one hand, it is true that these societies are divided, because of different levels of funding, into those where affluent men are housed well and those where workers have only managed to get the most modest cottages for themselves. What's more, the consequences of the First World War in a ruined central Europe have made the independent construction of these dwellings impossible. So, these societies (in Vienna, for example) have subordinated all that they still do to the work of municipal and state governments, which have taken on the role of making up for the terrible losses in the availability of housing. On the other hand, a great number of men, brought together by a persistent lack of food during and after the war, have become interested in ideas of self-sufficiency and have cherished the idea of leaving rented tenements in the cities and going back to nature. So, this idea of becoming complete men once more, of bridging the gap between city and countryside, is making progress and is at least *one* small utopia working towards a good life.

The anarchists had wanted to work more grandly in this area. Peter Kropotkin, in his constructive articles in *La révolte*, collected in *La Conquête du Pain* (1892), did nothing more than provide the grounds of and the reasons for his personal utopia, of which we also have an exquisite fragment in the article in English: "The Industrial Village of the Future" (October 1888), part of *Fields, Factories and Workshops: or, Industry Combined with Agriculture and Brain Work with Manual Work* (1901). This combination of city and countryside, of intellectual and manual work, of decentralized industry and intensive agriculture has created the basis for social and political harmony. It has rendered each locale autonomous as far as its fundamental needs are concerned, so any exchange with other locales would be limited to objects of minor importance. And so, no superiority of one locale over another would be created. This is the essence of the Kropotkinesque utopia. It would be desirable if this were so, but there is no proof that it will happen in such a way.

An anarchist who wanted to get to the bottom of these experimental ideas was Gustav Landauer, who was assassinated on May 2, 1919.

He understood, first, there had to be a constructive means to achieve cooperation. (See his anonymous *Ein Weg zur Befreiung der Arbeiterklasse* [A Way to Free the Working Class, 1895].) Later, Landauer expanded on his ideas in "Dreissig sozialistische Thesen" ["Thirty Socialist Theses"] (1907) and his great *Aufruf zum Sozialismus* [Call to Socialism] (*Der Sozialist*, the organ of the Sozialistischer Bund association, January 15, 1909 onwards; 1911 in book form; new ed., 1919). His goal at the time was the creation of free agricultural and industrial associations. These would be localized, scattered, and adaptative to particular circumstances. In practicing his diverse ideas for social organization through these associations, Landauer showed that much as he respected Kropotkin, he respected Proudhon just as much too. He would have left it up to experience to determine any preference among communism, collectivism, and mutualism. There was a framework, then, for experimentation on a grand scale. Landauer even hoped to find a practical means in the winter of 1918–1919 to create these associations, but the catastrophe which killed him intervened, and no one has yet continued his work.

I will conclude this part of the discussion with a letter from Kropotkin to comrades in the north of England (at Clousden Hill on the outskirts of Newcastle-on-Tyne) who had founded a small colony. His letter summarizes the difficulties that men like him, constructors of theories, experience with trying practically to apply their ideas to present circumstances within a capitalist society in order for social revolution to occur. This letter is to be found in *Les temps nouveaux* (May 9, 1896). He regrets seeing his friends withdraw from the work of propaganda and creating real freedom in order to devote themselves to an effort, perhaps abortive, that might lead to complete disillusionment. He thinks it will be good to stay on the outskirts of the great cities in order to enjoy their resources and not to become isolated in remote areas. There is no need to clear virgin land by hard work, he says. It would be worthwhile, he argues, to open up new forms of production and consumption by intensive cultivation, by perfected horticulture, by the production of early fruits and vegetables in greenhouses. It would even be worthwhile to give up collective family life in isolated group houses given the economics of supplies, firewood, and lodging. Instead, it would be better to scatter in groups among families and friends.

Any display whatsoever of authoritarian behavior, from Kropotkin's perspective, would be a sign of collapse. Decision-making should be done in the way peasants decide things: by discussing a question until they arrive at unanimity. Women's domestic chores should be reduced to the minimum and gradually replaced by machines wherever possible. What matters above all is the size of the enterprise. It should be done on a grand enough scale.

In order to arrive at a definitive result, a city of at least 20,000 inhabitants should be organized. Lodging, furniture, food, and clothing should be conveniently distributed, and groups would take care of everyone's artistic, scientific, and literary needs for free. Kropotkin continues:

> If we were to start with less than nothing, misery would lie in wait for us and we will break apart; moreover, the initial work on the land is hard for city workers. If the colony prospers, newcomers will appear: the uprooted and the less skilled. Here's a major stumbling block: they cannot be refused admission, but if everyone is admitted one runs the risk of being swamped. One doesn't want to be discouraging but it is important to forewarn.

This then, more or less, is how the man who encouraged every libertarian effort, vacillated on this occasion; he felt he was struggling against difficulties that were too great, that the forces which could unite at this time were too small to triumph. I am sorry that I have not seen what Élisée Reclus wrote in "Les colonies anarchists" [Anarchist Colonies] (*Les temps nouveaux* [July 7, 1900]) about the theatrical work [by Lucien Descaves and Maurice Donnay titled] *La Clairière* [The Clearing], which dramatized what happens to a fatally disunited colony.

An Italian anarchist, Giovanni Rossi (born in Pisa in 1855), wrote *Un comune socialista* [A Socialist Commune] (1876; published 1878). It's a utopia about a village, well written and practical. It ends in anarchistic communism but is based in the beginning on an act of voluntary benevolence by a landlord. It was Rossi who inspired and undertook the founding of the Cecilia colony in the Paraña region of Brazil from 1890 to 1894. There, peasants and Italian workers, anarchists for the most part, cleared the virgin land. Their story is described by Rossi and others and probably in more detail than any other anarchist colony in the collection *Utopie und Experiment: Studien und Berichte*] [Utopia and Experiment: Essays and Reports] (1897). This work was put together with great care by our Swiss comrade, Alfred Sanftleben (and by Rossi). It is a book worth the bother of re-reading, as I am just doing almost 30 years after it was published. There, one sees communism in its most libertarian forms practically applied, not at all in order to experiment with a preconceived utopian ideal but—as Rossi says on page 210—to observe how men conduct themselves if nothing but living freely unites them. Rossi declares that this free anarcho-communist life is possible, but that initiative has to be shown by an intelligent and hard-working minority. He argues that there would be clashes and very little kindness at first, but that practice would awaken the natural sociability of men. It would create a new ethics whereby the family as the center of egoism, which presents a major obstacle, would spontaneously and gradually dissolve. Such a dissolution would prepare the ground for the intended ideal. (This is a loose summary of pages 216–217 in the book.) Dr. Rossi summarized his final ideas in the utopia "Il Paranà nel secolo XX" [Paranà in the Twentieth Century], which appeared for the first time, in German, as pages 267–309 of this book by Rossi and Sanftleben. I do not know if it was printed anywhere else [other than Zürich]. It is a remarkable work which describes very well, for instance, this period of independent social life, of the repudiation of the State, and of the politics of free association that would precede an effective social revolution. For, in the period when anarchy is achieved, communism will be tied in with a system of groups formed according to their capabilities so that the group establishes its own rhythm of working—whether more intense or less efficient— and, so, the frictions which arise, as in the Cecilia colony, when the skilled and the unskilled, the hard-working and the lazy, work together would be prevented. It is one of the most thoughtful works on the subject.

There are few other anarchist utopias in these years or a little later: *La nueva Utopia* [The New Utopia] by Ricardo Mella and *El siglo de oro* [The Century of Gold] by M. B. are to be found in the *Segundo certamen socialista* [Second Socialist Convention] (1890: 201–227 and 229–237). There's Pietro Gori's *La leggenda del primo maggio. Documento pro-postero* [The Legend of the First of May: A Document for Posterity] (1905). Jean Grave, of course, wrote *Terre libre* [Free Land] (1908; translated into Spanish, also in 1908, by Anselmo Lorenzo in *Publicaciones de la Escuela Moderna* [Publications of the Modern School]). He also wrote *Les aventures de Nono* [The Adventures of Nono] (1901; translated by Anselmo Lorenzo in 1907 as "the second reading book" of Francisco Ferrer Guàrdia's Modern School) to interest children in communism and liberty. There is Lambro Canzani's *Uno sguardo dell'avvenire* [A Look to the Future], (1903) (which was printed by) Domenico Zavattero [1875–1947], a very well-known propagandist of the period. Henri Zisly describes naturism in the *Voyage au beau pays de Naturie* [Voyage to the Beautiful Land of Naturie] (1900).

Among individualist authors whose lives one could consider as representative of their ideas, there's John Henry Mackay and his *Die Anarchisten: Kulturgemälde aus dem Ende des XIX Jahrhunderts* [The Anarchists: A Picture of Culture at the End of the Nineteenth Century] (1911) and his *Die Freiheitsuche: Psychologie einer Entwicklung* [The Search for Freedom: The Psychology of Its Development] (1920) with that search being considered as a utopian construction. The thorny questions about monetary exchange which individualist American and English authors stir up are discussed in Seymour F. Norton's *Ten Men of Money Island, or the Primer of Finance* with an appendix by Henry Seymour (1891). The individualist and believer in voluntaryism, Auberon Herbert, has described his ideas in utopian form in his newspaper *Free Life* (1890). The strictly anti-socialist individualist J. H. Levy has published a small-sized and brief book, *An Individualist's Utopia* (1900?). I do not know this book published in the United States in 1893, *A Cityless and Countryless World. An Outline of Practical Cooperative Individualism* by Henry Olerich. Tolstoy uses the utopian genre in his short story "Ivan, le sot et ses deux frères" [Ivan the Fool and His Two Brothers] (1886) and elsewhere. A breath of liberty inspires *Die Eigenen: ein Tendenzroman für freie Geister* [Individuals: A Didactic Novel for Free Spirits] (1903) by Emil F. Ruedebusch (from the United States), who was also the author of *The Old and the New Ideal. A Solution to That Part of the Social Question Which Pertains to Love, Marriage, and Sexual Intercourse* (1897).

Experimental socialism of differing shades was realized during this era above all in the United States and also by Australians. These experimental socialists sometimes grounded their work on utopian writings by a founder, but I do not know this diverse literature except in its most developed forms when it appears, for example, in a periodical for propaganda purposes. Here, I should mention *The Integral Co-operator* from Enterprise, Kansas (1890); *The Credit Foncier of Sinaloa* in Hammonton, New Jersey (beginning in 1885); *Kaweah Commonwealth* in California (around 1890); *The Fairhope Courier*, in Alabama; *The Grander Age*, in Co-opolis, Missouri; *The Co-operator* (Brotherhood Colony) in Washington State, which later became *The Self-Helper* in Vancouver (British Columbia) (1913), and so on. The most notable colony from another time was Topolobampo in Mexico; later there was Ruskin in Tennessee, a colony that, for a long time, produced the periodical *The Coming Nation*. The name Ruskin reminds me that I should mention that its social ideas inspired some men in England to group together into a social guild.

The anarchists who grouped themselves in a colony in the extreme west, in Washington State, for a long time published the periodical *Discontent*, beginning on May 11, 1898. After March 11, 1903, there was the *Demonstrator*, replaced on November 15, 1910 by the *Agitator*, which was finally moved to Chicago where it was called *The Syndicalist* (January 1, 1913). In England, constructive and experimentalist socialist ideas were propagated by the writings of J. Bruce Wallace and the periodical *Brotherhood*, first published in Ireland in 1887, and subsequently in London for many years. These ideas were also propagated by the *Nationalisation News* from 1890 to 1893, which Bellamy's utopia had inspired. One marginal example of these socialist ideas, begun by Thomas Davidson, was the New Fellowship, which published *The Sower* and *Seedtime* from 1889 to 1898. We should even mention *New Australia*, a periodical in New South Wales; the *Cosme Monthly* and *Cosme* in Paraguay (publications from the Australian workers united in a colony in Paraguay); a project in New Zealand ("Wainoni"); *The Daisy Colony Scheme*, by Allen Clarke in Manchester; the project of the Van-Eeden Colony in North Carolina in the United States in 1912, and so on.

Moving on to the socialist utopias in the years after Bellamy: there were plenty, but none moved men to achieve their goals to the degree that the independent utopias or intentional communities just discussed had done in a limited way. This is understandable since the statist systems appeal to an electorate or, strictly speaking, to universal revolution but not to forces which are individual or united in groups. It is this way *everywhere*: in the absence of a leader who shakes things up a little from time to time. No one offers a steadying hand or things only advance imperceptibly. So, Oswald Koehler describes, without a utopian narrative, *Die sozialidemokratische Staat* [The Social-democratic State] (1891). Dr. S. Schorr discusses *Zur Theorie des Zükunftsstaates* [The Theory of the Future State], reprinted from the periodical *Deutschen Worte* [German Words] (April 1896). Atlanticus (Dr. Ballod) published *Ein Blick in den Zukunftsstaat. Produktion and Konsumtion im Sozialsstaat* [A Look at the Future State. Production and Consumption in the Social State] (1898). The preface was by Karl Kautsky, who also dealt with the distribution of the products of labor in a study for the *Jahrbuch für Socialwissenschaft* [The Social Science Yearbook] (1881). The Swiss socialist, Pastor Paul Pflüger, wrote *Der Schweizerische Sozialstaat. Eine Umschau im Jahre 1950* [The Swiss Social State. A Glimpse in the Year 1950] (1899). There are two Hungarian utopian works, in 1896 and 1907, that I do not know how to read. I should mention a statist socialist utopia in Japanese, *Shinshakai* [The New Society]. (See *La chronique des livres* [The Chronicle of Books], 25 February 1904: 193–198.) Carlo Monticelli wrote and published *II primo giorno del socialismo* [Socialism's New Day] (1904). Eugène Fournière, in the *Revue socialiste* (1899), published "Le rêve de Pierre Davant" [Peter Davant's Dream].

Works by more isolated socialists include, for example, the book *Si, étude sociale d'après demain* [Yes. A Social Study of the Day after Tomorrow] by Auguste Chirac (1893); *Un peu plus tard* [A Little Later], by Edmond Potonié-Pierre (1893), a feminist work; *La cite de l'egalite* [Equality City] by Olivier Souêtre (1896); *Les deux naufrages* [The Two Shipwrecks] (1905) by "Kamidel," followed by his *Dorotchim ou la gloire de Sodome* [Dorotchim, or the Glory of Sodom] in three parts (1909), and other similar writings. All of these were published in Nancy, France. The elderly socialist J. C. Claudel was their author, and also wrote a similar pamphlet on the occasion of the difficulties of 1878. This pamphlet (*Le sort réservé aux empereurs et rois* [The Fate Reserved for Emperors and Kings, 1878]), which was published in Brussels, caused a bit of an outcry. The police pounced on the pamphlet and its author in order to lay hands on the center of intrigue and regicide, but the pamphlet was no more than socialist exposition. It concluded that, in a reasonable society, emperors and kings should work like the rest of the world. There are other works too: *Etapes sociales (La Clairière)* [The Stages of Society (The Clearing)] in the little magazine *La jardin de France* [The Garden of France] (1910), edited by Hubert-Fillay. In languages other than French, we have Gustav Bolle's *Sozial: Eine Erzählung aus dem Staate der Sozialdemokratie* [Social: A Tale about the State of Social Democracy] (1891); Joseph Angerbauer's self-published *Tischlein, deck dich für Alle! Eine Betrachtung* [Little Table, Cover Yourself for Everyone's Sake! A Meditation] (1908); Josef Rotter's *Im Jahre 1999* [In the Year 1999] (1894; translated from the Dutch). I am not familiar with Carl Bolle's *Die Kosmier* [Cosmos] (1898), a communist utopia of which no more than the first volume exists, and I cannot speak precisely about a great Dutch utopia of which I remember no more than the word "Elpis" ["Hope" in Classical Greek] used in the title.

I cannot now recall a number of socialist utopias which were socialist to one degree or another. The *Twentieth Century* journal, published in New York and very advanced in its thinking for the time, brought out Samuel H. King's "The Journal of a Scientist during a Voyage to the Planet Mars." Lewis Henry Berens and Ignatius Singer anonymously published *The Story of My Dictatorship* (1894), which explains in the form of a utopia Henry George's Land Tax ideas. Havelock Ellis, the famous scientist, published *The Nineteenth Century. A Dialogue in Utopia* (1900). The socialist C. W. Wooldridge published *The Kingdom of God Is at Hand* (1900). H. Brockhouse, a member of the independent workers' party, published (in West Bromwich) a 15-page pamphlet, *Hopetown, an Industrial City as It Is and as It Could Be* (1905). And there are many more: the anonymously published *Christopolis: Life and Its Amenities in a Land of Garden Cities* (1903); Albert Kimsey Owen's *A Dream of an Ideal City* (1897); Frederick W. Hayes' *The Great Revolution of 1905: or, the Story of the Phalanx* (1893); William Dean Howells' *A Traveler from Altruria, Romance* (1894); Upton Sinclair's *The Industrial Republic: A Study of the America of Ten Years Hence* (1907); Jack London's *The Iron Heel* (1907), which is a history of the American social revolution; A. Bancroft Firmin's "The Altrurian Era... (a conference given in the year 2007)," which appeared in the magazine *Altruria* in September 1907. In languages other than English, there was Charles Richet's *Dans cent ans* [In One Hundred Years] (1892) (in the *Revue scientifique* [Scientific Review; 1891, 1892]) and discussed by F. S. Merlino in the *Societé nouvelle* [New Society], published in Brussels in May 1892, and Bertha von Suttner's *Das Maschinenalter: Zukunftvorlesungen über Unsere Zeit* [The Age of the Machine: Lectures about the Future of Our Times] (1889). Von Suttner was a well-known pacifist, and the book was originally published anonymously.

Now, we take up the utopias of pure fantasy although there are some social ideas in them and an enormous diversity of understanding about what society is. One of the most beautiful is W. H. Hudson's *A Crystal Age* (1887). Hudson was an English author who lived for a long time in Argentina and wrote of the ornithology of that country; he loved nature and his utopia reveals that love. Then there are these: W. Grove's *The Wreck of a World* (1889); the anonymous *Dawn of the Twentieth Century: 1st January 1901* (1888); Henry l'Estrange's *Platonia: A Tale of Other Worlds* (1893?); Henry Robert Heather Bigg's *The Human Republic* (1891); John Macnie's *Looking Forward, or, The Diothas* (1890), written under the pseudonym of Ismar Thiusen; Chauncey Thomas's *The Crystal Button: or, the Adventures of Paul Prognosis in the Forty-ninth Century* (1891); Ignatius Donnelly's *Caesar's Column* (1891), a very popular book in its time and antisocialist; Kenneth Folingsby's *Meda: A Tale of the Future* (1891); G. MacIver's *Neuroomia: A New Continent* (1894) (the preface's byline is New South Wales); Andrew Acworth's antisocialist *A New Eden* (1896?); Leonard A. Magnus's *A Japanese Utopia* (1905); and Godfrey Sweven's *Limanora: The Island of Progress* (1903). There are a large number of [other] similar works published in England that I have not mentioned.

In France there are, for example, from this fantasy genre (which is very often against socialism rather than supportive of it) the following: Alain Le Drimeur's *La Cité future* [The City of the Future] (1890); Neulif's *L'uthopie contemporaine: notes de voyage* [A Contemporary Utopia: Notes of a Voyage] (1888); Jean Erbal's *En l'an 2050!!!* [In the Year 2050!!!] (1889); Maurice Spronck's *L'an 330 de la république: xxii siècle de l'ère chrétienne* [The Year 330 of the Republic: The Twenty-Second Century of the Christian Era]) (1894); A. Vilgensofer's *La terre dans cent mille ans. Roman de moeurs. I. L'île enchantée* [The Earth in One Hundred Thousand Years. A Novel of Manners. Volume 1: The Enchanted Isle] (1893); Marc Thury's *Visite imaginative à un camp de travail le 1er mai 1922* [An Imaginary Visit to a Work Camp on the First of May 1922] (1902); André Mazade's *Au pays de liberté* [In the Country of Freedom] (1900); Georges Delbruck's *Au pays de l'harmonie: beauté, harmonie, amour* [In the Country of Harmony: Beauty, Harmony, Love] (1906); two utopias by the bookseller Albert Quantin, *Histoire prochaine. Roman socialiste* [Forthcoming History. A Socialist Novel] (1910), and *En plein vol: vision d'avenir* [In Full Flight: A Vision of the Future] (1913); and many others.

Besides these, there are *L'anno 3000* [The Year 3000; 1897] by Paolo Mantegazza (an author almost forgotten now); *Die Insel Mellonta* [The Island of Mellonta] (1883) by the well-known spiritualist Lazar B. Hellenbach; Hans Hardt's *Im Zukunftsstaat* [In the Future State] (1905); Dr. Joseph von Neupauer's *Österreich im Jahre 2020. Socialpolitischer Roman* [Austria in the Year 2020. A Sociopolitical Novel] (1893); *Im Reiche der Homunculiden* [In the Kingdom of the Homunculi] (1910) by the Viennese author Rudolf Hawel; Emil Gregorovius's *Der Himmel auf Erden in den Jahren 1901 bis 1912* [Heaven on Earth in the Years 1901 to 1912] (1892); George W. Bell's *Mr. Oseba's Last Discovery* (1904); and *Balmanno, the City of Our Quest and Its Social Problems* (1906), published anonymously in Paisley, Scotland. There are very curious astronomical novels by Paul Scheerbart that hide a satirical intent, such as *Die grosse Revolution. Ein Mondroman* [The Great Revolution. A World Novel] (1902), and there are others of this sort, more speculative though, by Kurd Lasswitz. There is also, in the same vein, Francisco Piria's *El socialismo triunfante. Lo que será mi país dentro de 200 años* [Socialism Triumphant. What My Country Will Be after 200 Years] (1898). The novels of Zola became more and more novels of argument, such as *Fécondité* [Fecundity] (1899) and *Travail* [Work] (1901). The latter is really a social rather than a socialist utopia even though it is filled with Fourierism.

There are utopian novels which are beautiful in appearance but pessimistic in outlook with a deep lack of faith in socialism. Among these are Paul Adam's *Lettres de Malaisie* [Letters from Malaysia] (1898)—much later titled *La cité prochaine. Lettres de Malaisie* [The Next City: Letters from Malaysia] (1908). There are also the works of the Russian writer Konstantin Sergeevich Mereschkowski, one of which is called *Das irdische Paradies. Ein Märchen aus dem 27. Jarhundert. Eine Utopie* [The Earthly Paradise. A Tale of the Twenty-seventh Century. A Utopia] (1903) as well as the philosopher Gabriel Tarde's *Fragment d'histoire future* [Fragment of the History of the Future] (1904). This work was translated into English as *Underground Man* (1905) as it is about a man living underground and reduced to merely existing in caves.

Then there are those utopias and anti-utopias which focus on women: Mrs. George Corbett's *New Amazonia: A Foretaste of the Future* (1889); Henri Desmarest's *La Femme future* [The Woman of the Future] (1900); Lady Florence Dixie's *Isola or The Disinherited* with observations by G. J. Holyoake (1903); Fernand Kolney's *L'amour dans cinq mille ans* [Love in Five Thousand Years] (1928); Mathéma's self-published *L'île d'Eve* [Eve's Isle] (1907); Walter Besant's *The Revolt of Man* (1882); Jacques Constant's *Le Triomphe des suffragettes. Roman des temps futurs* [The Triumph of the Suffragettes. A Novel of Future Times] (1910); a theatrical piece by Cicely Hamilton and Christopher St. John, *How the Vote Was Won* (1909); and others. The motif of Lysistrata is presented in George Noyes Miller's *The Strike of a Sex* (1891); Marie Desprès' *La grève des femmes* [The Women's Strike] (1895); and, in a similar vein, Camille Périer's *La grève des amoureux* [The Lovers' Strike] (1866). *Lysistrata* itself was interpreted in Paris by Mrs. Gabrielle Rüjane in a version by Maurice Donnay, *Lysistrata: comédie en quatre actes en prose* [Lysistrata. A Prose Comedy in Four Acts] (1892). Another *Lysistrata* had also been done by François Benoît

Hoffmann in the Year X of the Republic (1802), but it was banned. Its title was *Lisistrata, ou, les Athéniennes: comédie en un acte et en prose, mêlée de vaudevilles, imitée d'Aristophane* [Lysistrata, or the Athenians. A One-Act Farcical Comedy in Prose in Imitation of Aristophanes]. There is F. J. Gould's *The Agnostic Island* (1891), a freethinkers' work; Mrs. Noémie Dide produced *Fantaisie anticalviniste* [Anti-calvinist Fantasy] (1909).

One form of utopia is Jesus Christ being faced with the present misery and social iniquities. There are, for example, Ernest Gégout's *Jésus* (1897); Francesco Paolini's *Una visita di Gesù Cristo* [A Visit from Jesus Christ] (1908), written in the style of *If Christ Came to Chicago* and others of that kind. In 1849, the Fourierist Victor Meunier published the valuable pamphlet *Jésus-Christ devant les conseils de guerre* [Jesus Christ before the Councils of War] in the Librairie phalanstérinne [The Phalanstery Library] series. It is one of the very few socialist publications of the time that also published material in Italian, for there is an Italian version of Meunier's pamphlet titled *Gesù Cristo avanti un consiglio di guerra* (1850). Eleven years later, there was a widespread satirical poem, *Le Christ au Vatican* [Christ in the Vatican], which in many editions was credited to Victor Hugo, but the author was actually the French republican Jacques-Antoine Chappuis.

There are very strange pieces of fiction too. For example, L. P. Gratacap's *The Evacuation of England* (1908), which follows what happens after the Gulf Stream changes direction. J. H. Rosny supposes that there are beings who are not humans but crystal rays in *Xipéhuz* (1888). Ray Nyst wrote a prehistoric tale in *La caverne* [The Cave] (1909) just as George Sand had already written *Les amours de l'age d'or. Evenor et Leucippe* [Love in the Golden Age. Evenor and Leucippe] (1855). There is also Louis Estève's *La nouvelle Abbaye de Thilème* [The New Abbey of Thilème] (1906) just as there had already been Charles Asselineau's *Le paradis des gens de lettres* [The Paradise of Men of Letters] (1862).

War is fought against some times, as in O. Wichers von Gogh's *Krieg dem Kriege: dramatisches Zukunftsbild* [War of Wars: A Dramatic Picture of the Future] (1893), published in Zürich by a socialist publisher. The end of war has, however, been much more often foretold, described as happening in the future, desired in various forms. I have not wanted to record the religious, mystic, occult fictions because no one has faith in them now and because all religions are based on no more than a popular utopia gone astray and disguised by the priesthood to their benefit. The modern occultists have started to play the same game by putting their faith in fictions. One of the mystics of this genre was Thomas Lake Harris with his *Great Republic, a Poem of the Sun* (1867, second ed., 1891). A political and nationalistic utopia which bore fruit was Theodor Herzl's *Der Judenstaat* [The Jewish State] (1896). It inspired the Zionist movement and the British interest in the present State of Palestine.

Some other books in utopian form, satires of one type or another, are, for example, Theophilus M'Crib, B. A.'s *Kennaquhair: A Narrative of Utopian Travel* (1872); *Among the Têtchas of Central Asia* (1886); St. Loe Strachey's *How England Became a Republic* (1891); A. Bart-Claye's *Vers la cité future* [Towards the City of the Future] (1905); Frederic Bonhomme's *La humanité pacifique* [Humanity at Peace] (1907); M. G. Conrad's *In purpurner Finsternis. Romanimprovisation aus dem dreissigsten Jahrhundert* [In Purple Shadows. An Improvisational Novel of the Thirtieth Century] (1895), and so on.

I leave out the numerous antisocialist publications done on the orders of the bourgeoisie and its political parties, the fictions against Bellamy, and the many works that come close to being insipid such as the liberal, antisocialist German Eugen Richter's *Sozialdemokratische Zukunftsbilder* [The Socialdemocratic Vision of the Future] (1892), against which Franz Mehring (Nuremburg, 1892) and others wrote in defense of socialism. There were clumsy and wicked publications against socialism in England and in France in those years, too.

Other countries had social literature that was less intense, more tranquil, fresher also; I know little about them, but if there had been important utopias published in the 15 or 20 years after Bellamy in 1888 they would probably have been translated into the major European languages and I would have had some knowledge of them.

Utopia, which occupied the front rank for some time through Bellamy's *Looking Backward*, 1889–1890, has not been able to maintain its position and has crumbled once more, maintaining, nonetheless, a frequency and diversity that has not lessened.

Chapter 6

THE TWENTIETH CENTURY: 1900–1925

I come now to utopias written from the turn of the century until the First World War. This period I see as characterized above all by the *numerous* utopian publications of H. G. Wells.

This man of great talent has written more utopias than any other writer, except Jules Verne—whom I cannot take seriously. Wells knew how to persuade the public through fantasy combined with a well-respected talent for sociology. However, he abused the poor utopia that had created his reputation by writing one after another, and still he continued to write them as they had become a way of making money for him. The public indulged in the game of reading them just as at another time they might play with a kaleidoscope. Another version of utopia is found in each new book from Wells. Utopia, however, doesn't deserve this treatment, for in the most difficult times it has been a way in which an individual fantasy finds a voice and makes itself heard. The utopian, as an honest man, is only *one* voice. Most often they make their confession to the public just *once* through a utopia. Then, in later works, they explain their idea, develop their idea, or retire from writing. On occasion, utopian writers do lose their faith and can only regain it by writing a new utopia. Utopias are often written, as it were, with the *heart's blood* and are preceded—if they are worth anything—by laborious thought. A utopia establishes its fundamental idea and then set dresses it, as appropriate, with a fantastic framework so as to make it attractive to the public. This was, as the previous chapters have shown, a creative habit of old, and the process was respected until Wells came along. Bellamy wrote his first, then his second book, and then one hundred explanatory articles before retiring and dying. By contrast, Wells wrote a new utopia almost every year. It is the utopia commercialized, paid for, exploited. It is exploited, ironically, when so many other utopians felt inspired to try to put an end to exploitation and make the world free and beautiful. This relationship is mirrored by the decline in intellectual life in the years before the war, years that saw the commercialization and brutalization of culture—and that process had to end in catastrophe. I have surveyed the most absurd utopias that could be devised, but even they preserve the respect held for the tenacity of people of good faith, however foolish they may be. However, I find no pleasure in following the very clever, but utterly mercurial—even spineless—imagination of H. G. Wells. Brilliant author he may be, but he has lowered the utopian genre to the commercial vulgarity characteristic of our times.

At the same time, the constituent elements of utopia have not escaped a similar decline. It is true that an unprecedented number of the inventions dreamed up by utopians have been realized: people fly through the air and swim beneath the sea; they speak and listen over great distances; they are on the eve of transmitting power remotely in such a way as almost to give life to machines and to automatons; they have commercially exploited almost every corner of the globe; they know how to check disease and to mechanize production and supply; they use radio to broadcast worldwide; they watch marvelous things at the cinema; they poison each other every day with asphyxiating gases if they are not already sick. And what purpose has this inventiveness served? All of this invention has been used exclusively to establish an absolute capitalist tyranny along with the destruction that has resulted from it, destruction which suits the economic powerbrokers of the globe and the nationalist conquerors who are basically their tools. In this way are they able to spread evil for its own sake.

And all of this process serves only to perfect militarism, to spread capitalism far and wide, to use up the globe's last natural resources. Capitalists, in the end, control the natural riches of the land in the interest of the parasites and their minions while the masses continue in their role of "voluntary" servitude. Science prostitutes itself to capitalism and militarism; it works to achieve nothing more than increasing capitalism's power to dominate and destroy. And artists and the intelligentsia, what do they do? They all go along with the supposedly irresistible flow by producing work for the cinema and the radio; in this way, they all do nothing more than brutalize the enslaved masses. So, where would any interest lie in progress, in discovery, in invention, in thought? For, whatever the discovery, whatever the achievement of a utopian ideal might be, one knows that tomorrow will bring a more destructive weapon, that an idea will be more vulgarized in a commercial sense until it is ripe for cinema and radio, where anything goes—absolutely anything. The message put out against all of this noise is timid, modest, weak. It does not even seem to acknowledge the terrible fall from grace of the modern world.

Until that grandiose achievement in Russia: the triumph of socialism. A utopia amongst utopias, one scarcely dreamed of by even the most daring. And what has it turned into? Well, that immense country—which forms an integral part of two continents, which could have used its natural resources and open spaces to become self-sufficient and to feed a large part of the population of the globe—that immense country could have become a social laboratory in which all of the ideas behind a theory (one hypothesis) and its expression in a social utopia (another hypothesis) could have been examined, put to the test, with the necessary strategies in place and on the correct scale. The socialists and anarchists of the world could have shown up to live there in harmonious groups and to observe through the evolution of each the relative value of their various social concepts. None of this was achieved, however. The fanatics of a single hypothesis or utopia, Marxism, have created an absolute monopoly and set themselves up as the keepers of the country, as bitter enemies of everyone else, and, when necessary, the eradicators of *any other* socialist or anarchist concept and the jailers and executioners of its representatives. These Marxists oppose authority and the capitalist monopoly, but they do so not in the cause of liberty and happiness for all but in order to create their own strict, fiercely guarded monopoly. Then, as with a contagion, liberty prospers nowhere. The people have seen happiness and hope fade away for who knows how long.

This period was still utopian at its beginning, but later utopias were born of skepticism and desperation. However, in order not to prejudice the question, I want to talk now about the different groups of utopias from the time of Wells to the war years and on to the current period of decadence. I will do so as far as I can, but I have been unable to keep myself current because my access to materials has been limited since 1914 and I cannot now go back to learn more.

H. G. Wells, born in 1866 and the author of bizarre fantasies such as *The Invisible Man* (1897), strides onto the field of utopian thought with *The Time Machine* (1895). This book was followed by *The War of the Worlds* (1898), *The First Men on the Moon* (1901), *Mankind in the Making* (1903), *Anticipations of the Reaction of Mechanical and Scientific Progress upon Human Life and Thought* (1904), *The Food of the Gods* (1904), *A Modern Utopia* (1905), *In the Days of the Comet* (1906), *The War in the Air* (1908), *The World Set Free* (1914), and many others. Towards the end of the nineteenth century, Wells had joined the Fabian Society, an organization so dominated by George Bernard Shaw and Sidney Webb that Wells never assimilated into it. He always remains attached to a socialism on which he does not know how to stamp his own originality even though he has given form to so many ideas. He cleverly throws out ideas and stirs the pot, but it is not known which are truly his own. So, the influence his talent should have wielded is absent.

To me, Bertrand Russell appears to be very different from other utopian thinkers in that, without adopting a utopian form, he studied the future—in *The Prospects of Industrial Civilization* (1923)—on the basis of the present and the past, and such forecasts, supported as they are by sound evidence and logical conclusions, necessarily have the stamp of utopia. They are comparable to the moving visions of the future which the anarchist Ernest Coeurderoy has presented in a book with the odd title of *Hurrah!!! ou la révolution par les Cosaques* [Hurrah!!! or the Cossack Revolution] (1854). It is on this terrain that a wide-ranging study would have to begin. It would need to verify Russell's hypotheses and undertake its investigation in the spirit of liberty which Russell, lost in the authoritative orgies of those years, hardly took into account. Here utopian forecasting, the serious study of the facts and possibilities of evolution and a proud confidence in liberty, would need to be united so as to produce a first-rate study in the name of freedom of the outcome in the present situation and the foreseeable future.

At a time when French unionism, which arose around 1905 under the inspiration of Fernard Pelloutier, was gaining ground, Émile Pouget and Émile Pataud wrote *Comment nous ferons la Révolution* [How We Will Bring about the Revolution] (November 1909). Pouget was one of Pelloutier's well-known associates and editor at one time of, among other things, the famous *Le père peinard* [The Cushy Father] (1889–1894), and Pataud was also a highly respected thinker. A second edition of *Comment nous ferons* appeared in 1911 with a preface by Kropotkin. There was also an English translation in 1913 and a Russian translation in 1920 in the journal *Golos Truda* [The Voice of Labor] with a new introduction by Kropotkin. This second introduction by Kropotkin (dated June 1920) is his final word on utopia as revolutionary unionism. Kropotkin thought well of *Comment nous ferons* and held Pouget in high regard. Pataud also wrote the copy for an issue of *L'assiette au beurre* [The Butter Plate]: "Le Grand Soir" [The Great Evening] about the moment of the revolution. This journal was published in Paris and featured striking satirical engravings; the issue is number 475 and is dated May 7, 1910.

Pouget and Pataud's book would compare with the purely anarchist communist utopia of Sébastien Faure's *"Mon communism" (le bonheur universel)* [My Communism: Universal Happiness], translated as *Mi Comunismo: la felicidad universal* and published in Buenos Aires by *La protesta* in 1922. When its constructive ideas are applied to Argentina, a country that physically, historically, and by its geographic position differs enormously from France, the result is different utopian hypotheses. These you find in the well-received utopian writings of Pierre Quiroule: *Sobre la ruta de la anarquia, novela libertaria* [On the Road to Anarchy, a Novel about Freedom] (published in 1912, but written in 1909); *La ciudad anarquista americana* [The American Anarchist City] (published in 1914 by *La protesta*), and *En la sonada tierra del ideal* [In the Dreamland of the Ideal] (April 1924). Nothing is more useful in a utopia than its localization, its adaptation to each country, because as much as we are internationalists in ideas and feelings, we are equally always children of our environment for the forms and the subtleties of any practical application of an idea. The utopia that combines the ideal and the practical, will be truly u-topian—without place—if it wants only to please and inspire; it will be adapted to the environment if it aspires to the supreme success which a utopia can hope for: realization. The type of utopia of nowhere, beautiful and inspiring but not real, is *Les pacifiques* [The Peaceful Ones] of Han Ryner (Henri Ner), published in 1914 several weeks before the war. It mixes the essential anarchy of a distant age with the classic terrain of a great number of imaginary writings based on Plato's Atlantis.

The utopian achievements of these last 20 years by tentative anarchists have been slight and largely of a psychological sort rather than economic. However, some efforts at free community life without the means of production being held in common have been undertaken in the New York area and have had a practical influence. A theatrical piece by Lucien Descaves, often performed in Paris in 1903, shows the audience the intimate life of a colony. It had an effect. Soon after, *La clairière* [The Clearing] was performed at Vaux, near Château-Thierry in the Aisne region, and later at Aiglemont in the Ardennes. "A free style" (a term often adopted since 1902) was talked of in Provence, an "African hive" in Tunisia in 1912, and so on. There was a wide range of efforts associated with a brother of Emile Henry's, with George Butaud (and his Bascon colony), and others. All were done on a very small scale. The magazines and newspapers run by E. Armand after 1901 (*L'ère nouvelle* [The New Era]; *Hors du troupeau* [Apart from the Herd]; *Réfractaires* [The Resistance]; and, since 1922, *L'en-dehors* [Outside], which is still published in Orléans) contain abundant information on the experimental groups in France and almost everywhere else.

Now, there are men who have clearly separated themselves from society as it exists, men who need to live among comrades who are free, men who always know how to create a milieu of freedom by limiting their resources. Apart from these sorts of groups in France, all over America, in Germany, and elsewhere, there was, above all, the Dutch Blaricum colony in Holland as well as a few others in Belgium. The earlier writings of Frederik van Eeden, those of T. Luitjes, of Felix Ortt, the newspapers *Vrede* [Peace] and *De Pionier* [The Pioneer]—the former founded in 1898 and the latter in 1903—represent the beginnings of Dutch experimentation. *Der Genossenschaftspionier* [The Cooperative Pioneer] and *Die neue Gemeinschaft* [The New Community] (1900–1902), in which Gustav Landauer took part, bear witness to various German efforts. Landauer then published his essay "Durch Absonderung zur Gemeinschaft" [Through Separation to

Community] (1901), which talks of creating a community of those who have separated themselves from bourgeois society. There are the more recent efforts of Nicolai Scheierman, a Russian and author of *A Vision of the New Living Life* which prepares the way for the International Brotherhood of Service of Love in Freedom (1923). That more or less describes the scale and strategies of these enterprises which were hardly allowed to grow at all and definitely did not constitute economic levers to break the capitalist system. Instead, they consisted of men, women, and children—free in spirit, separated from prejudice, habituated to practical solidarity—who became joyful sparks of the great future light that could yet illuminate the darkness around them and who will be precious elements of any future reconstruction of society.

We move on to some socialist utopias of the present time, a very incomplete list: Robert Blatchford's *The Sorcery Shop. An Impossible Romance* (1907); A. Bogdanov's *Etoile rouge*; [Red Star]; J. Lichtneckert's *Der sozialdemokratische Welt-Staat mit Gemeigentum und Eigenproduktion* [The Social-democratic World State with Collective Property and Private Production]; Lucien Deslinières's *Le Maroc socialiste* [Socialist Morocco] (1912); from the same author with J. Marc-Py, *La résurrection du Docteur Valbel* [The Resurrection of Doctor Valbel]; Berthold Otto's *Der Zukunftstaat als sozialistische Monarchie* [The Future State as a Socialist Monarchy]; Emile Masson's *Utopie des iles bienheureuses dans le Pacifique en l'an 1980* [The Utopia of the Prosperity Islands in the Pacific in the Year 1980], a beautiful utopia; Alfons Petzold's *Severinde: Ein Alter Abenteurer-Roman* [Severinde: An Old Adventurer's Novel] (1923). Petzold was an Austrian poet and socialist; his book was probably based on the utopia of the Severambes (1675). There is also Jakob Vetsch's *Die Sonnenstadt: ein Bekenntnis und ein Weg. Roman aus der Zukunft für die Gegenwart* [The City of the Sun: An Avowal and a Way. A Novel from the Future for the Present] (1923).

Joseph Popper-Lynkeus's *Die allgemeine Nährpflicht als Lösung der soziale Frage* [The Universal Civil Service as a Solution to the Social Problem] (1912) is a very detailed project which has been publicized by much propaganda. The author implies that work, regulated by the state, from all men between the age of 18 and 30 years of age and all women between 18 and 25 years, could produce what they would need for the rest of their lives, and those who would want to could later earn more by taking on private jobs at their own discretion. This idea somewhat brings to mind the idea of *Le pain gratuit* [Free Bread] (1896) proposed in the book of the same title by Victor Barrucand, an anarchist of the time. The book contains critical observations of Kropotkin, Reclus, and several other anarchists: the idea is always that by one or another such steps of universal usefulness, enormous misery could be abolished and man could enter into the fight for existence with more equal possibilities of success. The Saint-Simonians counted on this method to arrive at the abolition of the *right of inheritance*, and Bakunin accepted this idea in full in order to achieve for man that which is called *equality from the moment of birth* for everyone.

Written in biblical style, the anonymous *Josua. Ein frohes Evangelium von künftigen Tagen* [Joshua, A Happy Evangelist of Future Days] (1912) foretells a revolution in the spirit of radical unionism. Its author, it is said, was a professor of philosophy at an Austrian university. On this point, I remember John Ballou Newbrough's strange and original book *Oahspe, A Light of Kosmon* (1910), essentially a bible of a sect called *Suomi-Oahspe Association-Roane*, Kosmon Year 62. It is full of utopian elements, but is also modeled, perhaps, on Mormon writings. Suomi means Finland; the text is in English; the book is American. I did not find any other information about this sect, a sect which I found curious and different from a good number of strange publications that are simply eccentric or crazy. In this one, there is the germ of an idea. Just as biblical in style is a small revolutionary pamphlet [by Ferdinand Beck], *Die Offenbarungen* [Revelations], published in Herisau in Switzerland in 1849, a socialist revolutionary echo of the commotion of 1848. There is also *Des Seig bei Jena... Die Letzte Schlacht; eine zunkünftige Begebenheit* [The Victory at Jena... The Last Battle; a Future Event], published by "Die Einigekeit" [Unity] (a syndicalist and antimilitaristic group) as well as a popular Russian anarchist tale, *Comment les paysans sont resté sans autorités* [How the Peasants Lived without a Government]. This account is signed by Sten'ka Zajac [or Zaets]. I do not know the original edition, but there are editions in Russian (in *Golos Truda*), in Bulgarian by 1912, and in Yiddish (Buenos Aires, 1923). No doubt, the major part of this propaganda literature from the last 10 years is unknown to me. I am familiar with neither Nariota's [or Nariosa's] *Riflessioni di un uomo delle caverne rivenienete nel secolo XX* [Reflections of a Caveman Awakening in the Twentieth Century] (Spezia, *Il Libertario* [Liberty], 1916) nor G. Cartella Gelardi's *I naufraghi del sogno* [The Ruins of the Dream] (Rome, 1920). Do these belong to the utopian genre? A[lfred]Cless's "Ein Zukunftbild der Menschheit" [A Vision of Humanity] (1893) is by an American anarchist but written in German.

At times the future of socialism has been spoken of at length in parliaments as in the German Reichstag from January 31 to February 7, 1893, and in the French Chamber of Deputies in the discussion between Jaurès, Vaillant, and Clemenceau from 1906. There exist special editions of those debates. One could even consult César de Paepe's "Silhouette d'une société collectiviste" [Outline of a Collectivist Society] in *La revue socialiste* [The Socialist Review] (Paris) for 1888 and Henri Brissac's "La société collectiviste" [Collectivist Society] in the same magazine in 1891.

There is a great deal of work about La Familistère [Social Palace] in Guise (Aisne), a large complex of workers' housing and factories. It was founded by one of the disciples of Fourierism, Jean-Baptiste André Godin, on the principle of worker participation, a sort of building model described sometimes as a socialist cooperative. This was a living utopia in the 1860s–1870s. The journal associated with the cooperative was *Le devoir* [Duty]. Godin's *Solutions sociales* [Social Solutions] is the principal exposition of its ideas. It is impossible to follow the projects and achievements of the participants or benefactors without feeling the allure of utopian thought. *Labour Copartnership*, published in London beginning in 1894, is one of the chronicles of this movement. At the same time, it is impossible to record all the more recent socialist colonies. The newspaper *The Llano Colonist*, of Leesville, Louisiana, has appeared for the last eight or nine years and gives information about these movements. Those which most emphasize individual freedom are recorded in *L'en-dehors* published in Orléans/Paris, France.

Anatole France has described Paris in 2270 in *Sur la pierre blanche* [On the White Rock] (1903), but his skepticism kept him to satiric fantasies like *L'île des pingouins* [The Island of Penguins] (1908) and to strange ideas such as those in *La révolte des anges* [The Angels' Rebellion] (1914). A utopia of an individualist dictatorship, H.-L. Follin's *La révolution du 4 septembre 19 ...* [The Revolution of 4 September 19 ...] (1921), is by one of the principal authors of that sort of rigidly bourgeois individualism so removed from the social individualism summarized and exemplified in E. Armand's *L'initiation individualiste anarchiste* [The Launch of Individualist Anarchism] (1923). There are even outlines of revolution, of acts of rebellion and of conspiracy, and how to be prepared for them, descriptions of violent strikes, of social cataclysms. Louise Michel's novel, *Le monde nouveau* [The New World] (1888) is full of the characteristics of this genre, and she contemplated pursuing these dreams, but it didn't happen—at least in the book. On the last page of *Le monde nouveau* one reads of "singular changes on one of the nearest planets. What are they? They are signals. The global International is beginning .... Look, we are going to respond." Emile Verhaeren's *Les aubes* [Dawns] (1918), the works of Han Ryner, and many other books contain visions of future struggle without stopping to look for solutions or definitive statements.

I move on now to the utopian writings that are outside the realms of socialism and anarchy, and that represent very diverse social concepts. So, for example, there are Emile Thirion's *Neustria, Utopie individualiste* [Neustria, an Individualist Utopia] (1901); Jean Jullien's *Enquête sur le monde futur* [Enquiry into the World of the Future] (1909); and R. H. Benson's *Im Dämmerschein der Zukunft* [The Glow of the Future] (1912), translated from English and an obviously clerical utopia by a Catholic priest. There is "What Will Posterity

Say of Us?" signed "The Hermit of Prague." It takes the form of a conference held in Darwin's living room in 1912; it appeared in the great magazine of evolutionary science, *Bedrock*. There is Wm. T. Burkitt's *The Coming Day. A Tale of Inevitable Social and Industrial Progress* (1913). There are three books from the young Polish author who died in the war, the titles when translated into German are *Auf silbernen Gefilden. Ein Mond-Roman* [On Silver Fields. A Novel about the Moon] (1903), *Der Sieger* [The Victor] (1910), and *Die alte Erde* [The Old Earth] (1911) (which I have not read). There are also Jean de Laby's *La sociéte future* [The Society of the Future] (1920) (which is not set in a utopian framework), and Henri Crozat's *La cité idéale ou l'urbanisme social rationnel* [The Ideal City or Rational, Social Urbanism] (1920), and others.

The more one gets into this subject, the more one notices that the *fictive framework* is no more than an accessory to the utopia; it's considered old fashioned by many authors. Then there are the makers of entire systems—singletons—and their number is legion. If a catalog were composed of the ideas put forth in all utopias, it would be necessary to add the ideas in these numerous books and even more numerous pamphlets with their unique ideas of every type and shade of meaning as examples of utopia. However, I leave out this large group of works although some have already slipped into the lists already presented.

There are also some utopian writings from diverse countries. In Romania, Braescu has written *Scurta* [a city] *in 100 years* (ca. 1890), perhaps socialist. On the island of Jamaica, in 1833, a periodical of advanced thought, the *Isonomist* (1833) [edited by Augustus Beaumont], published a strange dialog about a future age. It was reproduced in *The Gauntlet* (London), December 8, 1833, by its editor, the radical Richard Carlile. A utopia set in Greenland, in the language of that country, is Mathias Storch's *Singnagtuyag* [The Dream]. Storch was an Eskimo pastor. The novel presents a dream of local reforms adapted to that country. It is mentioned in a Danish newspaper in 1916. *A Constitution for the Kingdom of Heaven on Earth* appeared in Melbourne, Australia, in about 1915. [It was published anonymously.] *Como se hizo la revolucion* [How to Make a Revolution] (signed by Pedro Donamaria) is a study that replaces a great many theoretical articles stuffed with repetition (because a new theory cannot be found for every new article). It was published in *La voz del chauffeur* [The Voice of the Chauffeur] (Buenos Aires, March 1922), and there are others.

At times the anarchists have entertained themselves by ridiculing the social democrats in the form of utopian satire—as Max Baginski did in *Freiheit* (New York), September 24, 1894, and an Englishman in *The Torch* (London) in August 1895. The manifestations of utopia were not finished yet, however. After the First World War, Gustave Dupin (of Ermenonville) produced *Les Robinsons de la paix* [The Robinsons in Peacetime] (1920).

The tales of imaginary travels and so on became more and more numerous and fantastic. I could mention some stories by Edgar Allan Poe, such as "Hans Phaall—A Tale" (1835). There are, for instance, Max Haushofer's *Planetenfeuer* [Planet Fire] (1899) and George Sutherland's *Twentieth Century Inventions. A Forecast* (1901). There are diverse novels from J. H. Rosny. There are Louis Gastine and Léon Perrin's *Dans l'azur* [Into the Blue] (1909), an aviation novel written to support the idea of peace in the sky; Louis Gastine's *Énigme dans l'espace* [Riddle in Space] (1909) and *Le roi de l'espace* [The King of Space] (19??); and Max Pemberton's *The Impregnable City: A Romance* (1900). There are Ewald G. Seeliger's *Der Schrecken der Völker* [The Terror of the People] (1908); Edgar Wallace's *The Four Just Men* (1905); Jean de la Hire's *L'homme qui peut vivre dans l'eau* [The Man who Could Live Underwater] (1908), and a sequel, which moved to one of the planets; Ricciotto Canudo's *La ville sans chef* [A City without a Leader] (1910); André Couvreuer's *Une invasion de macrobes* [Invasion of the Macrobes] (1910); and Hector Fleischmann's *L'explosion du globe* [The Explosion of the Globe] (1910?). There are earlier examples too: William Westall's *A Queer Race. The Story of a Strange People* (1887); Delaval North's *The Last Man in London* (1887); and even J. Fenimore Cooper's *Mark's Reef; or, The Crater* (1847), and so on.

These novels, from an inoffensive genre in another time, acquired a very particular characteristic in the years before the war of 1914. Influenced by militarism (which gradually reawakened after its apparent eclipse during the Dreyfus affair), by various war scares, by aviation and its destructive possibilities, and by suspicion about sinister machinations [behind the scenes], this fantastic literature indulged in the common game of creating an atmosphere of mystery to prepare the spirit to expect anything. So, this literature got mixed up in profaning the utopian framework—that of future wars—with the crumbling visions of countries. In sum, they have deadened the nerves in order to prepare the world for war. This evolution is not unknown in the theater, in serious novels, and in political articles. The utopian genre does not lack them either. All of this, socialists and pacifists have ignored or misjudged because they have not believed in its existence, but the effects of this gradual poisoning have been no less great. The world would not have peacefully and with absolute fatalism submitted to war if its nerves had not been prepared for that evil by these injections of homicidal and fratricidal poison during these years.

I pass over this painful period and that of the War where, in Europe and, speaking for myself, my vision was limited by the boundaries of a single country in which, in the postwar period, one major party was maintained and perpetuated in power. As far as I can tell, in Europe two sorts of utopian literature have been published after 1918, and what has been published has depended on whether a country was victorious or defeated. In the victorious countries, utopias have hastened to leave the ruined Europe of their generation. They have fled to completely distant regions, and—those I know at least—have hardly worried about two pressing questions: How to undo the effect of terrible acts and how to restore the lives of ruined peoples? In the defeated countries, utopia has been disoriented, unstable, and despairing. It has hidden in every nook and cranny of morbid fantasy: seeing no way out, it has created monstrosities.

There is still this important factor: the Russian Revolution and the aborted revolutions in Germany, in Hungary, and in Finland. Above all, Russia professes a socialism that is no such thing while all these socialists and social democrats, too, are neither, but they still claim the label. If liberty, anarchy, revolutionary syndicalism would only raise their voices high, but they are enfeebled and resigned. So, apart from episodes of violence born of desperation, they do nothing, and reaction takes hold of their spirits. Then utopia is affected too. Still, it does not manage to sing like birds in the winter. What makes itself heard is eccentricity, unhealthy fiction. There have been exceptions, so much the better, but in general the result is deplorable.

I cite here some books that I have seen discussed but have not had occasion to read: Alfred Bratt's *Die Welt ohne Hunger* [The World without Hunger] (1916); Max Brod's *Das grosse Wagnis* [The Great Wager] (1919); Herbert Eulenberg's *Die Insel. Ein Spiel* [The Island. A Game] (1918); Norbert Jacques' *Piraths Insel* [Pirate's Island] (1918); F. X. Kappus's *Die lebenden Vierzehn* [The Fourteen Survivors] (1918); Annie Francé-Harrar's *Feuerseelen* [Souls on Fire] (1920); Claude Farrère's *Die Todgeweihten* [The Doomed] (1921) (and the French original, *Les condamnés à mort* [Those Condemned to Death] (1920)); Hans Christoph's *Die Fahrt in die Zukunft* [The Trip to the Future] (1922); Maurice Renard's *Die blaue Gefahr* [The Blue Danger] (1922) and the French original, *Le péril bleu* (1911); Georg Korf's *Die andere Seite der Welt* [The Other Side of the World] (1921); Kurt Lasswitz's *Auf Zwei Planeten* [On Two Planets] (1897); Fritz Brehmer's *Nebel der Andromeda* [The Andromeda Nebula] (1920); Egmont Colerus's *Antarktis* [Antarctica] (1920) as well as his *Sodom* (1920), *Weisse Magier* [White Magicians] (1922), and *Der dritte Weg* [The Third Way] (1921)—and so many others of this genre that seems to exhaust all of the possibilities and yet always finds new ones. And then there is the play *W. U. R.* (Werstands Universal Robots) (1921) about automated workers as imagined by the Czech Čapek brothers, as well as two works by Octave Joncquel and Théo Varlet in the two-part *L'epopée Martienne* [The Martian Epic] series: *Les titans de ciel* [The Titans of the Sky] (1921) and *L'agonie de la terre* [The Agony of the Earth] (1922), and so on.

There are, then, as we look back one last time, categories of works close to utopian, which express, for example, fears and nightmares that play on popular awareness and people's hopes. There have always been a great many prophets, visions, and predictions. People who want to guess the consequences of a depreciation in gold—or imagine what would happen if as unique an element as gold could be chemically broken down—could read a Dane, Otto M. Moeller, and his *Gold und Ehre* [Gold and Glory] (1896). That novel is a fiction of this type. Henri Allorge's "La famine de fer (en l'an 2432)" [The Iron Famine (in 2432)] (*La grande revue*, February 10, 1913) describes that year. There is a legend of a last great battle of the peoples of the world, and it is studied in Friedrich Zurbonsen's *Die Sage von der Völkerschlacht der Zukunft "am Birkenbaum"* [The Legend of the Battle of the People of the Future "at the Birch Tree"] (1897). Johannes Zemmrich with *Toteninseln und verwandte geographische Mythen* [The Islands of the Dead and Similar Geographical Myths] (1891) examines the Amazons; the rebellion and fall of the angels; the trips to a promised land such as that by St. Brendan; Eldorado; Bimini; Ophir; all of the dreamed-of lands, Schlaraffenland (the land of Cockaigne); the genre called Lügendichtung (tall tales), which reached their apogee in Münchhausen and later versions; Atlantis; the center of the Earth. All of these locations were the object of dreams, the lands of fantasy that always spin and parade through human thought, doing so more powerfully even than fact. And there are Shakespeare's *The Tempest* and Prospero's island; Grimmelshausen's *Simplicissimus* [The Simplest], a German novel of the seventeenth century, which is made up of utopian elements; and Schnabel and Tieck's *Insel Felsenburg* [Rock Island Castle] (1731–1743). The last of these forms a transition from the Robinsonade to a social utopia. Everywhere one encounters utopia, it has been altered by counterclaims, by eliminating the utopian element from literature. Literature will be much the poorer without it.

Just as utopias have proclaimed social ideals, the most noble ideas of freedom, so peace was also foreseen in noble utopian visions such as the Abbot of Saint-Pierre's *Projet [pour render la] paix perpétuelle* [Project (to Bring about) Perpetual Peace] (1712), and the study by Immanuel Kant titled *Zum ewigen Frieden* [Towards Eternal Peace] (1795). A rare work in this genre is titled *Etrennes de l'empereur de la Chine aux souverains de l'Europe pour l'année 1782* [A New Year's Gift from the Emperor of China to the Sovereigns of Europe in the Year 1782] (1782).

Shall I say a few things about the study of utopia?

Utopia was not lost sight of in earlier times as can be seen in, for example, Pierre Bayle's *Dictionnaire historique et critique* [Historical and Critical Dictionary] (1697) and in Garnier's large collection of *Voyages imaginaires* (1787–1789).

Since then, the economic and political sciences—because they emphasize history and realism—have underrated utopia. Among the first scholars who paid attention to utopia once more was G. C. Lewis in England. He has a chapter on ideal models in politics in his book *A Treatise on the Methods of Observation and Reasoning in Politics* (1852). Later, the German economist Robert von Mohl discussed the great utopias but without having the least sympathy for the ideas they present. Etienne Cabet, before and after having written *Icarie*, read utopias and spoke about them during his exile in London. After him, François Villegardelle and others did so in the 1840s. Then there was nothing new about utopias until 1891 when Professor F. Kleinwächter published, in Vienna, *Die Staatsromane* [Novels about the State]; Arthur von Kirchenheim later wrote *Schlaraffia politica, Geschichte der Dichtungen von besten Staat* [Political Idealism: History of the Workings of the Best State] (1892). It is obvious there were several weak pamphlets about some utopias, pamphlets intended to refute socialism, by A. Gehrke, M. Brasch, and others. The first who discussed this subject at some length—apart from the historians of socialism—was Professor Andreas Voigt and his *Die Sozialen Utopien. Funf Vorträge* [Socialist Utopias. Five Lectures] (1906).

I do not think there has been a serious study of the utopian genre as it appears in other countries with the exception, perhaps, of a recent book by an American: *The Story of Utopias*, by Lewis Mumford (1922). This book only spends time on a very small number of utopias, just 20 to 30. The other critics I have talked about discuss even fewer utopias. They focus on ten or 15 or 20, and I have talked about all of these in this study. They do not know about other utopias, but they pretend to by scorning them. So, they restrict themselves to a narrow circle of the 12 or 15 generally recognized utopias. This judgment includes Mumford, who has hardly described a larger magic circle of works traditionally seen as utopian. He does not advance the discussion of utopia much further at all. It is amazing to see the utopian materials of which he is ignorant.

The only ones who know about utopias are amateurs, collectors, and socialists free in spirit and long lived, who discover them little by little. One collector from Vienna, now dead, had gathered together the best collection of works of this genre; it was dispersed by a bookseller who published a catalog of 1850 items in 112 pages in March 1912. I know this catalog well; it is full of many original publications of every genre. The utopian literature it contains amounts, perhaps, strictly counted, to a third of the total, or about 600 titles. I know of another collection which, calculated in the same way, contains, perhaps, 400 or 500 titles which do not replicate the titles from the catalog of 1912. I know of a large number of titles of utopias from other sources. This knowledge allows me to say that with only these materials one could probably establish the existence of 1,000 to 1,200 utopias in various genres and in multiple editions and translations—and by undertaking a true bibliographic investigation one could arrive at even more. So, it can be seen that the [legitimate] study of utopias cannot be done on the basis of 20 or 30 examples when 300 to 500 would have to be known about.

Mr. Mumford's book is a nice enough description, but it is often useless even though it sometimes says very fine things. So, it boldly defines the nationalist utopia, and puts Mazzini in this category. Mumford does not promote anarchism or internationalism but sees into the depths of the question of how these terms are related with extraordinary subtlety. Nationalist utopias were created and then they were achieved in the real world. We have seen the results of that achievement. These pages from Mumford deserve to be quoted verbatim, but it would take up too much space in this chapter. I also do not have the book with me to quote from.

Here, I end my brief look at a genre of literature that some readers would, perhaps, not have believed was so extensive. Utopia has always existed, and it exists still. It will not die. It has been a strong medium for propaganda when it has value. When the ideas in a utopia are worth little but are presented attractively, it has been able to mislead the world: Christianity, nationalism, fictions that were believed in as necessary to achieve—to impose—faith. The people will always have their dream, their utopia, and every person has her or his own. There is not, then, any reason to look down upon or scorn this genre. On the contrary, if we knew how to create and propagate a powerful utopia, the world would help us to achieve it, so it falls to us to create it and to march forward with it. Only once did this happen—on May 1, 1890. On that day, the people were sure of what they wanted and their imaginations were deeply moved. It would have gone further, but the socialists were not prepared to support it. Since then, the imagination of the people has never been touched again, not by the Russian Revolution, not by the death of Ferrer. There has been an impulse to change now and then, but nothing has had universal appeal.

I do not say that all of the world should write utopias—God protect us! But in the gap between utopia and experiment and science, between the knowledge and the experience necessary for one or for the other, there are connections. Utopia is not identical to an energetic game, or to pure and simple fantasy, for frequently it also rests on reason, on knowledge, on experience. And it is a creation, a willed act. Criticism will modify it, even pour scorn on it. So much the better. It is the act of creating utopia which is essential; however, utopia does not work directly. It works through the spirit, through the intellect, through the fantasies we all hold on to. We use these powers very little in life.

Let us coordinate our ideas and establish, each for herself or himself, *my* utopia; then those who can should search for the most effective methods loudly to express their concept of utopia. Doing so will yet lead to something. One day, from here or from there, someone will come to prominence and will write for us a beautiful utopia. This person will know how to find the missing link between the present and the future, between our dreams and our present selves. She or he will find a way and will create a path forward to a free and limitless utopia.

23 January 1925
M. Nettlau

Note [by Nettlau]

It is obvious that this essay could not inform the reader of the contents, ideas, genre, and many special characteristics of the hundreds of utopias mentioned. This essay was meant above all to give a snapshot of the categories and interconnections in this great literature down the centuries. All the detailed work remains to be done by examining the various works and the historical details they bring with them. This work will establish above all the *connections* among utopias. In part, these derive from the originality of their plans, but very often these plans are constrained by a major utopian work or defined in opposition to one. This interdependence is very interesting to witness next to the isolation and independence which one finds in utopian literature just as often. I could not tackle all this in this preliminary sketch. M.N.

NOTES

Page iii

The title page of *Esbozo*. The 1934 IMAN edition states that the Spanish version is based on a German manuscript: "Trad. del alemán por D. Abad de Santillán." I have, however, found no manuscript in German for Nettlau's work despite extensive searching. It is likely that the publisher, IMAN, simply assumed that since German was Nettlau's first language, he will have written the manuscript in that language. Nettlau, however, wrote the manuscript in French—in all likelihood because it was the second language that both he and de Santillán shared and knew best. This shared language allowed de Santillán to translate the manuscript into Spanish for publication in 1925 and 1934. It may also be that de Santillán was in no way involved in the 1934 republication. That would make the mistake about a German manuscript easy to understand.

Page xxi

"He lives with a widow." Lucy Ross in her translation of Muñoz's *Cronologia* incorrectly says that Nettlau married this unnamed widow: "He marries a widow, mother of a thirteen-year-old girl" (8). Muñoz actually writes: "Une su vida a la de una mujer viuda, madre de una niña de trece años' (15–16). "Living with" or literally "uniting one's life" ("una su vida") is not the same as marriage; the latter would be "El se casó." I have seen this startling claim of marriage mentioned by Ross nowhere else in the scholarship on Nettlau. Indeed, the Rocker biography tells a very different story: "In the spring of 1914, he [Nettlau] had rented [Ger.: "eingemietet"] a room with a widow and her thirteen-year-old daughter. He lived there peacefully in the company of his books, his magazines, and his canaries until the invasion of Austria by the Nazis" (Ger. version, 1978, p. 210; my translation). It may be that Muñoz misunderstood Rocker, and Ross simply compounded the error.

Nettlau had relationships with women (often prostitutes), but after the death of Thérèse Bognar, he seems not to have formed a long-term romantic alliance again. His work was his first love.

Page xli

There is an online color reproduction of the 1934 IMAN edition of *Esbozo* at Max Nettlau—Esbozo de historia de las utopías: https://materialesfopep.files.wordpress.com.

Page 1

Biographical Sketch. The 1934 edition labels this section a Prologue. I have renamed it, logically and functionally, a Biographical Sketch. This sketch (or prologue) does not appear anywhere in the 1925 manuscript or the 1925 serial publication. It may be that MN was better known to the readers of *La protesta* than to those who bought the IMAN edition.

Page 10

Theocritus. MN writes "Therekrates," but there is no Ancient Greek poet of this name.
Plato's *Laws*. Plato's last and longest dialog in 12 books. The date of the work is unknown, but it is generally considered a late composition.

Page 11

Laurens. MN calls the author "l'abbé Dulaurens." The subtitle of *Etrennes* is *Poeme heroi-comique en XVII chants* (Heroic-comic Poem in 17 Cantos).
Mitra. I assume that MN is referring to the fourth-century cult of Mithrism, a Roman mystery cult with Iranian origins.

Page 13

Encyclopédists. Members of the Société des gens de lettres ("Society of Men of Letters"), a French writers' society. They contributed to the development of the *Encyclopédie* from June 1751 to December 1765 under Diderot and le Rond d'Alembert's direction.
Perrault. MN writes "Perreaux." MN is likely thinking of Perrault's "Sleeping Putto" (1882).
Count of Gabalis. *M. le comte de Gabalis: ou, entretiens sur les sciences secretes* (M. le Comte de Gabalis: or, Conversations on the Secret Sciences) (1670) was written by Abbé Nicolas-Pierre-Henri de Montfaucon de Villars (1635–1673). The eponymous "Comte de Gabalis" is an occultist who explains the mysteries of the world to the author.

Page 17

de Bergerac. The alternative title is *Histoire comique: contenant les états et empires de la Lune*.

Plockhoy. Plockhoy wrote two pamphlets relevant to MN's discussion: *The Way to the Peace and Settlement of These Nations* and *A Way Propounded to Make the Poor in These and Other Nations Happy*. Both date from 1659 although MN gives the date as 1658.

Page 18

The History of the Sevarites or Severambi. MN remarks:

> A complete version in French was published with the title of *Histoire des Sevarambes, peuples qui habitent une partie du troisième continent, communément appellé la terre australe* (The History of the Sevarites, a People who Live in a Part of the Third Continent Commonly Called the Southern Land) (1677–1679). There was (among others) a Dutch translation in 1682; German editions in 1689, 1717, and 1783; and an Italian translation in 1730. It is a massive work and was printed many times, the last time, I think, as Volume 5 in the great collection of *Voyages imaginaires*, published between 1787 and 1789 (ts. fl. 24; my translation from the French).

Nettlau is correct and refers to the massive compilation of utopias titled *Voyages imaginaires, songes, visions, et romans cabalistiques*, edited by (among others) Charles Garnier, and published in Paris and Amsterdam between 1787 and 1789. MN also cites later editions of *Histoire des Sevarambes* (in 1693 [Paris: C. Barbin], in 1732 [Amsterdam: Alexander Mortier], and in the *Voyages imaginaires* collection). These later editions were published with the title *Les aventures de Jacques Sadeur dans la decouverte et le voyage de la terre austral* (The Adventures of Jacques Sadeur in the Discovery of and Voyage to the Southern Land).

Fénelon. *Les aventures de Télémaque* recounts episodes omitted from Homer: the travels and education of Odysseus's son, Telemachus.

Rebmann. "Abenazar's kleine Republik" describes an anarchist-communist idyll in his longer account titled *Hans Kiekindiewelts Reisen in alle vier Weltheile und den Mond* (Hans Kiekindiewelt's Travels in All Four Parts of the World and on the Moon) (1794).

Histoire de Calejava. According to J.-M. Quérard's *La France littéraire, ou dictionnaire bibliographique* 3:348: "Cet ouvrage a été déttuit par l'auteur lui-même. Il n'en reste qu'un seul exemplaire." ("This work was destroyed by the author himself. Only one copy of it exists" [my translation].) WorldCat makes it clear that this is not the case although it is certainly a rare book. It was republished in Paris in 1970.

Page 19

Europaeus. "Lucius Cornelius Europaeus" was the pseudonym of the writer of *La monarchie des solipses* (1721), who was actually either Melchior Inchofer or Giulio Clemente Scotti.

Voyages imaginaires. The series exists in 36- and 39-volume versions. The publisher is unknown. It is divided into three groups and a three-volume supplement. The series is given over to imaginary voyages, dreams and visions, and cabalistic novels. The supplement covers the story of shipwrecks.

Page 21

Bougeant. Bougeant's work forms Volume 26 of Garnier's *Voyages imaginaires, songes, visions, et romans cabalistiques*.

L'abbe Maillot's *Voyage*. This book by l'abbe Maillot to which Nettlau refers is likely Nettlau's own as the only known copy is housed in the International Institute of Social History (IISH) in Amsterdam. Nettlau sold his vast library to the Institute when he became impoverished as a result of the hyperinflation that occurred in Germany and Austria after World War I.

Page 22

Jost de Villeneuve. Nettlau, in describing Villeneuve's work, provides the author's pseudonym only: M. de Listonai.

The *Statuts*. The *Statuts du bourg d'Oudun, composé de la famille R**, vivant en commun* consists of 44 articles appended to *Le paysan perverti*.

Page 23

A Journey to the Land of Ophyr. For a discussion of this work, see Marek Příhoda's essay.

Resnier. Guillaume Resnier's *Republique universelle, ou l'humanité ailée, réunie sous l'empire de la raison* (1788) was written under the pseudonym of Reinser II.

Page 28

"Ruvarebohni." "Ruvarebohni" is simply a French anagram of "vrai bonheur," that is, "truly happy."

Page 29

Sonnenfels. MN may be thinking of his *Über die Abschaffung der Tortur* (On the Abolition of Torture) (1775) given MN's own work on this subject.

Pezzl. MN may be thinking of his novel *Faustin, oder das philosophische Jahrhundert* (Faustin, or the Philosophical Century) (1783), which was a deliberate imitation of Voltaire's *Candide*.

Albrecht. MN may be thinking of his political novel *Die Affenkönige oder die Reformation des Affenlandes. Ein politischer Roman in zwei Büchern* (The Monkey Kings or the Reformation of Monkey Country. A Political Novel in Two Books) (1788) or his play *Die Kolonie* (The Colony) (1793).

Abdera. This town was a major Greek polis on the Thracian coast in the Classical era. The polis lay less than ten miles east-northeast of the mouth of the Nestos river and almost directly opposite the island of Thasos. The city that developed from it became of major importance in ancient Greece. After the 4th century CE, it declined, contracted to just its acropolis, and was abandoned.

Biberach (or Biberach an der Riss). This location is a town in southern Germany. It is the capital of the Biberach district in the Upper Swabia region of the German state of Baden-Württemberg.

Schildbürgers. The inhabitants of the fictional town of Schilda. They are the main protagonists in a whole series of short stories, the Schildbürger pranks. They are among the best-known German collection of joke stories in the form of novels. Their author is most likely to be Johann Friedrich von Schoenberg (1543–1614).

Krähwinkel. A real village in North Rhine-Westphalia. Krähwinkel is situated next to Theisbitze, and close to Viehgasse.

Page 31

John Trotter. His novel, *Travels in Phrenologasto* (1825), was written under the pseudonym of Gio. Battista Balscopo with the additional subterfuge that it was supposedly a translation from the Italian.

Page 34

MN is technically correct in giving Thoreau's full name as David Henry Thoreau. He was christened such, but changed his name to the more familiar Henry David Thoreau after finishing college. He did so for unknown reasons.

Page 35

The Book of Platonopolis. This book was, in fact, incompletely published in serial form over three issues. The Communitarian Library was actually called The Communist Chronicle, or Promethean Magazine.

Page 36

Petzler. With Petzler's 1897 utopia, it is likely MN is referring to *Grosse Jubiläumsfeier und imposanter Triumphzug in Erinnerung des hundertjährigen Bestehens de social-demokratischen Staatseinrichtung in Britannien* (Major Anniversary Celebrations and Impressive Triumphal Procession to Commemorate the Centenary of the Social-democratic State Institution in Britain).

Page 37

Considerant. I have been unable to trace the German translation of Considerant's work on Herschel.
Coeurderoy. MN wrote a "Notice biographique sur Ernest Coeurderoy (1825–1862)" for the three-volume edition of Coeurderoy's work published in three volumes in Paris in 1910 by Stock.
Guillaume. MN is probably referring to Guillaume's pamphlet titled *Idées sur l'organsation sociale* (Ideas about the Organization of Society). There is no work by Guillaume titled *Une commune sociale*.

Page 39

Theophile Gautier's "Paris future." I have been unable to find this essay in the collection cited by MN: *Le diable à Paris* (1845).

Page 40

"The Hungarian novelist." MN follows the title with [1952]. It's unclear why. The information about the Hungarian edition of the book is as follows: *A jövő század regénye* (A Novel of the Coming Century), 1873.

"Heliomanes." An unidentified pseudonym for the author of *A Journey to the Sun* (1866).

Sibbern. The work MN is referring to by Sibbern is almost certainly *Meddelelser af Indholdet af et Skrivt fra Aaret 2135* (Messages Written from the Year 2135).

"The pages of the copy in the British Museum have not been cut." MN will likely have done the majority of his research for *Esbozo* in the British Museum Reading Room. Such a resource would have had the sort of bibliographical information about authors, titles, and editions that distinguishes *Esbozo* as an historical account.

Page 43

Chapter 5. The fifth section is preceded by a note from MN to Abad de Santillán. It is dated January 19, 1925. It begins with a two-line heading: "V (to follow)." It reads as follows:

> There will be two chapters to come: 1887 to 1925 (quite long)—and some final comments (short). It's necessary to verify the details for these—so I cannot write these chapters quickly. Pierre Quirole has been kind enough to send me his utopias and other writings; I will speak about his utopian writings in their place in chapter V. I would like, in order to please him and since he's someone who loves this genre, to put at the head of the article "to Pierre Quirole," as is often done. If it's possible, I ask you to put his name. If the state of hostilities makes this impossible, don't do it—I can't render an opinion and it's of no importance to me. If it will only do harm, then *don't*—but how can I know? I do not want to make an issue of this, believe me, for an act of comradeship should never harm someone. Do as you wish—and over there the presses have refused to run for three months—or have they not?—the gods alone know.

This note does not, of course, appear in either the 1925 or the 1934 printed editions. The 1925 serial publication is, however, dedicated "A Pierre Quirole," so de Santillán did as his friend requested. It is also clear from the note that MN sent *Esbozo* to de Santillán in two batches.

Page 50

La clairière. *La clairière* premiered at the Théâtre Antoine on April 6, 1900, and was revived on March 12, 1909.

Page 52

Free Life. This title was a weekly paper with a small circulation. It began in 1890. It soon became a monthly paper titled *Organ of Voluntary Taxation and the Voluntary State*. This paper ran until 1901.

Olerich. Olerich's book describes social conditions on Mars and is supposedly told by a Martian.

The Old and the New. The first edition of *The Old and the New* was a work in German titled *Freie Menschen in der Liebe und Ehe. Ein Versuch, die Menschen glücklicher und besser zu machen* (Free People in Love and Marriage. An Attempt to Make People Happier and Better). It was published in 1895.

Credit Foncier. This newspaper actually belongs to the Topolobambo Colony in Mexico although based on the paragraph following the one in which Nettlau cites the work he seems to be unaware of this fact.

The Coming Nation. This newspaper was published at the Ruskin colony in Ruskin (about 50 miles west of Nashville) between 1893 and 1902. See Francelia Butler's "The Ruskin Commonwealth" for more details.

Page 54

"Elpis." I have been unable to find this work although there are a couple of journals from the late nineteenth century that begin with the word.

Altruria. As well as the location for Howells' novel, Altruria was a short-lived utopian commune in Sonoma County, California. It was based on Christian socialist principles and was founded by Edward Byron Payne in 1894. It finished as a commune by 1896.

Page 56

Hamilton and St. John. *How the Vote Was Won* was first performed in April 1909 at the Royalty Theatre in London.

Lysistrata. Donnay's play was first performed at the Grand Théâtre, Paris, on December 22, 1892.

Lisistrata. Hoffmann's version of the famous story was first performed on January 15, 1802 at the Théâtre Feydeau.

Page 57

If Christ Came to Chicago. MN's reference is to W. T. Stead's book of that title. That book has a subtitle "A Plea for the Union of All Who Love in the Service of All Who Suffer."

Hugo. WorldCat cites Victor Hugo's authorship as uncertain. The earliest dated edition I have been able to locate is a London 1862 edition published by the Librairie et agence de l'imprimerie universelle. It is 14 pages long. The earliest may be an eight-page version published by Librairie Populaire s. a. An 1880 edition cites the author simply as "un artiste en renom" (a renowned artist).
Rosny (pseud.). *Les Xipéhuz* may have been the work mainly of the elder Boex brother, Joseph Henri Honoré.
Les amours de l'age d'or. The date is not definitely 1855. The publisher, based on the contents page of the book, is P. Briez. The place of publication based on the same page is Abbeville. The subtitle appears to date from 1871.

Page 58

M'Crib. The title page of the edition includes the epigraph: "Non sine spe melioris uevi" ("Not without hope of a better time").
Among the Têtchas. The Library of Congress holds a copy. The book is cited in *The English Catalogue of Books* 4.14 as follows: "Among the Têtchas of Central Asia, 12mo, 1s (Gem Library), Southern Pub. Co. 1886." The book is reviewed in *The Saturday Review of Politics, Literature, Science, and Art* (London) 61.1600 (June 26, 1886: 902) as follows:

> *Among the Têtchas of Central Asia* (Southern Publishing Co.) is neither a very deft nor a very delicate excursion in satirical romance. The narrative lacks plausibility, the humour is somewhat flat, and the satire decidedly rough. In the land of the Têtchas the supremacy of women is complete. They hold all official appointments, possess a House of Oratory—in which the Silencer is a chief dignitary—a College of Eloquence, temples of law, medicine, and so forth, and are ruled by an old lady known as the Grand Lam. There is, of course, a university, though without a professor of logic, which curious circumstance leads to a remark of the author that is a fair sample of his wit, "'Our girls,' says his guide, the head of the institution, 'could not master the premises of a syllogism—they never went beyond the major.' 'They seldom get beyond a captain in England,' I replied."

The book was also reviewed in *The Literary World* June 18, 1886: 595, col. 2: "The work is decidedly clever; but, as will be gathered from the above remarks, extremely far-fetched."

Bart-Claye. The title, *Vers la cité future*, is followed by an epigraph: "Il faudrait cependant que leur royaume fût un peu de ce monde" (Their kingdom had to be a little bit of this world).

1889–1890. It is not clear by this pair of dates if MN means that *Looking Backward* was published during these years (it was actually published in 1888), or if that was the period of the novel's popularity (it actually lasted much longer as MN implies earlier in the sentence). I suspect MN meant the date of publication and was writing it down as an approximation from memory.

Page 59

heart's blood. MN uses the German expression here: *mit dem Herzblut*.

Page 62

Golos Truda was a Russian-language anarchist newspaper founded by working-class Russian expatriates in New York City in 1911. The newspaper moved to Petrograd during the Russian Revolution in 1917. It ceased publication in 1929 having been suppressed by the Stalinist regime.

L'assiette au beurre. A French magazine emphasizing satire and anarchism and published weekly between 1901 and 1912 and monthly (albeit intermittently) between 1921 and 1925. It ceased publication in 1936. The title of the magazine literally means "butter plate" but has the connotation of the English expression about political corruption, "pork barrel."

Page 63

"A theatrical piece." This comment is probably a reference to Maurice Donnay and Lucien Descaves' *La clarière* (The Clearing), first published in 1900.

Emile Henry. The brother of Emile Henry is Jean-Charles Fortuné Henry (1869–1931). He was an important figure in anarchist circles and founded an intentional community (Colonie l'Essai) in Aiglemont in the Ardennes.

L'ère nouvelle. *L'ère nouvelle* ran from 1901–1911. *Hors du troupeau* was published in 1911 only. *L'en-dehors* from 1922–1939.

Blaricum colony. A colony of Christian anarchists in Blaricum, Belgium. It was founded in 1900 and ended in 1904 after there was local opposition to the colonists as foreigners and vegetarians.

Vrede. Actually, the name of a printing company which moved from The Hague to Blaricum in 1902. It printed *De Pionier*, which Felix Ortt edited.

Die neue Gemeinschaft. An anarcho-communist commune (1900–1904) organized by Julius and Heinrich Hart, and Gustav Landauer in Berlin. The commune was influenced by the Garden City movement and the ideas of William Morris. It is sometimes referred to as bohemian.

Page 64

Etoile rouge. I have been unable to locate this translation. WorldCat cites a version from the 1900s, which was published in Paris in a journal by the Organization juive révolutionnaire. The first publication in book form was in 1908 in St. Petersburg. MN also cites editions in Russian (1918), Ukrainian (1923), and German (1923). There is a 1984 English version (*Red Star: The First Bolshevik Utopia*) translated by Charles Rougle and edited by Loren R. Graham and Richard Stites. It was published by Indiana University Press in Bloomington.
Le Maroc socialiste. MN cites a subtitle for this work: *A Project for Socialist Colonization*.
Die Sonnenstadt. MN refers to the famous utopia titled *La città del sole* (The City of the Sun). This work was written by Tommaso Campanella in Italian in 1602 and first published in Latin in 1623. The first published Italian version, edited by Norberto Bobbio, was published by G. Einaudi in Turin in 1941. There is a good bilingual (Italian and English) edition *La città del sole: dialogo poetico; The City of the Sun: A Poetical Dialogue* published in 1981.

Page 65

Saint-Simonians. Those who were inspired by the ideas of Claude Henri de Rouvroy, comte de Saint-Simon. His ideas suggested growth in industrialization and in scientific discovery would profoundly change society. Temporal and spiritual power would evolve into a productive society grounded in useful work, the basis of any true equality.
Suomi-Oahspe. I have been unable to find information on the "Suomi-Oahspe Association Roane." It may be that it is entirely fictional.
Offenbarungen. MN indicates that there is an 1849 edition published in Herisau, Switzerland. I have been unable to locate this edition. In the Bibliography, I have cited a book of the same title by Ferdinand K. Beck. It may be the one MN is thinking of, but it hardly seems socialist. I suspect it is more likely that MN is thinking of *Delenda Austria!: Die Auflösung Österrreiches al seine Notwendigkeit unserer Zeit* (Destroy Austria! The Dissolution of Austria as a Necessity in Our Time). It was written by Louis Vogel and published in 1849 in Herisau by M. Schläpfer. As the title suggests, it is markedly more revolutionary.

Die Einigekeit. *Die Einigekeit* was a German newspaper. It appeared from June 19, 1897 to August 8, 1914. It was the organ of the radical socialist Free Association of German Trade Unions (FVdG). Its original editor was Gustav Kessler, but he was replaced by Fritz Kater after his death in 1904.

Comment les paysans. I have been unable to locate this popular Russian anarchist tale. I have been unable to locate the edition in Yiddish. The edition published in St. Petersburg is actually Croatian. The title in English would be: *What Happens When Men Are Left without Leadership, A Fairy Tale*. As to the Bulgarian version, I have been able to locate one other version (by Sten'ka Zaets). It was published in Sofia, Bulgaria in 1923.

Cless. The only citation in WorldCat is to a review of *Ein Zukunftsbild der Menschheit* (A Vision of the Future of Mankind) in *Verlagsmagazin* (Publishers' Magazine) vol. 20. Cless's essay originally appeared in *Neue Zeit: Revue des geistigen und offentlichen Lebens* (The New Age: Review of Intellectual and Public Life) 11 (1892–1893). The magazine was published in Stuttgart and was the journal of the German Social-Democratic Workers' Party.

Page 66

Labour Copartnership. MN indicates this journal began in 1894. Its purpose is described in the Notes and Memoranda section of *The Quarterly Journal of Economics* 9.1 (Oct. 1894): 96. It was also published between 1902 and 1905.

The Llano Colonist. This newspaper was published in 1921 in Llano, California and in New Llano, in Leesville, Louisiana between April 1921 and December 1937 under the editorship of Job Harriman.

Benson. *Im Dämmerschein der Zukunft* was published simultaneously by the Benziger Brothers in Germany and in New York. It is a translation of Benson's *The Dawn of All* (1911).

Page 67

"young Polish author." The young Polish author is Jerzy Żulawski (1874–1915). He was a writer, philosopher, and translator, most famous for his science-fiction work *Trylogia Księżycowa* (Lunar Trilogy) written between 1901 and 1911.

Braescu. I have not been able to locate *Scurta dans cent ans* (ca. 1890).

Isonomist. This journal was begun and ended in 1833. It was a daily newspaper edited by Augustus Hardin Beaumont (a member of the legislature) and published in Kingston, Jamaica. I have not managed to locate the work which MN mentions.

The Gauntlet. The summary of the information from the *Isonomist* as reprinted in *The Gauntlet* is titled "Ourselves in Prospect," No. 44 (Dec. 8, 1833): 690. MN is incorrect to say it was "reproduced" ("reproduit"); it was excerpted.
Storch. The work MN mentions is titled *En Grønlænders drøm*. It was published in Copenhagen in 1915. I have not been able to find the book in Greenlandic under the title *Singnagtuyag*.
Como se hizo la revolución. I have not been able to locate this reference.
Freiheit. An anarchist journal (1879–1910) founded by Johann Most and published in London and, later, in New York.
The Torch. *The Torch of Anarchy* (1891–1896) was a newspaper edited by Olivia, Helen, and Arthur Rosetti, the adolescent children of William Rosetti (the Pre-Raphaelite) and Lucy Maddox Brown. See Christopher Draper's history of the newspaper: radicalhistorynetwork.blogspot.com/2018/02/the-torch-of-anarchy-1891-1896.html.

Page 68

de la Hire. The sequel to which MN refers is *Le mystère des XV* (The Mystery of the XV). It takes place on Mars, and was published serially in 1911 and in book form in 1922. *L'homme qui peut vivre dans l'eau* was published serially in 1909 in *Le matin* and in book form in 1910, 1922, and 1926. WorldCat only has a record for the 1926 publication.
A Queer Race. MN cites 1892 as the year this book was published. WorldCat cites 1887. There is no 1892 edition. The entire book is available at books.google.com.

Page 69

Auf zwei Planeten. In the French manuscript, MN wrote "*Zwischen zwei Welten* (Between Two Worlds) par Kurd Lasswitz" (fl. 58). This title and author combination does not appear to exist. MN may be misremembering the correct title of Lasswitz's novel (which he cited earlier in the manuscript), published in 1897: *Auf zwei Planeten*. There *is* a book titled *Zwischen zwei Welten*. It was written by Evgenij Nikolaevic Posel'janin, but it was not first published until 1926, a year after MN's account of utopian history was written.
The Martian Epic. The two parts of the Martian epic by Joncquel and Théo Varlet were published in an English adaptation by Brian M. Stableford, *The Martian Epic: The Titans of the Heavens. The Agony of the Earth* (Encino, CA: Black Coat Press, 2008).

Page 70

Zurbonsen. Zurbonsen elaborates on a Westphalian legend that the Byzantine Emperor would create his kingdom in Jerusalem. He would hang his shield in a birch tree and give up his kingdom to God. With the Antichrist's arrival, the emperor would take up his shield once again, fight the holy war, and establish a new kingdom of God. The scene is depicted in Karl Goetz's cast-bronze medal titled "die letzte Schlacht am Birkenbaum" ("the last battle at the birch tree") (1923). See https://karlgoetz.com/galleries/WWI/pages/K-298.html. WorldCat incorrectly spells "Birkenbaum" as "Birkenbaume."

St. Brendan. Brendan of Clonfert (ca. 484–ca. 577 CE) was one of the early Irish monastic saints and one of the Twelve Apostles of Ireland. He is also referred to as Brendan the Navigator, Brendan the Voyager, Brendan the Anchorite, and Brendan the Bold. He is best known for his legendary voyage in search of the Garden of Eden, a voyage dated to the first decades of the sixth century CE.

Münchhausen. A fictional German nobleman created by Rudolf Erich Raspe (1736–1794) in *Baron Münchausen's Narrative of His Marvellous Travels and Campaigns in Russia* (1785). The book was first published in London in English and then translated into German in 1786 by Gottfried August Bürger (1747–1794). Raspe was a German writer, scientist, and librarian. Bürger was a German poet, well known in particular for his ballad *Lenore*.

Insel Felsenburg. This novel was first published in 1731. There were sequels in 1732, 1736, and 1743.

Page 71

Lewis. The chapter in *A Treatise on the Methods of Observation and Reasoning in Politics* is "On Ideal Models in Politics."

Mohl. It is unclear to what book by Robert von Mohl MN is referring. It may well be his *Encyclopädie der Staatswissenschaften* (Encyclopedia of Political Science) (1851).

Gehrke. In referring to one of the "weak pamphlets" "intended to refute socialism," MN likely means Gehrke's *Communistische Idealstaaten* (1878). Gehrke's book covers Plato's ideal republic, More's *Utopia*, Campanella's *The City of the Sun*, and Cabet's *Voyage to Icaria*.

Mumford. The pages to which MN refers in his discussion of Mumford's analysis of Mazzini's ideas are sections 10–15 of *The Story of Utopias* (pp. 221–234). Mumford initially characterizes Mazzini's ideas as a Hans Andersen fairy tale "clapped together" but a "beautiful fabrication of the National State" (222). Then, however, Mumford goes on to offer a fine critique over nearly

13 pages of the underpinnings of the utopia of nationalism. He ends with an assertion with which MN would likely have agreed:

> We may perhaps approach our social institutions a little more courageously when we realize how completely we ourselves have created them and how, without our perpetual "will to believe" they would vanish like smoke in the wind (234).

Page 72

May 1, 1890. MN refers to International Workers Day, created to commemorate the Haymarket massacre in Chicago on May 4, 1886, a bloody event which grew out of a general strike—on May 1 of that year—in support of an eight-hour working day. The massacre included the police firing live rounds at workers. Seven police officers and at least four civilians died; 60 police officers and 115 civilians were injured. Hundreds of workers and those who sympathized with the cause were later arrested and summarily tried. Four were executed by hanging. On the following day (May 5, 1886), in Milwaukee, Wisconsin, the state militia fired live rounds at strikers. Seven were killed including a bystander feeding chickens in his garden.

"The death of Ferrer." Francisco Ferrer (1859–1909). Executed in 1909 by a Spanish firing squad.

Page 73

Note. MN finishes the French manuscript with a note appended to the final sentence. I have reproduced it verbatim at the end of this edition of *Esbozo*. This Note appears in a similar guise at the end of the Spanish serial publication in 1925 but at the *beginning* of the Spanish book version of 1934. MN then follows this note with some postscripts (which do not appear anywhere in either Spanish version):

> When do you need the *Prologue* to Bakunin V: Chartism and An[archism]?
> I will begin Bakunin's Biography II in February.
> Received letter and ten [word missing? possibly "pounds"] and thank you ***very much***.
> I spoke of the German Bakunin book with Dr. Karl Federn; if one day there is a package from him, you know he has my trust. I will *explain* shortly—
> Received [Bakunin's?] Works in Spanish; marvellous; best wishes.

Appendix A
SELECT NETTLAU BIBLIOGRAPHY

With this short list of Nettlau's works, I have been guided by several considerations. First, I have mentioned here those works which scholars most frequently cite as important to Nettlau's development as a thinker or to the history of anarchism as an idea. Second, I have cited those works which I found most useful to my own understanding of Nettlau's remarkable career as an anarchist. Third (albeit with two exceptions), I have only listed those works which are relatively easy to access in academic libraries.

Bibliographie de l'Anarchie. Brussels: Bibliothèque des "Temps Nouveau," 1897.
A Contribution to an Anarchist Bibliography of Latin America. 1931. Trans. Paul Sharkey. London: Kate Sharpley Library, 1994.
"Death of Karl Marx." *The Commonweal* 4.113 (Mar. 10, 1888): 79.
Die historische Entwickelung des Anarchismus. New York: Freiheit, 1890.
Élisée Reclus. Anarchist und Gelehrter (1830–1905). Berlin: Verlag "Der Syndikalist," 1928.
Ernest Coeurderoy. Leipzig: Hirschfeld, 1911.
Errico Malatesta. Das Leben eines Anarchisten. Berlin: Verlag "Der Syndikalist," 1922.
Eugenik der Anarchie. Ed. Rudolf de Jong. Wetzlar: Büchse der Pandora, 1985.
"The Evolution of Anarchism." *Freedom* 9.96 [93] (May 1895): 6–7.
Geschichte der Anarchie. Vol. 1: *Der Verfrühling der Anarchie.* Berlin: Verlag "Der Syndikalist," 1925. Vol. 2: *Der Anarchismus von Proudhon zu Kropotkin.* Berlin: Verlag "Der Syndikalist," 1927. Vol. 3: *Anarchisten und Sozialrevolutionäre.* Berlin: ASY-Verlag, 1931. Vol. 4: *Die erste Blütezeit der Anarchie: 1886–1894.* Vaduz, Liechtenstein: Topos Verlag, 1981. Vol. 5: *Anarchisten und Syndikalisten, Part 1.* Vaduz, Liechtenstein: Topos Verlag, 1984.
"La vida de Gustavo Landauer según su correspondencia." *La protesta – suplemento quincenal* (Buenos Aires) 8.309 (July 31, 1929): [353]–392.
"L'idée anarchiste. Son passé – son avenir." *L'idée anarchiste* (Paris) 1 (Mar. 13, 1924); 4–13 (Apr. 24–Nov. 15, 1924).
Max Nettlau Papers (1870–1944). 42 metres in extent. International Institute of Social History. ARCH01001.
Michael Bakunin. Eine Biographie. 3 vols. Privately printed, 1896–1900. Rpt. Milan: Feltrinelli, 1971. Mimeographed ms. 1290 fl.
Michael Bakunin. Eine biographische Skizze. Berlin: P. Pawlowitsch, 1901.
La Première Internationale en Espagne (1868–1888). 2 vols. Ed. Renée Lambaret. Dordrecht: D. Reidel, 1969.

Responsibility and Solidarity in the Labor Struggle. London: Freedom Office, 1900.

Revival of the Inquisition. Details of the Tortures Inflicted on Spanish Political Prisoners. London: J. Perry, 1897.

A Short History of Anarchism. Ed. and trans. Heiner M. Becker. London: Freedom Press, 1996. Originally published in Spanish in 1935.

Why We Are Anarchists. London: Office of "The Commonweal," 1894.

Appendix B

AN ANNOTATED GAZETTEER OF NETTLAU'S UTOPIANS

A

Abbot of St. Pierre. Charles-Irénée Castel, abbé de Saint-Pierre (1658–1743) was a French author who proposed an international organization to maintain peace. He influenced Rousseau and Kant.

Acworth. Andrew Acworth may have been a barrister and conveyancer.

Adam. Paul Auguste Marie Adam (1862–1920) was a French novelist, an early proponent of Symbolism in France, and one of the founders of the Symbolist review *Le symboliste*.

Albrecht. Johann Friedrich Ernst Albrecht (1752–1814) was a German physician and writer. He wrote over 80 novels and plays.

Allorge. Henri Allorge (also Henry Allorge and H. A.) (1878–1938) was a French poet and man of letters.

Amersin. Ferdinand Amersin (1838–1894) was an Austrian writer and physician. He wrote on political and philosophical subjects. He also wrote the science-fiction novel *Das Land der Freiheit* (The Land of Freedom) (1874).

Andreae. Johann Valentin Andreae (1586–1654) was a German theologian, Rosicrucian, and prominent member of the Protestant utopian movement.

Angerbauer. Joseph Angerbauer. Census records and city directories indicate Angerbauer was a laborer.

Aratus of Soli. Aratus of Soli (ca. 315–240 BCE) was the author of *Phenomena* and *Diosemeia*.

Aristophanes. Aristophanes (ca. 446–386 BCE) was a comic playwright in ancient Athens and a poet. Eleven of his 40 plays survive in virtually complete form.

Aristotle. Aristotle (384–322 BCE) was a Greek philosopher and student of Plato's. He was the founder of the Lyceum, the Peripatetic school of philosophy, and the Aristotelian tradition. His philosophy has arguably had more influence on Western thought than that of any other Ancient Greek's including Plato.

Armand. Émile Armand was the pseudonym of Ernest-Lucien Juin Armand (1872–1962), an individualist anarchist and a believer in polyamory and pacificism.

Arrhenius. Svante August Arrhenius (1859–1927) was a Swedish scientist. Originally a physicist, but often referred to as a chemist, Arrhenius was one of the founders of the science of physical chemistry.

Asselineau. Charles Asselineau (1820–1874) was a French writer, art critic, and close friend of Charles Baudelaire.

Auerbach. Berthold Auerbach (né Moses Baruch Auerbacher) (1812–1882) was a German-Jewish poet and author. He was the founder of the German *tendenzroman* ("purpose novel"), in which fiction is used as a means of influencing public opinion on social, political, moral, or religious questions.

B

Babeuf. François-Noël Babeuf (also known as Gracchus Babeuf) (1760–1797) was a French socialist, revolutionary, and journalist during the French Revolution. He was executed for his role in the Conspiracy of the Equals.

Bachstrom. Johann Friedrich (sometimes Jan Fryderyk) Bachstrom (1688–1742). He was a Polish writer, scientist, and theologian. His utopian novel (published in 1737) concerns a group of shipwrecked religious dissidents (the Inquiraner) living near an unnamed North-African mountain range. There complete religious freedom exists. Bachstrom was imprisoned at the urging of the Jesuits and died from strangulation.

Bacon. Sir Francis Bacon, Viscount St. Albans (1561–1626). He was an English philosopher, statesman, and essayist. His works are foundational to the scientific method and empiricism in general. The epigrammatic and simple style in his essays has also been influential in the creation of that genre.

Baginski. Max Baginski (sometimes Baginsky) (1864–1943), a German-American anarchist. He collaborated on Johann Most's *Freiheit* newspaper and became its editor in 1907.

Bakunin. Mikhail Alexandrovich Bakunin (1814–1876) was a Russian revolutionary anarchist, socialist, and founder of collectivist anarchism. He is considered among the most influential figures of anarchism and a major founder of the revolutionary socialist and social anarchist traditions.

Ballod. Carl Ballod (also Kārlis Balodis) (pen name, Atlanticus) (1864–1931) was a Latvian economist, statistician, and demographer.

Barbançois-Villegongis. The Marquis Charles-Hélion de Barbançois-Villegongis (1760–1822) was a French agronomist. He introduced merino rams to France and designed a new model plough.

Barmby. John Goodwyn Barmby (1820–1881) was an English utopian socialist and an influential supporter of Robert Owen in the late 1830s and early 1840s.

Barrucand. Victor Barrucand (1864–1934) was a French journalist and writer. He began as a libertarian; then he became a federalist; and, finally, he became a humanist.

Bart-Claye. A Bart-Claye. I have been unable to find any further information about this writer other than his 1905 book.

Basedow. Johann Bernhard Basedow (1724–1790) was a German educational reformer, teacher, and writer.

Bauernfeld. Eduard von Bauernfeld (1802–1890) was an Austrian dramatist and writer born in Vienna.

Bayle. Pierre Bayle (1647–1706) was a French philosopher, author, and lexicographer. He is commonly regarded as a forerunner of the Encyclopédistes of the mid-eighteenth century.

Beaumont. Augustus Hardin Beaumont (1798–1838) was a secondary figure of English radicalism and Chartism during the 1830s. He was briefly associated with the London Working Men's Association in its early stages and then went to the northeast of England where he founded the *Northern Liberator*.

Beaurieu. Gaspard Guillard de Beaurieu (1728–1795). I have been unable to find any information about this writer beyond his having been born in Saint-Pol in the Pas-de-Calais and dying in Paris.

Bebel. Ferdinand August Bebel (1840–1913) was a German socialist politician, writer, and orator. He was one of the founders of the Social Democratic Workers' Party of Germany (SDAP) in 1869.

Beck. Ferdinand Karl Heinrich Beck (1789–1862) was a German judge who played a key role in the beginnings of the constitutional movement in the Grand Duchy of Hesse in the years 1817 to 1820.

Bell. Andrew Bell (1753–1832) was a Scottish Episcopalian priest and educationalist who pioneered the Madras System of Education in schools and was the founder of Madras College, a secondary school in St. Andrews, Scotland.

Bell. Col. George William Bell (1832–1907) was born in the United States and was United States Consul in Sydney, Australia from 1894–1900. He lived there until his death. His utopian novel, *Mr. Oseba's Last Discovery*, was based on his 1903 trip to New Zealand.

Bellamy. Edward Bellamy (1850–1898) was born in Chicopee, Massachusetts. He was a romance and science-fiction writer, journalist, and political activist. His most famous works are *Looking Backward* (1888) and, to a lesser extent, its sequel: *Equality* (1897).

Bellers. John Bellers (1654–1725) was a Quaker and educational theorist.
Benda. Daniel A. Benda. I have been unable to find any information about this author.
Benson. Robert Hugh Benson (1871–1914) was a Roman Catholic priest and writer. He wrote what is considered one of the earliest dystopias: *Lord of the World* (1907).
Berens. Lewis (incorrectly Louis) Henry Berens (?–ca. 1913), was a businessman, political theorist, lecturer, and author in the early days of the colony of South Australia. He was a strong advocate for the single tax.
Berington. Simon Berington (1680–1755). He was an English writer, possibly a Catholic priest. His *Memoirs of Sigr Gaudentio di Lucca* (1737) is an early example of the "Lost World" motif in science fiction. It may be the first such example, too, to focus on the ancient Egyptians.
Besant. Sir Walter Besant (1836–1901) was an English novelist and historian.
Béthune. Chevalier de Béthune was a French author who may have been related to the influential Béthune family. The one book for which he is well known is *Relation du monde de Mercure* (1750), an early example of science fiction.
Bienvenu. Léon-Charles Bienvenu (pen name, Touchatout) (1835–1911) was a French journalist and writer known for his harsh satires on political and social life during the Second French Empire.
Bigg. Henry Robert Heather Bigg (1853–1911) was an English doctor and author.
Blatchford. Robert Peel Glanville Blatchford (1851–1943) was an English socialist campaigner, journalist, and author. He was also a prominent atheist, nationalist, spiritualist, and opponent of eugenics.
Bodin. Félix Bodin (1795–1837) was a French essayist, journalist, novelist, historian, and politician. His *Le roman de l'avenir* (1834) was an important precursor to science fiction and futurist literature.
Boétie. Étienne de la Boétie (1530–1563). He was a French magistrate, poet, political theorist, and friend of the essayist Michel de Montaigne. His "Discourse on Voluntary Servitude" influenced the neoclassical history of utopian thought.
Bogdanov. Alexander Aleksandrovich Bogdanov (né Alexander Malinovsky) (1873–1928) was a Russian physician, philosopher, science-fiction writer, and Bolshevik revolutionary.
Bolle. Carl (also Karl) August Bolle (1821–1909) was a German naturalist and collector.
Bolle. Gustav Adolph Erdmann Vitalis Bolle (pen names: G. Erdmann, G. Adolfi) (1842–1902) was a German teacher, playwright, and novelist.

Bölsche. Wilhelm Bölsche (1861–1939) was a German author, editor, and publicist. He was among the early promoters of nature conservation and popular science.

Bolzano. Bernard Bolzano (né Bernardus Placidus Johann Nepomuk Bolzano) (1781–1848) was a Bohemian mathematician, logician, philosopher, theologian, and Catholic priest of Italian extraction. He was known for his liberal views. His collected works occupy some 130 volumes.

Bonhomme. Frederic Bonhomme. I have been unable to find any information about this writer.

Bougeant. Guillaume-Hyacinthe Bougeant (better known as le Père Bougeant) (1690–1743) was a French Jesuit and historian who taught classics at the College of Caen and Nevers.

Bowman. Hildebrand Bowman may have been the pseudonym of John Elliott (1759–1834), an English sailor and writer. See Anne Brown's "'The First New Zealand Novel'?: John Elliott's 'Travels of Hildebrand Bowman' (1778)." However, both Rowan Gibbs in a 1994 article and Cliff Thornton in a 2000–2001 article have argued for other authors behind the pseudonym.

Boyer. Jean-Baptiste de Boyer, Marquis d'Argens (1703–1771) was a French rationalist, author, and critic of the Catholic church. He was also a close friend of Voltaire.

Braescu. Probably Gheorghe Brăescu (1871–1949), a Romanian writer of novels and sketches.

Brasch. I have been unable to identify the "G. Brasch" to whom MN refers.

Bratt. Alfred Bratt (1891–1918) was an Austrian writer, playwright, and lecturer.

Brehmer. Fritz Brehmer (1873–1952) was a German writer, translator, naval officer, and consul.

Bretonne. Nicolas Retif (or Restif) de la Bretonne (1734–1806) was a French novelist. He was extraordinarily prolific and wide-ranging in his interests, with some 200 books to his name.

Briancourt. Math (also Mathieu) Briancourt (1793–1882) was a French Fourierist.

Brissac. Henri Brissac (1826–1906) was a French journalist and political theorist.

Brockhouse. H. Brockhouse. I have been unable to find any information about this writer.

Brod. Max Brod (1884–1968) was a writer and theater and music critic with Austrian, Czechoslovak, and Israeli citizenship. He played an important role in preserving the legacy of Franz Kafka.

Brunt. Samuel Brunt (pseud.). I have been unable to locate any details about who wrote Brunt's satire on the infamous South Sea Bubble, one of the earliest instances (1711–1718) of financial speculation that gets out of hand.

Buckingham. James Silk Buckingham (1786–1855) was a Cornish-born British author, journalist, and traveler known for his contributions to Indian journalism. He was a pioneer among the Europeans who fought for a liberal press in India.

Bugnet. Nicolas Bugnet (1749–1822) was a French utopian writer.

Bulwer-Lytton. Edward George Earle Lytton Bulwer-Lytton (1803–1873) was an English writer and politician. His *Coming Race* has been profoundly influential in the history of utopian literature and, in particular, the "Hollow Earth" subgenre of the same.

Buonarroti. Filippo Giuseppe Maria Ludovico Buonarroti (more often known as Philippe Buonarroti) (1761–1837) was an Italian utopian socialist, writer, and agitator. He saw social development as moving from monarchy to liberalism to radicalism and, finally, to communism.

Burgh. James Burgh (1714–1775) was a British radical reformer and politician who advocated for free speech and universal suffrage.

Burkitt. William T. Burkitt. I have been unable to find any information about this writer.

Butaud. Georges Butaud (1868–1926), a French individualist anarchist. He founded a vegan colony with Sophie Zaïkowska in Bascon, near Château-Thierry in Aisne.

Butler. Samuel Butler (1835–1902) was an English novelist and critic. In other works, he examined Christian orthodoxy, evolutionary thought, and Italian art, and made prose translations of the *Iliad* and the *Odyssey*.

Byron. George Gordon Byron, 6th Baron Byron (1788–1824) was an English poet and peer, and one of the leading figures of the Romantic movement.

C

Cabet. Étienne Cabet (1788–1856) was a French philosopher and utopian socialist who founded the Icarian movement.

Campanella. Tommaso Campanella (also Giovanni Domenico Campanella) (1568–1639) was an Italian Dominican friar, philosopher, theologian, astrologer, and poet. His most famous work, *La città del sole* (1602) describes an egalitarian theocratic society where property is held in common. He also played an important role in the Protestant utopian movement of the Renaissance.

Campe. Joachim Heinrich Campe (1746–1818) was a German writer, linguist, educator, and publisher. He was a major representative of the German Enlightenment.

Canudo. Ricciotto Canudo (1877–1923) was a Franco-Italian writer, novelist, poet, philosopher, art critic, literary critic, film critic, musicologist, and screenwriter.

Canzani. Lambro Canzani. I have been unable to find any information about this writer.

Čapek. Karel Čapek (1890–1938) was a Czech writer, playwright, and critic. He introduced the word *robot* to the English language.

Carlile. Richard Carlile (1790–1843) was an important English agitator for the establishment of universal suffrage and freedom of the press in Great Britain.

Casanova. Giacomo Girolamo Casanova (1725–1798) was a Venetian adventurer and writer.

Catalde, de. I have been unable to find any further information about this writer.

Cathelineau. Alexandre Cathelineau. A pseudonym of the British author who has been variously identified as either James Hinton (1822–1875) or H. Cowen. This author also used the pseudonym Chrysostom Trueman.

Chappuis. Jacques-Antoine Chappuis. I have been unable to find any information about this writer.

Charlemagne. Charlemagne (747–814 CE) was successively King of the Franks, King of the Lombards, and King of the Romans. He united most of the countries and peoples of West and Central Europe under his leadership. His name is the French rendition of "Charles the Great."

Chesney. Sir George Tomkyns Chesney (1830–1895) was a British Army general, politician, and writer of fiction. His *The Battle of Dorking* (1871) was a founding work in the genre of invasion literature.

Chirac. Auguste Édouard Marie Victor Anaclet Chirac (1838–1910) was a French journalist, writer, playwright, Proudhonian socialist, and anti-Semite.

Christoph. Hans (né Johannes) Christoph (1901–1992) was a German artist.

Clarke. Allen Clarke (pen names: Ben Adhem and Teddy Ashton) (1863–1936) was an English journalist, playwright, short-story writer, and novelist.

Claudel. J.-C. Claudel (pen name, Kamidel [de Lucessefnoc]). I have been unable to find any information about this pseudonymous writer.

Clemenceau. Georges Benjamin Clemenceau (1841–1929) was a French statesman who served as Prime Minister of France from 1906 to 1909 and again from 1917 until 1920.

Cless. Alfred Cless (1852–?). The *Deutsche National Bibliothek* lists Cless as an anarchist and jurist. He also wrote under the pseudonym A. Martin.

Coeurderoy. Ernest Cœurderoy (1825–1862) was a medical doctor, a revolutionary journalist, and a French libertarian writer. He lived in exile for most of his life and committed suicide.

Colerus. Egmont Colerus von Geldern (1888–1939) was an Austrian writer.

Conrad. Michael Georg Conrad (1846–1927) was a German writer and philosopher. He was the publisher of *Die Gesellschaft* (Communal Life).

Considerant. Victor Prosper Considerant (1808–1893) was a French supporter of Fourierism, a philosopher, economist, and utopian thinker. Between 1855 and 1857, he founded the Fourierist intentional community of La Réunion in Texas near what is now downtown Dallas.

Constant. Jacques Constant. I have been unable to find any information about this writer.

Constantine. Constantine (ca. 272–337 CE) was a Roman emperor, also known as Constantine the Great. He reigned from 306 to 337 CE. He was the first emperor to convert to Christianity.

Cooper. James Fenimore Cooper (1789–1851) was an American writer of historical romances.

Corbett. Elizabeth Burgoyne Corbett (also known as Mrs. George Corbett) (1846–1930) was an English feminist writer.

Costa. Andrea Antonio Baldassarre Costa (1851–1910) was an Italian politician and socialist activist.

Couvreur. André Couvreur (1865–1944) was a French doctor who became a writer specializing in fantastic fiction.

Crozat. Henry Crozat. I have been unable to find any information about this writer.

Cyrille. V. Cyrille. I have been unable to find any information about this writer.

D

d'Aulnoy. Marie-Catherine Le Jumel de Barneville, Baroness d'Aulnoy (1650–1705) was a French novelist known for her literary fairy tales. She is generally considered to have invented the term "fairy tale" (i.e., "contes de fee").

d'Hupay. Joseph Alexandre Victor d'Hupay (1746–1818) was a French writer and philosopher deeply committed to the values of the Enlightenment. He may have been the first to coin the word "communism" in its modern sense.

Davidson. Thomas Davidson (1840–1900) was a Scottish-American philosopher and lecturer.

de Bergerac. Savinien de Cyrano de Bergerac (1619–1655) was a French novelist and playwright. He was the model for Edmond Rostand's most noted drama, *Cyrano de Bergerac* (1897).

de la Roche. Charles-François Tiphaigne de la Roche (1722–1774) was a French physician and author. His novels often mix science with cabalistic ideas.

de la Rue. François Joubert de la Rue (1695–ca. 1757) was a French Protestant in exile even as he pretended to be a "savage" traveling through France.

de Parny. Évaneste de Parny (1753–1814) was a French poet best known for his early and ground-breaking *Poésies érotiques* (1778).

Defoe. Daniel Defoe, né Foe (1660–1731), was an English writer, journalist, and pamphleteer, most famous in the utopian tradition for his novel *Robinson Crusoe* (1719).

Déjacque. Joseph Déjacque (also Dejacques) (1821–1864) was a French anarcho-communist poet, philosopher, and writer.

Delbruck. Georges Delbruck. I have been unable to find any information about this writer.

Descottes. G. Descottes. I have been unable to find any information about this writer.

Desfontaines. Abbé Pierre François Guyot-Desfontaines (1685–1745) was a French journalist, translator, and popular historian. He is best remembered now for this contribution to changing the focus of French literary criticism and journalism.

Deslinières. Lucien Deslinières (1857–1937) was a French journalist, socialist, and writer.

Desmarest. Henri Desmarest. I have been unable to find any information about this writer.

Desnoyers. Louis Claude Joseph Florence Desnoyers (1802–1868) was a French journalist and writer, author of novels for young people, and founder (in 1837) of the Société des gens de letters.

Despres. Marie Despres was the pseudonym (and maiden name) of Mme Philippe-Balthazar-Georges Raynal de Tissonière.

Dickens. Charles John Huffam Dickens (1812–1870) was an English writer and social critic. He was one of the most famous Victorian novelists.

Dide. Mrs. Noémie Dide. I have been unable to find any information about this writer.

Diderot. Denis Diderot (1713–1784) was a French philosopher, art critic, and writer. He co-founded the Encyclopédie and was a prominent Enlightenment figure.

Dixie. Lady Florence Caroline Dixie (née Douglas) (1855–1905) was a Scottish writer, war correspondent, and feminist.

Dixmerie. Nicolas Bricaire de la Dixmerie (ca. 1730–1791) was a French man of letters.

Donamaria. Pedro Donamaria. I have been unable to find any information about this writer.

Doni. Anton Francesco Doni (1513–1574) was an Italian writer, publisher, and translator. His *I mondi* (1652) was inspired by More's *Utopia* (1516). Doni himself had published More's work in an Italian translation in Venice in 1548.

Donnay. Charles Maurice Donnay (1859–1945) was a French dramatist.

Donnelly. Ignatius Loyola Donnelly (1831–1901) was an American congressman, populist writer, and fringe scientist.

Drimeur. Alain Le Drimeur. I have been unable to find any information about this writer. The name is likely a pseudonym.

Du Laurens. Henri Joseph Du Laurens (1719–1793) was born in Douai, France. He was a defrocked monk, poet, and novelist.

Dupin. Gustave Dupin (1861–1933) was a French glassmaker and peace activist. He was one of the founders of the Société d'études pour la recherche des responsabilités de la guerre (The Society for Research into Responsibility for the War). He co-founded the newspaper *La plèbe* (The Plebs) (in 1918) and edited the monthly magazine *Vers la vérité* (Towards the Truth) (1923–1924).

E

Ellis. Henry Havelock Ellis (1859–1939) was an English physician, eugenicist, writer, progressive intellectual, and social reformer who studied human sexuality.

Empedocles. Empedocles (ca. 494–434 BCE) was a Greek philosopher who predates Socrates. He originated the cosmogonic theory of the four classical elements.

Engels. Friedrich (sometimes anglicized as Frederick) Engels (1820–1895) was a German philosopher, critic of political economy, historian, political theorist, and revolutionary socialist. He was also a businessman, journalist, and political activist. His father was an owner of large textile factories in Salford, England and Wuppertal, Germany. He used some of this money to support the publication of his and Marx's ideas.

Ephorus. Ephorus (ca. 400–330 BCE) was an ancient Greek historian from Cyme in Aeolia known for his 29-volume universal history.

Erbal. Jean Erbal. I have been unable to find any information about this writer.

Erskine. Thomas Erskine, 1st Baron Erskine (1750–1823) was a British lawyer and politician who served as Lord Chancellor of the United Kingdom for a year. In his retirement, he wrote *Armata* (1817), a strange tale of a man sailing to the moon upon a highway of ocean.

Estève. Louis Estève (1876–1955) was a French individualistic anarchist. He studied at the University of Toulouse and was a poet, novelist, and essayist.

Etzler. John Adolphus Etzler (1791–1846?) was a German engineer and inventor who immigrated to the United States in 1831 with a vision of creating a technological utopia.

Euhemerus of Messene. Euhemerus (late fourth-century BCE) was a Greek mythographer.

Eulenberg. Max Herbert Eulenberg (1876–1949) was a German writer and militant humanist.

F

Fabien. Jacques Fabien. I have not been able to find any information on this writer. He is not to be confused with the Jacques Fabien Gautier d'Agoty (1716–1785), who was a French anatomist, painter, and printmaker.

Fabre. Jean-Henri Casimir Fabre (1823–1915) was a French naturalist, entomologist, and author known for the lively style of his popular books on the lives of insects.

Farrère. Claude Farrère was the pseudonym of Frédéric-Charles Bargone (1876–1957), a French naval officer and writer of more than 75 novels.

Faure. Sébastien Faure (1858–1942) was a French anarchist, freethought activist, and a proponent of synthetic anarchism.

Fazy. James Fazy (né Jean Jacob Fazy) (1794–1878) was a Swiss politician who served on the Council of States (1848–1872) and the National Council (1857–1866). He was the author of the Genevan Constitution of 1847.

Federn. Karl Federn (1868–1943) was an Austrian lawyer, writer, and translator.

Fénelon. François de Salignac de la Mothe-Fénelon (1651–1715) (usually abbreviated simply to François Fénelon) was a poet and theologian, and later Archbishop of Cambrai.

Fessler. Ignaz Aurelius Fessler (1756–1839) was a Hungarian ecclesiastic, politician, historian, and freemason. This is likely the person referred to by MN.

Fichte. Johann Gottlieb Fichte (1762–1814) was a German philosopher who espoused a philosophical idealism founded on an intense subjectivity. He (not Hegel) developed the famous thesis-antithesis-synthesis model of reasoning and argument.

Firmin. Albert Bancroft Firmin. I have been unable to find any information about this writer.

Flammarion. Nicolas Camille Flammarion (1842–1925) was a French astronomer and author of more than 50 books on many different subjects.

Florian. Jean-Pierre Claris de Florian (1755–1794) was a French fabulist, novelist, and poet. His *Numa Pompilius* (1786) was a deliberate imitation of Fénelon's work on Telemachus.

Flürscheim. Michael Flürscheim (1844–1912) was a German economist and geologist. See Lyman Tower Sargent's "Michael Flürscheim: From the Single Tax to Currency Reform" (2010).

Foigny. Gabriel de Foigny (ca. 1630–1692) was born in Lorraine, France, and later moved to Geneva. He began as a Franciscan; he became a Protestant.

Folingsby. Kenneth Folingsby. I have been unable to find any information about this writer. The name may be pseudonymous. The writer is likely Scots.

Follin. Henri Léon Follin (pen name, de Léon Hendryk) (1866–). I have been unable to find any further information about this writer.

Fontenelle. Bernard Le Bovier de Fontenelle (1657–1757) was a French author who popularized the study of the sciences during the Enlightenment.

Forrest. Henry John Forrest (1822–1899) was an English novelist, typesetter, proofreader, and journalist.

Fourier. François Marie Charles Fourier (1772–1837) was a French philosopher and one of the founders of utopian socialism. Fourier is credited with having originated the word "feminism" in 1837.

Fournière. Eugène Fournière (1857–1914) was a French writer and politician, deputy for Aisne from 1898 to 1902.

France. Anatole France (né François-Anatole Thibault) (1844–1924) was a French poet, journalist, novelist, and French man of letters. He won the 1921 Nobel Prize in Literature.

Franklin. Alfred Louis Auguste Poux (pen name, Alfred Franklin) (1830–1917) was a French librarian, historian, and writer. He specialized in the history of Paris.

Friederich. Johann Konrad Friederich (also using the pseudonyms Carl Strahlheim and Karl F. Fröhlich) (1789–1858) was a German writer, editor, journalist, military officer, and adventurer. His utopian writings were remarkably predictive of the contemporary world. He died in poverty in Le Havre, France.

G

Garnier. Charles Georges Thomas Garnier (1746–1795) was a French lawyer and writer.

Gastine. Louis Jules Gastine (1858–1935) was a French writer who often wrote about air travel and technology.

Gautier. Jules Pierre Théophile Gautier (1811–1872) was a French poet, novelist, and art critic.

Gégout. Charles Joseph Ernest Gégout (1854–1936) was a French anarchist, and founder and editor of *L'attaque* (Attack).

Gehrke. Dr. Albert Gehrke (1840–1911) was a teacher and educator. He was born in Straussenberg, worked in Rudolstadt, and died in Berlin.

Geiger. Carl Ignaz Geiger (né Kaspar Ignatius Joseph Anton Geiger) (1756–1791) was a German lawyer, writer, and radical Enlightenment thinker. He wrote several satires and the utopian short novel to which MN refers.

George. Henry George (1839–1897) was an American political economist, journalist, and social reformer. He is best known as the exponent of a single-tax solution to the equitable funding of government.

Gerlardi. Giuseppe Cartella Gelardi (1885–1962) was an Italian painter, accountant, and poet.

Godin. Jean-Baptiste André Godin (1817–1888) was a French industrialist, writer, political theorist, and social innovator.

Godwin. Francis Godwin (1562–1633) was an English historian, science-fiction author, and Bishop of Llandaff and of Hereford.

Godwin. William Godwin (1756–1836) was an English journalist, political philosopher, and novelist. He is considered one of the first exponents of utilitarianism and the first modern proponent of anarchism.

Goethe. Johann Wolfgang von Goethe (1749–1832) was a German poet, playwright, novelist, scientist, and critic. He is considered the greatest and most influential writer in the German language; his work has had a profound and wide-ranging influence on Western literary, political, and philosophical thought from the Enlightenment to the present day.

Gori. Pietro Gori (1865–1911) was an Italian lawyer, journalist, intellectual, and anarchist poet.

Gould. Frederick James Gould (1855–1938) was an English teacher, writer, and secular humanist.

Gouvest. Jean-Jacques Maubert de Gouvest (1721–1767) was—successively—a monk, an artillery officer, an historian, a journalist, and a man of letters. He is better known for having led a colorful life than for his written works.

Gratacap. Louis Pope Gratacap (1851–1917) was an American naturalist, museum curator, and writer who began with essays such as "The Ice Age" (1878).

Grave. Jean Grave (1854–1939) was an important activist in the French and international anarchist movements. He was the editor of major anarchist periodicals, and wrote dozens of pamphlets and a number of important anarchist books.

Gregorovius. Emil Gregorovius. I have been unable to find any information about this writer.

Grimmelshausen. Hans Jakob Christoffel von Grimmelshausen (1621/22–1676) was a German writer best known for his 1669 picaresque novel *Simplicius Simplicissimus* (German: *Der abenteuerliche Simplicissimus*) and the accompanying Simplician Scriptures series.

Grousset. Jean François Paschal Grousset (pen names: André Laurie, Philippe Daryl, Tiburce Moray, and Léopold Virey) (1844–1909) was a French politician, journalist, translator, and science-fiction writer.

Grove. William Grove was the pseudonym of Reginald Colebrooke Reade (1853–1891). Reade was an architect, surveyor, and manager of a school. He was the author of both *The Wreck of a World* (1889) and, a year before that, *A Mexican Mystery*.

Guàrdia. Francesco Ferrer i Guàrdia (commonly known as Francisco Ferrer) (1859–1909) was a radical freethinker, anarchist, and educator behind a network of secular, private, libertarian schools in and around Barcelona. His execution, following a revolt in Barcelona, propelled Ferrer into martyrdom.

Gueudeville. Nicolas Gueudeville (1652–1721). He was a defrocked Benedictine monk who became a radical journalist and pamphleteer. He represents a precursor of Rousseau's socialism.

Guillaume. James Guillaume (1844–1916) was a leading member of the Jura federation, the anarchist wing of the First International. Later, Guillaume took an active role in the founding of the Anarchist St. Imier International.

H

Hall. Joseph Hall (1574–1656) was an English bishop, satirist, and neo-Stoic.

Haller. Albrecht von Haller (1708–1777) was a Swiss anatomist, physiologist, naturalist, encyclopedist, bibliographer, and poet. He is sometimes thought of as the founder of modern physiology.

Hamilton. Cicely Mary Hamilton (née Hammill) (1872–1952) was an English actress, writer, journalist, suffragette, and feminist.

Hardt, Hans. Paul Albrecht (pen name, Hans Hardt) (1863–ca. 1935) was a German writer.

Harrar. Annie France-Harrar (1886–1971) was an Austrian writer and scientist.

Harrington. James Harrington (also Harington) (1611–1677) was an English political theorist best known for *The Commonwealth of Oceana* (1656), a work which describes a utopia in the wake of the execution of Charles I in 1649.

Harris. Thomas Lake Harris (1823–1906) was an Anglo-American preacher, prophet, poet, and vintner. He was the leader of a series of communal religious experiments which culminated with a group called the Brotherhood of the New Life in Santa Rosa, California.

Harting. Pieter Harting (1812–1885) was a Dutch biologist and naturalist, born in Rotterdam. He made contributions in a number of scientific disciplines, and is remembered for his work in the fields of microscopy, hydrology, botany, and biostratigraphy. *Anno 2066* appears to have been his only work of fiction under the name of Dr. Dioscorides.

Haushofer. Max Haushofer (1840–1907) was a German poet and professor of economics and statistics. He was a member of various Munich literary circles.

Hawel. Rudolf Hawel (1860–1923) was an Austrian writer.

Hawthorne. Nathaniel Hawthorne (1804–1864) was an American novelist and short-story writer. He joined the transcendentalist utopian community at Brook Farm in 1841. He left later that year although his Brook Farm adventure became an inspiration for his novel *The Blithedale Romance* (1852).

Hayes. Frederick William Hayes (1848–1918) was an English architect, painter, playwright, and author.

Heinse. (Johann Jakob) Wilhelm Heinse (1746–1803) was a German author mainly remembered for *Ardinghello und die glückseligen Inseln* (Ardinghello and the Fortunate Isles) (1787), a novel which allows him to expound on his views on art and life, the plot being laid in the Italy of the sixteenth century.

Hellenbach. Lazar Freiherr von Hellenbach (also Lazar Baron von Hellenbach and Lazar Freiherr Hellenbach von Paczolay) (1827–1887) was an Austrian politician, philosophical and socio-political writer, and one of the most famous occultists of his time.

Hemyng. Samuel Bracebridge Hemyng (1841–1901) was an English lawyer and popular novelist.

Henlau. J. A. Henlau wrote under the pseudonym of Justus Feminis. I have been unable to find any further information about this writer.

Henry. The anarchist MN refers to is Jean-Charles Fortuné Henry (1869–1931) rather than his brother (Joseph Felix "Émile" Henry). See https://criminalgenealogy.blogspot.com/2021/03/jean-charles-fortune-henry-his-brother.html.

Herbert. Auberon Edward William Molyneux Herbert (1838–1906) was a British writer, theorist, philosopher, and individualist. He served as an MP for Nottingham from 1870 to 1874.

"The Hermit of Prague." I have been unable to find any information about this pseudonymous writer.

Hertzka. Theodor Hertzka (also Hertzka Tivadar) (1845–1924) was a Jewish-Hungarian-Austrian economist and journalist.

Herzl. Theodor Herzl (1860–1904) was an Austro-Hungarian Jewish journalist, playwright, political activist, and writer who was the father of modern political Zionism. Herzl formed the Zionist Organization and promoted Jewish immigration to Palestine in an effort to form a Jewish state.

Hesiod. Hesiod (ca. 750–650 BCE) was an ancient Greek poet and contemporary of Homer. His poetry is an important source for understanding Greek mythology.

Hire. Jean de la Hire was the pseudonym of Adolphe d'Espie (1878–1956), a prolific writer of popular fiction in several genres.

Hobbes. Thomas Hobbes (1588–1679) was an English philosopher best known for *Leviathan* (1651), in which he expounds an influential formulation of social-contract theory.

Hoffmann. François-Benoît Hoffman (1760–1828) was a French playwright and critic, best known today for his operatic librettos.

Holberg. Ludvig Holberg (1684–1754) was a writer, essayist, philosopher, historian, and playwright born in Bergen, Norway. He played a central role in the formation of Danish and Norwegian literature.

Holland. Annes Johan Vitringa (pen names: Jan Holland; Jochem van Ondere; "Een Spiritist") (1827–1901). He published some 11 books between 1876 and 1888. He was born in Hardewijk, Netherlands and studied at Gronigen and Leiden universities. He began as a teacher, became a rector, and for the last years of his life was a journalist for the cause of the Roman Catholic church.

Holyoake. George Jacob Holyoake (1817–1906) was an English secularist, co-operator, and newspaper editor.

Howard. Sir Ebenezer Howard (1850–1928) was an English urban planner and founder of the garden-city movement.

Howells. William Dean Howells (1837–1920) was an American realist novelist, literary critic, and playwright.

Hubert-Fillay. Hubert-Fillay (also Hubert Fillay) (1879–1945) was a French regional writer.

Hudson. William Henry Hudson (also Guillermo Enrique Hudson) (1841–1922) was an Anglo-Argentine author, naturalist, and ornithologist.

Hugo. Victor-Marie Hugo (1802–1885) was a French poet, novelist, essayist, playwright, and dramatist of the Romantic period.

Hume. David Hume (né Home) (1711–1776) was a Scottish Enlightenment philosopher, historian, economist, and essayist. He is best known today for his highly influential system of philosophical empiricism.

I

Iambulus (also Jambulus). Iambulus (fourth-century BCE) was a Greek merchant and likely the author of a utopian work about the "Islands of the Sun." Only a fragment of the work survives in Diodorus Siculus's *Bibliotheca historica*. Iambulus is also mentioned in Lucian of Samosata's *Alethe diegemata* (*A True Story*), which dates from the second century BCE.

Inchofer. Melchior Inchofer (also Imhofer) (ca. 1584–1648). He was an Austrian-Hungarian Jesuit. His best-known, utopian, work (*La monarchie des solipses* [1721]) was published anonymously and may actually be by Giulio C. Scotti.

J

Jacques. Norbert Jacques (1880–1954) was a Luxembourg novelist, journalist, screenwriter, and translator who wrote in German.

Jaunez-Sponville. Pierre Ignace Jaunez-Sponville (1750–1805) was a French writer active under the First Empire.

Jaurès. Auguste Marie Joseph Jean Léon Jaurès (usually simply Jean Jaurès) (1859–1914) was a French socialist leader.

Jókai. Móric Jókai de Ásva (also Maurus or Mauritius Jokai or Mauritius) (1825–1904) was a Hungarian nobleman, novelist, dramatist, and revolutionary. He was an active participant and a leading figure in the Hungarian liberal revolution of 1848 in Pest.

Joncquel. Octave Joncquel. I have been unable to find any information about this writer.

Jullien. Jean-Thomas-Édouard Jullien (often simply Jean Jullien) (1854–1919) was a French playwright and theatre critic.

Junius. Junius was the pseudonym of a writer who contributed a series of letters to the *Public Advertiser* (1769–1772). The identity of the writer is not categorically known, but it may have been Sir Philip Francis (1740–1818), an Irish-born British politician and pamphleteer.

Junqua. Pierre-François Junqua (1821–1899) was an erstwhile Catholic priest twice jailed for hostility to his former religion. He became an editor of the journal *La renovation religieuse et sociale* in Belgium, and espoused a triple communism: of origin, production, and consumption. He later became a bookseller in Paris. See https://maitron.fr/spip.php?article62596 for more information.

K

Kampffmeyer. Bernhard Kampffmeyer (1867–1942) was a socialist and activist who sympathized with anarchism. He and his brother, Paul Kampffmeyer, were involved in the labor movement and were a driving force behind the garden-city movement.

Kant. Immanuel Kant (1724–1804) was a German philosopher and one of the most important thinkers of the Enlightenment. His comprehensive and systematic works in epistemology, metaphysics, ethics, and aesthetics have made him one of the most influential figures in modern Western philosophy.

Kappus. Franz Xaver Kappus (1883–1966) was an Austrian military officer, journalist, editor, and writer who wrote poetry, short stories, novels, and screenplays.

Kautsky. Karl Johann Kautsky (1854–1938) was a Czech-Austrian philosopher, journalist, and orthodox Marxist theorist.

Kelly. Harry May Kelly (1871–1953) was an American anarchist and lifelong activist in the Modern School movement.

King. Samuel H. King. I have been unable to find any information about this writer.

King Arthur. He was a legendary British leader who, according to medieval histories and romances, led the defense of Britain against Saxon invaders in the late fifth and early sixth centuries CE. Where history ends and legend begins is impossible to tease out as his story has seen numerous literary accretions over the centuries. Most of his knights of the Round Table were famed for their purity and courage.

Kirchenheim. Heinrich Adolf Paul Arthur von Kirchenheim (né Koscielski) (1855–1924) was a German lawyer.

Kleinwächter. Friedrich (von) Kleinwächter (1838–1927) was an Austrian economist.

Klopstock. Friedrich Gottlieb Klopstock (1724–1803) was a German poet. One of his major contributions to German literature was to move it away from the use of French models—as is evident from *Die deutsche Gelehrtenrepublik* (1774), his scheme for the regeneration of German letters.

Koehler. Oswald Koehler. I have been unable to find any information about this writer.

Kolney. Fernand Pochon de Colnet (pen name, Fernand Kolney) (1868–1930) was a French writer well known for his Malthusian approach to the problems of overpopulation.

Korf. Georg Korf was an accountant and novelist.

Kropotkin. Pyotr Alexeyevich Kropotkin (1842–1921) was a Russian anarchist, socialist revolutionary, economist, political scientist, and philosopher who advocated for anarcho-communism.

L

L'Estrange. Henry l'Estrange. I have been unable to find any further information about this writer beyond the name being pseudonymous.

Laboulaye. Édouard René Lefebvre de Laboulaye (commonly known as Édouard Laboulaye) (1811–1883) was a French jurist and politician.

Laby. Jean de Laby. I have been unable to find any information about this writer.

Lancaster. Joseph Lancaster (1778–1838) was an English Quaker and public-education innovator. He developed a monitorial system of primary education which was applied in the nineteenth century to growing industrial centers in England.

Landauer. Gustav Landauer (1870–1919) was one of the leading German theorists on anarchism at the end of the nineteenth century and the beginning of the twentieth. He was an advocate of social anarchism and an avowed pacifist. In 1919, he was briefly Commissioner of Enlightenment and Public Instruction in the short-lived Bavarian Soviet Republic during the German Revolution of 1918–1919. He was assassinated when this republic was overthrown.

Lang. Andrew Lang (1844–1912) was a Scottish poet, novelist, literary critic, and contributor to the field of anthropology. He is best known as a collector of folk and fairy tales.

Lasswitz. Kurd Lasswitz (pen name, Velatus) (1848–1910) was a German author, scientist, and philosopher. He has been called "the father of German science fiction."

Lawrence. James Henry Lawrence (1773–1840) was a British writer best known for his utopian novel, *The Empire of the Nairs, or the Rights of Women* (1811). He was influenced by the writings of Mary Wollstonecraft and William Godwin. Lawrence in turn influenced the writing of Percy Bysshe Shelley.

Le Hon. Henri Le Hon (also Lehon) (1809–1872) was a Belgian seascape painter, physicist, and soldier.

Leczcinski. Stanisław I Leczcinski (also Leszczyński) (1677–1766) was twice King of Poland. He died after his silk bedclothes caught fire at his palace in Lunéville. It is hard to know if the work referred to by MN was ghost written.

Lee. Thomas Lee (1831–1889? Also 1830–1904) was an English publican and plasterer active as a writer between 1886 and 1888.

Léo. Victoire Léodile Béra (pen name, Andre Léo) (1824–1900) was a French novelist, journalist, and feminist. She took her pen name from her two twin sons' names.

Leroux. Pierre Henri Leroux (1797–1871) was a French philosopher and political economist.

Lesconvel. Pierre de Lesconvel (also Hervé Pezron de Lesconvel) (ca. 1650–1722). He was a French historian and writer whose utopian novel, *Idée d'un regne doux et heureux* (1703), was deeply influenced by Fénelon's *Télémaque*.

Lesguillon. Hermance Lesguillon (née Lasdrin) (pen names: Madame Hermance and Hermance Sandrin) (1800–1882) was a nineteenth-century French poet and novelist.

Lévis. Pierre Marc Gaston de Lévis (1764–1830), second duke of Lévis, was a French politician, aphorist, and deputy to the National Constituent Assembly. During the French Revolution, he escaped to England. Two of his three sisters and his mother were sent to the guillotine.

Levy. Joseph Hiam Levy (1838–1913) was an English author and economist, and an important figure in the Personal Rights Association.

Lewis. Sir George Cornewall Lewis (1806–1863) was a British statesman and man of letters. He is best known for preserving neutrality in 1862 when the British cabinet debated intervention in the American Civil War.

Lichtenberger. André Lichtenberger (1870–1940) was a French sociologist and novelist. He wrote about socialism and utopianism among other foci.

Lichtneckert. Josef Lichtneckert. I have been unable to find any information about this writer.

Limanowski. Bolesław Limanowski (1835–1935) was a Polish socialist, historian, and journalist. He was also a tireless promoter of Agrarianism.

Linton. Eliza Lynn Linton (1822–1898) was the first female salaried journalist in Britain and the author of more than 20 novels. Many of her essays took a strong anti-feminist viewpoint.

Lithgow. John Lithgow was likely Scottish by birth and possibly a clerk in a factory. He emigrated to the United States in 1795. He began publishing his ideas in 1799 under the pseudonym of "Timothy Telltruth." He was for a short time the editor of *The Temple of Reason* wherein he expressed his deist principles. He may well have returned to Britain in about 1805.

Locke. John Locke (1632–1704) was an English philosopher and physician, widely regarded as one of the most influential of Enlightenment thinkers. Considered one of the first of the British empiricists, he is equally important to social-contract theory.

London. John Griffith London (né John Griffith Chaney) (1876–1916) was an American novelist, journalist, and social activist.

Longley. Alcander Longley (sometimes Langley) (1832–1918) was a social activist who organized secular utopian communities and published newspapers which promoted the communitarian cause during a career that lasted more than 40 years.

Lorenzo. Anselmo Lorenzo Asperilla (1841–1914) was a crucial figure in the early Spanish anarchist movement. He was known as "the grandfather of Spanish anarchism."

Lucian of Samosata. Lucian of Samosata (ca. 125–180 CE) was a Greek satirist. His *True Story* is considered the first example of science fiction.

Luitjes. Tjerk Luitjes (1867–1946) was an anarchist based in Gronigen who published under the pseudonym Travailleur. See in particular his book titled *Over de grondprincipen van christendom en anarchie als tegenstelligen* (On the Fundamental Principles of Christianity and Anarchy as Opposites) (1900; 1902).

Lycurgus. Lycurgus flourished in the first half of the ninth century BCE. He was a legendary lawgiver of Sparta who promoted the Spartan virtues of equality, military fitness, and austerity.

M

M'Crib. T. M'Crib was the pseudonym of Henry B. Lee. I have been unable to find any further information about Lee.

Mably. Gabriel Bonnot de Mably (also known as Abbé de Mably) (1709–1785) was a French philosopher, historian, and popular writer.

Mackay. John Henry Mackay (1864–1933) was a Scots anarchist, intellectual, and writer. He was born in Scotland to a German mother and a Scots father. He was raised in Germany. A noted homosexual, he died soon after the rise to power of the virulently homophobic Hitler in 1933. He may have committed suicide, or his death may have been due to natural causes.

Macnie. John Macnie (pen name, Ismar Thiusen) (1836–1909) was a Scottish educator who came to the United States in 1867. He taught at the University of North Dakota. *Looking Forward* was his only work of fiction. Some sources incorrectly cite 1844 as the year he was born.

Magnus. Leonard A. Magnus (1879–1924) was an English linguist, author, translator, and textual scholar who specialized in Russian literature.

Maillot. L'abbé Maillot was a priest in the town of Villers in France.

Mantegazza. Paolo Mantegazza (1831–1910) was an Italian neurologist, physiologist, and novelist.

Marc-Py. Marcel Jean François Py (pen name, J. Marc-Py) (1884–1946) was a French man of letters.

Maréchal. Sylvain Maréchal (1750–1803) was a French essayist, poet, philosopher, and political theorist. His ideas presaged utopian socialism and communism as well as utopian anarchism.

Marivaux. Pierre Carlet de Chamblain de Marivaux (often simply Marivaux) (1688–1763) was a highly influential French playwright and novelist.

Marriott. Joseph Marriott was a minister who contributed an essay titled "Community: A Vision" to Robert Owen's *The New Moral World* (1837). He also published *A Catechism on Circumstances, or, The Foundation Stone of a Community* (1840?). He may be the same individual as the Joseph Marriott who was removed from his Unitarian ministry in Lancashire or Cheshire in 1838. See J. P. Earwaker's *Local Gleanings*, p. 123.

Martineau. Harriet Martineau (1802–1876) was an English social theorist, who wrote from holistic, religious, and feminist angles. Unusually for a female writer at this time, she earned enough to support herself.

Marx. Karl Heinrich Marx (1818–1883) was a German philosopher, critic of political economy, economist, historian, sociologist, political theorist, journalist, and socialist revolutionary. Marx's political and philosophical thought has had an enormous influence on subsequent intellectual, economic, and political history.

Masson. Émile Masson (pen names: Brenn, Ewan Gweznou, and Ion Prigent) (1869–1923) was a Breton writer and intellectual.

Mathéma. I have been unable to find any information about this writer.

Mazade. André Mazade. I have been unable to find any information about this writer.

Mazzini. Giuseppe Mazzini (1805–1872) was an Italian politician, journalist, activist for the unification of Italy, and spearhead of the Italian revolutionary movement.

McIver. George McIver (né MacIver) (1859–1945) was a Scots-born author who emigrated to Australia in 1861.

Mehring. Franz Erdmann Mehring (1846–1919) was a German communist historian and revolutionary socialist politician. He was a senior member of the Social Democratic Party of Germany during the German Revolution of 1918–1919.

Mella. Ricardo Mella Cea (1861–1925) was an important writer, intellectual, and anarchist active in the late nineteenth and early twentieth centuries.

Mercier. Louis-Sébastien Mercier (1740–1814) was a French dramatist and writer. His novel *L'an 2440* (1771) is an early precursor of science fiction

Mereschkowski. Konstantin Sergeevich Mereschkowski (1855–1921) was a prominent Russian biologist and botanist.

Merlino. Francesco Saverio Merlino (1856–1930) was an Italian lawyer, anarchist, and theorist of libertarian socialism.

Meslier. Jean Meslier (1664–1729) was a French Catholic priest who wrote a book-length essay discovered after his death, an essay which promoted atheism and materialism.

Mettais. Hippolyte Mettais (1812–?) was a French doctor and writer.

Meunier. Victor Meunier (1817–1903) was a French scientific writer and militant socialist.

Meyern. Wilhelm Friedrich von Meyern (né Meyer) (1759–1829) was a German author, soldier, and diplomat. *Dya-Na-Sore* (1787) occupied five volumes in its third edition (1800).

Michel. Louise Michel Ecouter (pen name, "Enjolras") (1830–1905) was a French teacher, writer, feminist, militant anarchist, and Freemason. She was one of the major figures of the Paris Commune.

Miller. George Noyes Miller (1845–1904) was an American writer, usually of nonfiction texts about the Oneida community.

Mirbeau. Octave Mirbeau (1848–1917) was a French novelist, art critic, travel writer, pamphleteer, journalist, and playwright.

Moeller. Otto Martin Moeller (also Møller) (1860–1898) was a Danish writer and translator.

Mohl. Robert von Mohl (1799–1875) was a German jurist, a professor of political science and law, a politician, and later an ambassador in the service of Friedrich I, Duke of Baden.

Moilin. Jules Antoine (also Tony) Moilin (1832–1871) was a French physician and politician. He took part in the Paris Commune and was executed on May 27, 1871 in the Luxembourg Gardens in Paris.

Mondasse. Jean-Baptiste-Augustin Varennes de Mondasse. I have been unable to locate any further information about this writer.

Montaigne. Michel Eyquem de Montaigne (1533–1592) was one of the most significant philosophers of the French Renaissance. He is known for popularizing the essay as a literary genre and making it an extraordinarily important form of cultural expression.

Montesquieu. Charles Louis de Secondat, Baron de La Brède et de Montesquieu (usually referred to simply as Montesquieu) (1689–1755) was a French judge, man of letters, historian, and political philosopher.

Monticelli. Carlo Monticelli. This is likely the author of *Socialismo popolare* (1902). He was born in 1857.

More. Sir/St. Thomas More (1478–1535). He wrote the foundational book *Utopia* in 1516 in Latin. He was a vital counsellor to Henry VIII, but was executed on the monarch's orders for his refusal to sign the Oath of Supremacy and, thereby, accept that Henry was head of the Church of England. He was a quintessential humanist, diplomat, politician, and philosopher.

Morelly. Étienne-Gabriel Morelly (1717–1778) was a French utopian thinker and novelist.

Morris. William Morris (1834–1896) was a British textile designer, poet, artist, novelist, printer, translator, and socialist activist. He was a prime mover of the Arts and Crafts Movement.

Mosneron. Jean-Baptiste Mosneron de Launay (1738–1830) was a French politician and man of letters. He was arrested during the Terror, imprisoned in Luxembourg, and was only freed after the fall of Robespierre.

Most. Johann Most (1846–1906) was a German-American anarchist and newspaper editor. He was the author of nearly 30 books and pamphlets, most provocatively *The Social Monster: A Paper on Communism and Anarchism* (1890).

Mouhy. Charles de Fieux Mouhy (1701–1784) was a French novelist who also published works devoted to the history of theatre. His *Lamekis* (1735) is sometimes considered an early example of science fiction.

Mozart. Wolfgang Amadeus Mozart (1756–1791) was a brilliant and influential German Classical composer.

Mumford. Lewis Mumford (1895–1990) was an American historian, sociologist, and literary critic. His book on utopia has been tremendously influential in the field.

N

Nariota/Nariosa. I have been unable to find any information about this writer.

Neulif. I have been unable to find any information about this writer. The name is likely a pseudonym.

Neupauer. Josef von Neupauer (1806–1902) was an Austrian politician and science-fiction author.

Newbrough. John Ballou Newbrough (1828–1891) was an American dentist who published a book titled *Oahspe: A New Bible* (1882). This book was purportedly new revelations from Jehovih [sic] created by automatic writing and directed towards "Faithists." A religion called Faithism and a number of intentional communities were founded based on the book.

North. Delaval North. I have been unable to find any information about this writer.

Norton. Seymour F. Norton (1841–?) was the proprietor and editor of the monthly *Chicago Sentinel* (1891–?). *Ten Men of Monkey Island* was possibly the most widely circulated of the many Populist pamphlets. One of Flürscheim's works was a response to it, and Flürscheim said that more than 500,000 copies of Norton's pamphlet had been sold.

Noyes. John Humphrey Noyes (1811–1886) was an American preacher, radical religious philosopher, and utopian socialist. He founded the Putney, Oneida, and Wallingford communities, and is credited with coining the term "complex marriage."

Nys. Ernest Nys (1851–1920) was a Belgian lawyer and a law professor at the University of Brussels. He was also a member of the Permanent Court of Arbitration.

Nyst. Ray Nyst (1864–1943) was a Belgian art critic interested in Futurism.

O

Offenbach. Jacques Offenbach (1819–1880) was a German-born French composer of the Romantic period. He wrote nearly 100 operettas. His incomplete opera *The Tales of Hoffmann* has been tremendously influential.

Olerich. Henry Olerich (1851–1927) was a utopian author from Nebraska who believed in the utopian possibilities of collective farming. As well as being the author of three utopian works, he was a lawyer, farmer, and teacher.

Oppenheimer. Franz Oppenheimer (1864–1943) was a German sociologist and political economist who also published on the fundamental sociology of the state.

Ortt. Felix Ortt (1866–1959) was a civil engineer and Christian anarchist. He wrote more than 30 books between 1896 and 1959. He was fascinated by parapsychology, spiritualism, and a concept he termed "pneumatic-energetic monism."

Otto. Berthold Otto (1859–1933) was a German socialist reformer and founder of a school in Berlin-Lichterfelde.

Owen. Albert Kimsey Owen (1848–1916) was a utopian reformer and founder of a co-operative community in Topolobampo, Sinaloa, Mexico.

Owen. Robert Owen (1771–1858) was a Welsh textile manufacturer, philanthropist, and social reformer. He has been extraordinarily influential in utopian socialism and the cooperative movement.

P

Paepe. César de Paepe (1842–1890) was a Belgian doctor and syndicalist.

Paine. Thomas Paine (né Thomas Pain) (1737–1809) was an English-born American political activist, philosopher, political theorist, and revolutionary. He wrote, most famously, *Common Sense* (1776), *The American Crisis* (1776–1783), and *The Rights of Man* (1791).

Panizza. Oskar Panizza (1853–1921) was a German psychiatrist as well as a playwright, novelist, poet, and essayist. He served a one-year prison sentence for *Das Liebeskonzil* because it was considered blasphemous.

Paolini. Francesco G. Paolini. I have been unable to find any information about this writer.

Pataud. Émile Pataud (1869–1935) was a French revolutionary trade unionist. He was secretary of the General Syndicate of Electrical Industries which he created with a few friends. It quickly became anarcho-syndicalist.

Patot. Simon Tyssot de Patot (1655–1738). He was a French writer and poet responsible for two important pieces of fantastic literature emphasizing, in one case, the "Lost World" motif, and, in the other, the "Hollow Earth."

Pechméja. Jean-Joseph de Pechméja (1741–1785) was a French man of letters.

Pellerin. Georges Pellerin (possibly, according to Brian Stableford, the pseudonym of Gustave Dupuynode [1817–1898]).

Pelloutier. Fernand-Léonce-Émile Pelloutier (1867–1901) was a French anarchist and syndicalist.

Pemberton. Sir Max Pemberton (1863–1950) was a journalist and popular English novelist, working mainly in the adventure and mystery genres.

Pemberton. Robert Pemberton (1788?–1879) was an Englishman of obscure birth, thought to be one of the illegitimate children of the court of George III. He published nothing until he was 60 and then brought out 11 books in 10 years. See Rockey (1981).

Pêrier. Camille Pêrier was the pseudonym of Mme Bentégeat (1824–1883).

Perrault. Léon-Jean-Bazille Perrault (1832–1908) was a French academic painter. He painted in many genres and was, in his time, immensely popular.

Perrin. This may be Léon Charles Perrin (1886–1978), who was mainly known as a sculptor. There is also a Léon Perrin (1853–1922), who appears to have been an academic scientist and doctor.

Pestalozzi. Johann Heinrich Pestalozzi (1746–1827) was a Swiss teacher and educational reformer who exemplified Romanticism in his views.

Petzler. Johann Aloys Petzler (1814?–1898) was a music teacher and well-known radical thinker. He published a number of utopias in German and English which go well beyond Chartism in their ideas. He claims to have shared a cell in France with Proudhon before being expelled to England.

Petzold. Alfons Maria Petzold (pen name, De Profundis) (1882–1923) was an Austrian writer.

Pezzl. Johann Pezzl (1756–1823) was a German writer and librarian during the Enlightenment.

Pflüger. Paul Pflüger. This may be the Paul Bernard Pflüger (1865–1947) who wrote *Einführung in die soziale Frage* (1910).

Phaleas of Chalcedon. Phaleas of Chalcedon (early fourth century BCE) was a Greek statesman who believed that all citizens of any model city should be equal in property and education. We have no written works by him. A contemporary of Plato, Phaleas was one of the utopian thinkers who flourished during a turbulent period of Athenian democracy. The sole surviving reference to him is in Book II of Aristotle's *Politics*.

Pick. Otto Pick (1887–1940) was a Czech poet and translator. He belonged to the German-speaking Jewish community in Prague and to the literary circle that included Max Brod, Franz Kafka, and Franz Werfel.

Pillot. Jean-Jacques Pillot (1808–1877) was a French revolutionary and republican communist. He was born in Vaux-Lavalette and died in the prison at Melun.

Piria. Francesco (also Francisco) Piria (1847–1933) was a Uruguayan entrepreneur, journalist, and politician of Italian origin. He was famous mainly for having created a seaside city in Uruguay that bears his name, Piriápolis.

Plato. Plato (428/427 or 424/423–348/347 BCE) was a Greek philosopher who founded the Platonist school of thought and the Academy, the first institution of higher learning in the Western world. He was a student of Socrates and best known now for the dialogic form of reasoning and the concept of *mimesis* or imitation.

Plockhoy. Pieter Corneliszoon Plockhoy (also Plockboy) (ca. 1625–ca. 1670) was a Dutch Mennonite and utopist who founded an intentional community at Lewes Creek on the Delaware Bay in 1663. The community was destroyed by an English raid in 1664.

Poe. Edgar Allan Poe (né Edgar Poe) (1809–1849) was an American writer, poet, editor, and literary critic. Poe is best known for his poetry and short stories, particularly his tales of mystery and the macabre.

Popper-Lynkeus. Josef Popper-Lynkeus (1838–1921) was an Austrian scholar, writer, and inventor. He was the uncle of Austrian-British philosopher Karl Popper.

Potonié-Pierre. Edmond Potonié (better known as Edmond Potonié-Pierre) (1829–1902) was a French pacifist. He was the founder of the Ligue du Bien Public and co-founder of the newspaper *Libre échange*.

Pouget. Émile Pouget (1860–1931) was a French anarcho-communist, who adopted tactics close to those of anarcho-syndicalism. He was vice-secretary of the General Confederation of Labour from 1901 to 1908.

Powderly. Terence Vincent Powderly (1849–1924) was an American labor-union leader, politician, and attorney, best known for being head of the Knights of Labor in the late 1880s.

Prat. Jules Gustave Prat (pen name, Jacques Ultor) (1823–1895) was a French lawyer.

Puisieux. Philip Florent de Puisieux (1713–1772) was a French lawyer, journalist, translator, and ambassador to France.

Q

Quantin. Albert Mane Jérôme Quantin (1850–1933) was a bibliophile, publisher, printer, and writer of utopian socialist fiction.

Quiroule. Pierre Quiroule was the pseudonym of Joaquín Alejo Falconnet (1867–1938), an anarchist writer who was born in France but lived in Argentina from an early age.

R

Rabelais. François Rabelais (ca. 1483–1553) was a French Renaissance writer, physician, humanist, monk, and Greek scholar. He is mainly known as a writer of satire, of the grotesque, and of bawdy.

Ramsay. Andrew Michael Ramsay (popularly known as Chevalier Ramsay) (1686–1743) was a Scots-born writer and a Christian Universalist. He was a protégé of Fénelon's. Ramsay's *Les voyages de Cyrus* imitates Fénelon's work on Telemachus.

Rebmann. Andreas Georg Friedrich von Rebmann (1768–1824) was a German lawyer and writer at the time of the French Revolution. He was born in Sugenheim, Bavaria, and died in Wiesenbaden, near Frankfurt.

Reclus. Jacques Élisée Reclus (1830–1905) was a French geographer, writer, and anarchist.

Reigny. Louis Abel Beffroy de Reigny (1757–1811) was a French dramatist and man of letters. His *Nicodème clans la Lune, ou la révolution pacifique* (1790), a three-act farce, is said to have been performed more than four hundred times.

Réjane. Gabrielle Réjane (née Gabrielle Charlotte Réju) (1856–1920) was a French actress.

Renard. Maurice Renard (1875–1939) was a French writer who specialized in science fiction, fantasy, and detective fiction.

Renouvier. Charles Bernard Renouvier (1815–1903) was a French philosopher. He sought to update Kantian liberalism and individualism for the socio-economic realities of the late nineteenth century.

Resnier. André Guillaume Resnier de Goué (1729–1811) was a brigadier general of the French Revolution, a writer, and one of the pioneers of aviation and gliding.

Rey-Dussueil. Antoine Rey-Dussueil (1798–1851) was a French journalist and novelist.

Reynolds. Dr. James Reynolds may be, as MN suggests, the author of *Equality, or A History of Lithconia* (1837). (The novel was published anonymously.) However, Michael Durey, in "John Lithgow's Lithconia: The Making and Meaning of America's First 'Utopian Socialist' Tract," convincingly identifies the author as John Lithgow.

Richet. Charles Richet (1850–1935) was a physiologist and editor of the *Revue scientifique* (from 1878 to 1902). He won the Nobel Prize in 1913 for his work on anaphylaxis. He was also a spiritualist and an amateur dramatist.

Richter. Eugen Richter (1838–1906) was a German politician and journalist. He was one of the leading advocates of liberalism in the Prussian Landtag and the German Reichstag.

Robin Hood. A legendary outlaw who may date back as far as the late thirteenth century. His historicity is much debated.

Rondelet. Antonin François Rondelet (1823–1893) was a French professor of philosophy and economics and a committed Catholic. He wrote particularly about education and the social organization of the family.

Rosny. J.-H. Rosny was a pseudonym for two brothers: Joseph Henri Honoré Boex (1856–1940) and Séraphin Justin Boex (1859–1948).

Rossi. Giovanni Rossi (1856–1943) was an Italian anarchist, collectivist, writer, and founder of utopian communities. He was a promoter of cooperative libertarian colonies, free love, and the emancipation of women. The experimental libertarian Cecília Colony, which he founded in Brazil in 1890, inspired several fictional treatments including a feature film, *La Cecilia*, in 1976.

Rotter. Josef Rotter (or Hotter). I have been unable to find any information about this writer.

Rousseau. Jean-Jacques Rousseau (1712–1778) was a Genevan philosopher and writer. His political philosophy influenced the progress of the Enlightenment throughout Europe as well as the development of modern political, economic, and educational ideas.

Rouzade. Léonie Rouzade (née Louise-Léonie Camusat) (1839–1916) was a French feminist, politician, journalist, and author. An active supporter of women's rights, she co-founded (with Eugénie Potonié-Pierre in 1880) the "Union des femmes," the first association of socialist women in France. As a writer, she published two utopian novels in 1872.

Ruedebusch. Emil F. Ruedebusch (1861–1940) lived in Mayville, Wisconsin. In 1906, he was the president of a "transvaluation society," the purpose of which was "to bring about the transvaluation of all values in matters of love and the relations of the sexes" ("Observations and Comments"). The same journal, *Mother Earth*, in which this comment appeared remarks that he was tried and heavily fined for his book *The Old and New Ideal*. *Mother Earth* considers him as "known in this country."

Russell. Bertrand Arthur William Russell, 3rd Earl Russell (1872–1970) was a British philosopher, logician, and social critic. He was a public intellectual, historian, social critic, political activist, and Nobel laureate.

Ryner. Han Ryner was the pseudonym of Jacques Élie Henri Ambroise Ner (1861–1938), a French individualistic anarchist. He was born in French Algeria and died in Paris.

S

Saint-Simon. Claude Henri de Rouvroy, comte de Saint-Simon (also simply Henri de Saint-Simon) (1760–1825) was a French political, economic, and socialist theorist who had a substantial influence on politics, economics, sociology, and the philosophy of science.

Sainte-Foy. Philippe-Auguste de Sainte-Foy, Chevalier d'Arcq (1721–1795) was a French soldier and man of letters. He was particularly known for his essays.

Sales. Jean Baptiste Claude Delisle de Sales (also Jean-Baptiste Isoard de Lisle) (1741–1816) was a French philosopher noted, in particular, for *The Philosophy of Nature: Treatise on Human Moral Nature* (1770).

Sand. George Sand was the pseudonym of Amantine Lucile Aurore Dupin (1804–1876). She was a French novelist and journalist. Her fame made her a major representative of European Romanticism. She wrote more than 60 novels and a dozen plays.

Sanftleben. Alfred G. Sanftleben (1871–1952) was a German immigrant influenced by the ideas of Rudolph Rocker and Gustav Landauer. He came to Los Angeles in 1900. He wrote articles for Most's *Freiheit* and other radical journals.

Sardat. Antoine-Rose-Marius Sardat (1794–18??) was a French writer. I have been unable to locate any further information about him.

Sarrazin. Adrien Jean Paul François Anne, Comte de Sarrazin (1775–1852) was a French writer.

Say. Jean-Baptiste Say (1767–1832) was a French economist who argued in favor of competition, free trade, and lifting restraints on business. He is best known for Say's Law—also known as the law of markets.

Scheerbart. Paul Karl Wilhelm Scheerbart (pen name, Kuno Küfer) (1863–1915) was a German author of speculative fiction and drawings.

Scheierman. Nicolai Aleksandrovič Scheierman (1869–). I have been unable to find any further information about this writer.

Schnabel. Johann Gottfried Schnabel (pen name, Gisander) (1692–ca. 1751) was a German writer best known for his novel *Insel Felsenburg*.

Schorr. Yeḳuti'el Zalman Shor (as identified by OCLC WorldCat Identities). I have been unable to find further information about this writer.

Scotti. Giulio Clemente Scotti (1602–1669) was an Italian, an erstwhile Jesuit, and, later, a professor of philosophy at Parma and, then, Ferrara.

Seeliger. Ewald Gerhard Seeliger (1877–1959) was a German novelist, a prolific writer who wrote novels mainly set at sea or around Hamburg.

Seriman. Zaccaria Seriman (1709–1784) was a wealthy Venetian writer of Armenian ancestry. His *Viaggi di Enrico Wanton* (1749) features a race of dog-headed monkeys living in or near Australia who are visited by a pair of shipwrecked men.

Seymour. Henry Albert Seymour (1860–1938) was an English secularist and individualist anarchist. He published the first English-language anarchist periodical in Britain.

Shaw. George Bernard Shaw (often simply, Bernard Shaw) (1856–1950) was an Irish playwright, critic, polemicist, and political activist. He wrote more than 60 plays. In 1925, he was awarded the Nobel Prize in Literature.

Shcherbatov. Prince Mikhailo Mikhailovich Shcherbatov (1733–1790) was a leading ideologue of the Russian Enlightenment. His view of human nature and social progress is akin to Swift's pessimism. He was known as a statesman, historian, writer, and philosopher. Shcherbatov's vision of the ideal state in his *Journey to the Land of Ophyr* (1784) depicts Peter I's westernizing reforms as having been reversed with the nobility and the serfs viewed in their "natural" (and inherently unequal) relations to each other.

Shelley. Percy Bysshe Shelley (1792–1822) was one of the major English Romantic poets, and a radical in his poetry as well as in his political and social views.

Sibbern. Frederik Christian Sibbern (often just F. C. Sibbern) (1785–1872) was a Danish philosopher.

Sinclair. Upton Beall Sinclair Jr. (1878–1968) was an American writer, muckraker, and political activist. He wrote almost 100 books in several genres. He won the Pulitzer Prize for Fiction in 1943.

Singer. Ignatius Singer (ca. 1853–1926) was a British writer and chemist as well as a speaker on scientific, economic, philological, and theological issues in the late nineteenth and early twentieth centuries. He was born in Hungary, settled in England, and spent some years in Australia and New Zealand.

Socrates. Socrates (ca. 470–399 BCE) was a Greek philosopher from Athens, and is credited, along with Plato and Aristotle, as being one of the founders of Western philosophy. He left behind no written documents containing his ideas.

Sonnenfels. Joseph Freiherr von Sonnenfels (1732–1817) was an Austrian and German jurist and novelist.

Souêtre. Ol(l)ivier Marie Souêtre (also Olivier Souvestre) (1831–1896) was a Breton poet and singer. He actively participated in the Paris Commune and the anarchist movement.

Spence. Thomas Spence (1750–1814) was an English Radical. He advocated for the common ownership of land as well as a democratic equality of the sexes. Spence was one of the leading revolutionaries of the late eighteenth and early nineteenth centuries.

Spronck. Maurice Spronck was a French writer and politician (1861–1921).

St. John. Christabel Gertrude Marshall (pen name, Christopher Marie St. John) (1871–1960) was a British campaigner for women's suffrage, a playwright, and an author.

Storch. Mathias Storch (1883–1957) was a Greenlandic priest, educator, and novelist. He published the first novel by a native Greenlander in the local language.

Strachey. John St. Loe Strachey (1860–1927) was a British journalist and newspaper proprietor.

Suleau. François-Louis Suleau (1758–1792) was a French royalist monarchist pamphleteer. He was murdered on 10 August 1792 by a mob during the French Revolution.

Sutherland. George Sutherland (1855–1905) was born in Dumbarton, Scotland and emigrated with his family at the age of 9 to Sydney, Australia. He began as a teacher and later became a highly respected journalist and historian.

Suttner. Bertha Sophie Felicitas Freifrau von Suttner (née Countess Kinsky von Wchinitz und Tettau) (1843–1914) was an Austrian-Bohemian pacifist and novelist. She was the first woman to be awarded the Nobel Peace Prize.

Sweven. John Macmillan Brown (pen name, Godfrey Sweven) (1845–1935) was a Scots-New Zealand academic, administrator, and promoter of education for women.

Swift. Jonathan Swift (1667–1745) was an Anglo-Irish satirist, author, essayist, political pamphleteer, and poet, most famous in the utopian tradition for *Gulliver's Travels*.

T

Tarde. Jean-Gabriel de Tarde (1843–1904) was a French sociologist, criminologist, and social psychologist.

Tchetschouline. Frédéric Tchetschouline. I have been unable to find out any further information about this writer except that he appears to have lived in Helsingfors in Finland.

Terrasson. Jean Terrasson (1670–1750) was a French writer, priest, member of the prestigious Académie Français, and later a professor of Greek at the College de France. His fantasy novel *Sethos* combined Masonic rites and Ancient Egyptian rituals.

Terson. Jean Terson (1803–1885) was a French Catholic priest converted by the Saint-Simonians in Carcassonne in 1831.

Theocritus. Theocritus (ca. 300 BC–250 BCE) was a Greek poet from Sicily and the creator of Ancient Greek pastoral poetry.

Thirion. Émile-Ambroise Thirion (also known as Émile Thirion) (1825–1906) was a French man of letters, playwright, and republican propagandist.

Thomas. Chauncey Thomas (1822–1898) was a Boston coach builder and writer.

Thomson. William Thomson (1746–1817) was a Scottish minister, historian, and writer. He often wrote under the pseudonym of Captain Thomas Newte.

Thoreau. Henry David Thoreau (né David Henry Thoreau) (1817–1862) was an American naturalist, essayist, poet, and philosopher. A leading transcendentalist, he is best known for his book *Walden* (a reflection on simple living in nature) and his essay "Resistance to Civil Government" (an argument for disobedience to an unjust state).

Thury. Marc Thury (1822–1905) was a Swiss psychical researcher, professor of physics and natural history at the University of Geneva, and a pioneer of investigations into telekinetic phenomena.

Tieck. Johann Ludwig Tieck (1773–1853) was a German poet, fiction writer, translator, and critic. He was one of the founding fathers of the European Romantic movement in the late-eighteenth and early-nineteenth centuries.

Tolstoy. Count Lev Nikolayevich Tolstoy (usually known as Leo Tolstoy) (1828–1910) was a Russian writer who is regarded as one of the greatest authors of all time. He received nominations for the Nobel Prize in Literature every year from 1902 to 1906 and for the Nobel Peace Prize in 1901, 1902, and 1909.

Trotter. John Trotter of the East India Company. He was born in Midlothian, Scotland, joined the East Indian Company in 1808, and worked for the company in Calcutta and Benares before retiring in 1842. He is likely the same John Trotter who was a temporary member of the board of customs, salt, and opium in 1807.

V

Vaillant. Marie Édouard Vaillant (1840–1915) was a French politician.

Vairasse. Denis Vairasse d'Allais (ca. 1630–1672) was a French Huguenot writer, best known for his utopian novel, *History of the Sevarites* (1675).

Van Eeeden. Frederik Willem van Eeden (1860–1932) was a Dutch writer and psychiatrist. He founded a Walden commune (inspired by Thoreau's *Walden*). See also his three-part essay "The Quest for a Happy Humanity" (*The World's Work* Aug.–Oct. 1911).

Varlet. Théo Varlet (pen name, Déodat Serval) (1878–1938) was a poet, a writer of science fiction and fantasy, and a translator.

Velde. Carl Franz van der Velde (1779–1824) was a German author of historical novels.

Verhaeren. Émile Adolphe Gustave Verhaeren Saint-Amand (1855–1916) was a Flemish poet.

Verne. Jules Gabriel Verne (1828–1905) was a French novelist, poet, and playwright. He is one of the most important early writers of science fiction.

Véron. Pierre Véron (1831–1900) was a French writer, journalist, and librettist.

Vetsch. Jakob Vetsch (pen name, Mundus) (1879–1942) was a Swiss dialect researcher and writer. He is best known for his utopia *Die Sonnenstadt*, whose ideology he called Mundism.

Veuillot. Louis Veuillot (1813–1883) was a French journalist and author who helped to popularize ultramontanism, a philosophy favoring Papal supremacy.

Vilgensofer. A. Vilgensofer. I have been unable to find any information about this writer.

Villedeuil. Pierre-Charles Laurent de Villedeuil (1831–1906). I have been unable to find further information about this writer.

Villegardelle. François Villegardelle (1810–1856) was a French economist and translator. He translated Campanella's *La città del sole* (1602) in 1840.

Villeneuve. Daniel Jost de Villeneuve. I have been unable to find any further information about this writer. The *BnF catalogue général* calls him an "auteur dramatique" (i.e., "playwright").

Vogt. This may be Dr. Oskar Vogt (1870–1959) given this scientist's socialist beliefs.

Voigt. Andreas Voigt (1860–1940 or 1941) was a German mathematician, economist, and politician.

Voltaire. François-Marie Arouet (pseudonym, Voltaire) (1694–1778) was a French Enlightenment writer, historian, and philosopher famous for his wit and his criticism of Christianity and of slavery. He advocated for very modern values: freedom of speech, freedom of religion, and separation of church and state.

Voss. Julius von Voss (1768–1832) was an extraordinarily prolific German author. *Ini. Ein Roman aus dem ein und zwanzigsten Jahrhundert* is generally regarded as the first German science-fiction novel.

Vuilmet (or Vailmet). I have been unable to find any information about this writer.

W

Wallace. John Bruce Wallace was a congregationalist minister who started a magazine called *The Brotherhood* in Limavady, Northern Ireland in 1887. Wallace was influenced by the views of Henry George and Edward Bellamy. In 1891, Wallace moved to London and took over a derelict church in Southgate Road, Hackney, naming it "The Brotherhood Church." The Church was organized as an anarchist, pacifist community.

Wallace. Richard Horatio Edgar Wallace (1875–1932) was a British writer. He was extraordinarily prolific, with 18 plays, 957 short stories, and over 170 novels to his name.

Wallace. Robert Wallace (1697–1771) was a minister of the Church of Scotland and a writer on population.

Waterhouse. Elizabeth (née Hodgkin) Waterhouse (1834–1918) was an English author and poet. Her work consisted mostly of religious studies and tracts written from a Quaker point of view.

Watteau. Antoine Watteau (1684–1721) was a French painter who revitalized the Baroque style by shifting it to the more naturalistic and less elaborate Rococo.

Webb. Sidney James Webb, 1st Baron Passfield (1859–1947) was a British socialist, economist, and reformer who co-founded the London School of Economics. He was an early member of the Fabian Society and wrote the original, pro-nationalisation Clause IV for the British Labour Party.

Weitling. Wilhelm Christian Weitling (1808–1871) was a German tailor, an inventor, a radical political activist, and one of the first theorists of communism. He gained fame in Europe as a social theorist before he emigrated to the United States.

Wells. Herbert George Wells (1866–1946) was an English writer who wrote more than 50 novels and dozens of short stories. His nonfiction output included works of social commentary, politics, history, popular science, satire, biography, and autobiography. He has been called the "father of science fiction."

Westall. William Bury Westall (1834–1903) was born in Old Accrington, Lancashire and was a businessman, journalist, popular novelist, and science-fiction writer.

Wetstein. Jacob Wetstein (fl. 1738–) was a Dutch publisher and printer active in Amsterdam.

Whiting. Sydney Whiting (1820–1875) was a barrister, poet, and novelist.

Wichers von Gogh. Otto Wichers von Gogh was the son of the actor Eugen Heinrich Oskar von Gogh and Katharina Therese Wichers. He first went to sea and later became an actor, probably with a traveling group. He was a socialist pamphleteer.

Wieland. Christoph Martin Wieland (1733–1813) was a German poet and writer. He is best remembered for having written the first Bildungsroman (*Geschichte des Agathon*) in 1766.

Wilkes. John Wilkes (1725–1797) was a British radical journalist and politician, a magistrate, essayist, and soldier. In 1776, he introduced the first bill for parliamentary reform in the British Parliament.

William Tell. A Swiss folk hero of the eighteenth century. An expert marksman, he symbolized resistance to autocratic rule.

Winstanley. Gerrard Winstanley (1609–1676) was an English Protestant religious reformer, political philosopher, and activist during the period of the Commonwealth of England. Winstanley was the leader of the True Levellers (or Diggers), a radical anti-enclosures group.

Wooldridge. Charles William Wooldridge (1847–1908) was an English doctor and author who lived in the United States after childhood.

Wright. Henry Wright (ca. 1852–1940) was, among other things, the translator of Eugen Richter's *Pictures of the Socialistic Future* (1893). He may have been associated with the London publishing firm of Houlston and Wright.

Z

Zajac. Sten'ka Zajac. I have been unable to find any information about this writer.

Zavattero. Domenico Zavattero (1875–1947) was an Italian anarchist editor, activist, and polemicist. He contributed to the anarchist periodical *Il Martello*.

Zemmrich. Johannes Zemmrich (1868–1944) was a German historian, teacher, and writer.

Zeno. Likely Zeno of Elea (ca. 495–430 BC), who was a pre-Socratic philosopher and vital in the history of dialectics and paradox.

Zisly. Henri Zisly (1872–1945) was a French individualist anarchist and naturist.

Zola. Émile Édouard Charles Antoine Zola (1840–1902) was a French novelist, journalist, playwright, and the best-known practitioner of the literary school of naturalism.

Zschokke. Johann Heinrich Daniel Zschokke (1771–1848) was a German, later Swiss, author and reformer who had an extensive civil service career, and wrote histories, fiction and other works which were widely known at the time.

Żulawski. Jerzy (1874–1915). He was a writer, philosopher, and translator, most famous for his science-fiction work *Trylogia Księżycowa* (Lunar Trilogy) written between 1901 and 1911.

Zurbonsen. Friedrich Zurbonsen (1856–1941) was a German historian, teacher, and writer.

Appendix C

LIST OF INTENTIONAL COMMUNITIES IN *ESBOZO*

Blaricum
Brotherhood
Cecilia Colony
Clousden Hill
Cosme
The Daisy Colony Scheme
Der Genossenschaftspionier
Die neue Gemeinschaft
Kaweah Commonwealth
La Familistere
Modern Times
New Fellowship
Oneida
Rappites
Ruskin
Shakers
Topolobampo
Van-Eeden Colony
Wainoni

Appendix D

LIST OF UTOPIAN NEWSPAPERS AND JOURNALS IN *ESBOZO*

Agitator
Blackwood's Magazine
Brotherhood
The Coming Nation
The Co-operator
Cosme Monthly
The Credit Foncier of Sinaloa
De Pionier
Demonstrator
Deutsche Worte
Discontent
The Fairhope Courier
The Grander Age
Hors du troupeau
The Integral Co-operator
L'en-Dehors
L'ère nouvelle
La chronique des livres
Labour Copartnership
Le devoir
Le jardin de France
The Llano Colonist
Nationalisation News
New Australia
New Moral World
Refractaires
Revue socialiste
Seedtime

The Self-Helper
Solutions sociales
The Sower
The Syndicalist
Temple of Reason
Twentieth Century
Vrede

BIBLIOGRAPHY

Acharya, M. P. T. "Max Nettlau as Biographer and Historian: An Appreciation of His Style, Method, and System." *We Are Anarchists: Essays on Anarchism, Pacificism, and the Indian Independence Movement, 1923–1953*. Oakland, CA: AK Press, [2019]. [155]–160.
Acworth, Andrew. *A New Eden. [A Novel]*. London: Ward & Lock, 1896. Internet Resource.
Adam, Paul. *La cité prochaine: lettres de Malaisie*. Paris: Bibliothèque des Auteurs Modernes, 1908. Print.
———. *Lettres de Malaisie: roman*. Paris: Revue Blanche, 1898. Internet Resource.
Adams, Matthew S. "The Possibilities of Anarchist History: Rethinking the Canon and Writing History." *Anarchist Developments in Cultural History* 2013.1 ("Blasting the Canon" special issue): 33–62.
Albrecht, Johann Friedrich Ernst. *Die Affenkönige oder die Reformation des Affenlandes. Ein politischer Roman in zwei Büchern*. N. p.: Im Verlag Georg Philipp Wucherers, 1788.
———. *Die Kolonie*. [Augsburg]: n.p., 1793.
Allais, Denis V., and A. Roberts. *The History of the Sevarites or Sevarambi, a Nation Inhabiting Part of the Third Continent Commonly Called Terræ Australes Incognitæ: With an Account of Their Admirable Government, Religion, Customs, and Language*. London: Printed for Henry Brome, 1675. Internet Resource.
Allorge, Henri. "La Famine de fer (en l'an 2432)." *La grande revue* 77 (Feb. 10, 1913): 547–551. Full text is available at the hathitrust: https://babel.hathitrrust.org.
Altena, Bert. "A Networking Historian: The Transnational, the National, and the Patriotic in and around Nettlau's *Geschichte der Anarchie*." *Reassessing the Transnational Turn: Scales of Analysis in Anarchist and Syndicalist Studies*. Ed. Constance Bantman and Bert Altena. New York: Routledge, 2014. [62]–79.
Amersin, Ferdinand. *Das Land der Freiheit. Ein Zukunftsbild in schlichten Erzählungsform*. Graz: Leykam-Josefsthal, 1874. Print.
———. *Gemeinverständliche Weisheitslehre (Wahrheits Klugheits und Geschmackslehre)*. Triest: Julius Dase, Commissions-Verlag, 1881. Internet Resource.
———. *Weisheit und Tugend des reinen Menschenthums. In den Formen der Lehre und der Dichtung gemeinverständlich Dargestellt*. Graz: Commissions-Verlag "Leykam-Josefsthal," 1871. Print.
Among the Têtchas of Central Asia. London: Southern Printing Company, 1886.
"The Anarchist Encyclopedia: A Gallery of Saints & Sinners." https://web.archive.org/web/20150224043814/http://recollectionbooks.com/bleed/Encyclopedia/NettlauMax.htm.
Andreæ, Johann V. *Reipublicæ Christianopolitanæ Descriptio*. Argentorati: Zetzner, 1619. Print.
Angerbauer, Joseph. *Tischlein, deck dich für Alle! Eine Betrachtung*. West Norwood: Selbstverlag, 1908. Print.
Arcq, Philippe-Auguste S.-F. *Lettres d'osman*. A Constantinople [i.e., Paris]: Publisher Not Identified, 1753. Internet Resource.

Argens, Jean-Baptiste B. *Lettres juives, ou correspondance philosophique, historique et critique, entre un Juif voyageur à Paris, et ses correspondans en divers endroits.* Lausanne et Geneve: Bosquet, 1739. Print.

Aristophanes. *The Ekklesiazusai.* Ed. David Stewart. Milton Keynes: Open University Press, 1979. Print.

Armand, Émile. *L'initiation individualiste anarchiste.* Paris: Éditions de L'en-Dehors, 1923. Print.

A[rthur]. L[ehning]. "Max Nettlau." *Bulletin of the International Institute of Social History* 5.1 (1950): 25–29. https://www.jstor.org/stable/44601109.

Asselineau, Charles, and Félix Bracquemond. *Le paradis des gens de lettres, selon ce qui a été vu et entendu, l'an du Seigneur MDCCCXLI* [sic pour *1861*]. Paris (Rue Richelieu, 97): Librairie de Poulet-Malassis, 1861. Print.

Atlanticus. *Ein Blick in den Zukunftsstaat: Produktion und Konsum im Sozialstaat.* Stuttgart: Dietz, 1898. Print.

Avrich, Paul. *An American Anarchist: The Life of Voltairine de Cleyre.* Princeton: Princeton University Press, 1978.

———. Introduction. *God and the State.* By Michael Bakunin. 1916. Toronto: Dover, 1970. [v]–xii.

Bachstrom, Johann F. *Das Bey zwey hundert Jahr lang unbekannte, nunmehro aber entdeckte vortreffliche Land der Inqviraner ... Nach allen seinen Sitten, Gebrauchen, Ordnungen, Gottesdienst, Wissenschaften, Kunsten, Vortheilen und Einrichtung umstandlich Beschrieben, und dem gemeinem Wesen zum besten Mitgetheilet.* Franckfurt, 1736. Internet Resource.

Bacon, Francis. *New Atlantis: A Work Vnfinished.* London: Printed by J. H. for William Lee, 1627. Print.

Bakunin, Mikhail. *The Revolutionary Catechism.* 1866. N.p.: Pattern Books, 2020.

Balmanno. *The City of Our Quest and Its Social Problems.* Paisley: Alexander Gardner, 1906. Print.

Barbançois-Villegongis, Charles-Hélion. *Le rêve singulier, ou la nation comme il n'y en a point,* Par M. De B. Tome Ier. Paris, 1808. Print.

Barmby, Goodwyn. "The Book of Platonopolis: Or, the Perfect Commonwealth. A Romance of the Future." In *The Communist Chronicle, or Promethean Magazine* 1.35–37 [1845]. Print.

Barrucand, Victor. *Le pain gratuit.* Paris: Chamuel, 1896. Internet Resource.

Bart-Claye, A. *Vers la cité future.* Paris: Société Française d'imprimerie et de libnairie, 1905. Print.

Bauernfeld, Eduard. *Die Republik der Thiere.* Wien: Verlag Nicht Ermittelbar, 1848. Print.

Bayle, Pierre. *Dictionnaire historique et critique.* Rotterdam: Reinier Leers, 1697. Print.

Beaumont, Augustus H. *Isonomist.* Kingston, Jamaica?: Augustus Hardin Beaumont, 1833. Print.

Beaurieu, Caspar G. *L'éleve de la nature.* Paris: Panckoucke, 1764. Print.

Bebel, August. *Charles Fourier: sein Leben und seine Theorien.* Stuttgart: J. H. W. Dietz, 1888. Print.

———. *Die Frau und der Sozialismus (Die Frau in der Vergangenheit, gegen wart und Zukunft).* Stuttgart: J. H. W. Dietz, 1891. Print.

Beck, Ferdinand K. *Die Offenbarungen und gebote Gottes über Deutschlands künftige Reichsverfassung.* Darmstadt: Wittich, 1849. Print.

Becker, Heiner M. Introduction. *A Short History of Anarchism.* By Max Nettlau. Trans. Ida Pilat Isca. Ed. Heiner M. Becker. London: Freedom Press, 1996. ix–xxiii.

———. "A Short Guide to Nettlau's Historical Work." *A Short History of Anarchism*. By Max Nettlau. Trans. Ida Pilat Isca. Ed. Heiner M. Becker. London: Freedom Press, 1996. 351–365.
Beffroy, de R. L.-A. *La constitution de la Lune: rêve politique et moral*. À Paris: Chez Froullé, 1793. Print.
———. *Nicodème dans la Lune, ou, la révolution pacifique: folie en prose et en Trois Actes, mêlée d'ariettes et de vaudevilles*. À Paris: Chez l'auteur, et au Théâtre Lyrique, 1791. Print.
Behrens, Lewis H., and Ignatius Singer. *The Story of My Dictatorship*. London: Bliss, Sands & Foster, 1894. Print.
Beitzinger, A. J. "Anarchism." *The New Catholic Encyclopedia*. Second ed. Detroit: Thomson/Gale, 2003. 383–385.
Bell, George W. *Mr. Oseba's Last Discovery*. Wellington, NZ: New Zealand Times Co., 1904. Print.
Bellamy, Edward. *Equality*. New York: D. Appleton, 1897. Print.
———. *Looking Backward, 2000–1887*. Boston: Ticknor and Company, 1888. Print.
———. "What 'Nationalism' Means." *Contemporary Review* July 1890: 1–18.
Bellers, John. *Proposals for Raising a Colledge of Industry of All Useful Trades and Husbandry*. London: Printed and Sold by T. Sowle, 1695. Internet Resource.
Benda, Daniel A., and H. G. Benda. *Die Felicier--geschichtliche Entwickelung eines Urvolks: 1*. Leipzig: Fleischer, 1827. Print.
Benson, Robert H. *Im Dämmerschein der Zukunft: Ein Roman in Traumbildern*. Ed. and trans. Rudolfine Ettlinger and Anna Ettlinger Einsiedeln: Verlagsanstalt Benziger, 1912. Print.
Bergerac, Cyrano de. *Histoire comique: contenant les états et empires de la Lune*. Paris: Charles de Sercy. 1657. Internet Resource.
———. *Les novvelles oevvres de monsievr de Cyrano Bergerac: contenant l'histoire comiqve des estats & empires du soleil, plvsievrs lettres, et avtres pieces diuertissantes*. Paris: Charles de Sercy, 1662. Print.
Berington, Simon. *The Memoirs of Sigr Gaudentio di Lucca: Taken from His Confession and Examination before the Fathers of the Inquisition at Bologna in Italy. Making a Discovery of an Unknown Country in the Midst of the Vast Deserts of Africa, as Ancient, Populous, and Civilized, as the Chinese*. Trans. E. T., gent. London: T. Cooper, 1737. Print.
Berneri, Marie-Louise. *Journey through Utopia*. London: Routledge & Kegan Paul, 1950.
Besant, Walter. *The Revolt of Man*. London: W. Blackwood and Sons, 1882. Print.
Béthune, Chevalier de. *Relation du monde de Mercure*. Genève: Chez Barillot & Fils, 1750. Internet Resource.
Bevir, Mark, ed. *Encyclopedia of Political Theory*. London: Sage, 2010.
Bienvenu, Léon. *Histoire de France tintamarresque*. 1868. Paris, 1886. Print.
Bigg, Henry R. H. *The Human Republic*. London: David Stott, 1891. Print.
Blatchford, Robert. *Merrie England*. London: Clarion Office, 1894. Print.
———. *The Sorcery Shop: An Impossible Romance*. London: Clarion Press, 1907. Print.
Bodin, Félix. *Le roman de l'avenir*. Paris: Lecointe et Pougin, 1834. Print.
Boétie, Etienne de la. *Discours de la servitude volontaire*. 1557. Institut Coppet, 2015. Internet Resource.
Bogdanov, Aleksandr A. *Der rote Stern: Ein utopischer Roman*. Berlin: Jugendinternationale, 1923. Print.
———. *Krasnaja Zvezda*. Leningrad, Moskva: Kniga, 1925. Print.
———. *Red Star: The First Bolshevik Utopia*. Ed. Loren R. Graham and Richard Stites. Trans. Charles Rougle. Bloomington: Indiana University Press, 1984.

Bolle, Carl. *Die Kosmier.* Bern, 1898. Print.
Bolle, G. *Sozial. Eine Erzählung aus dem Staate der Sozialdemokratie.* Berlin, 1891. Print.
Bolzano, Bernard. *Vom besten Staat.* 2019. Print.
Bonhomme, Frederic. *La humanité pacifique.* 1907.
Bougeant, Guillaume-Hyacinthe. *Voyage merveilleux du prince Fan-Férédin, dans la romancie.* Amsterdam: Née de la Rochelle, 1788. Internet Resource.
Bowman, Hildebrand. *The Travels of Hildebrand Bowman, Esquire, into Carnovirria, Taupiniera, Olfactaria, and Auditante, in New Zealand; in the Island of Bonhommica, and in the Powerful Kingdom of Luxo-Volupto on the Great Southern Continent. Written by Himself, Etc.* London: W. Strahan & T. Cadell, 1778. Print.
Bratt, Alfred. *Die Welt ohne Hunger. Roman.* Second ed. Berlin: Erich Reiss Verlag, 1916. Print.
Brehmer, Fritz. *Nebel der Andromeda.* Leipzig: Staackmann, 1920. Print.
Briancourt, Math. *Visite au phalanstère.* Paris: Librairie Phalanstèrienne, 1848. Internet Resource.
Bricaire, de L. D. N. *Le aauvage de Taïti aux Français: avec un envoi au philosophe ami des sauvages.* Londres: Lejay, 1770. Print.
Brissac, Henri. "La societe collectiviste." *La Revue socialiste* 14.82 (Oct. 1891): 446–465.
Brockhouse, H. *Hopetown. An Industrial Town, As It Is, and As It Might Be.* West Bromwich: Round, 1905. Print.
Brod, Max. *Das grosse Wagnis.* Leipzig: Kurt Wolff, 1919. Print.
Brown, Anne. "'The First New Zealand Novel'?: John Elliott's 'Travels of Hildebrand Bowman' (1778)." https://www.researchgate.net/publication/350960030_%27The_First_New_Zealand_Novel%27_John_Elliott%27s_%27Travels_of_Hildebrand_Bowman%27_1778. 2021 conference paper.
Brunt, Samuel (pseud.). *A Voyage to Cacklogallinia: With a Description of the Religion, Policy, Customs and Manners, of That Country, by Captain Samuel Brunt.* London: Printed by J. Watson and Sold by the Booksellers of London and Westminster, 1727. Internet Resource.
Buckingham, James S. *National Evils and Practical Remedies: With a Plan for a Model Town.* London: Peter Jackson, 1849.
Burazerovic, Manfred. "Max Nettlau: Der Lange Weg zür Freiheit." Diss. Universität Bochum, 1995. Berlin: OPPO-Verlag, 1996.
———. "Max Nettlau: Die Verantwortung des freien Menschen." *Anarchisten.* Ed. Wolfram Beyer. Berlin: OPPO, 1993. 88–100.
———. "Nettlau, Max." *Wegbereiter der Demokratie: 87 Porträts.* Ed. Manfred Asendorf. Stuttgart: J. B. Metzler, 2006. 162–164.
Burgh, James. *An Account of the First Settlement, Laws, Form of Government, and Police, of the Cessares, a People of South America: In Nine Letters.* London: Printed for J. Payne, 1764. Internet Resource.
Burkitt, Wm T. *The Coming Day: A Story of Inevitable Social and Industrial Progress.* London: Drane's Danegeld House, 1913. Print.
Butler, Francelia. "The Ruskin Commonwealth: A Unique Experiment in Marxian Socialism." *Tennessee Historical Quarterly* 23.4 (Dec. 1964): 333–342.
Butler, Samuel. *Erewhon, or Over the Range.* London: Trübner, 1872. Print.
———. *Erewhon Revisited: Twenty Years Later, Both by the Original Discoverer of the Country and by His Son.* London: Grant Richards, 1901. Print.
———. *Ergindwon, oder, jenseits der Berge.* Leipzig: J.A. Barth, 1879. Internet Resource.

Cabet, Étienne. *Icarie*. Paris: au Bureau du Populaire, 1849.
———. *Reise nach Ikarien*. Paris: Büreau des Populär, 1847. Print.
———. *Voyage en Icarie: roman philosophique et social*. Second ed. Paris: J. Mallet, 1842. Print.
———. *Voyage et aventures de Lord Villiam Carisdall en Icarie*. Paris: H. Souverain, 1840. Internet Resource.
Campanella, Tommaso. *La città del sole: dialogo poetico; The City of the Sun: A Poetical Dialogue*. Ed. Luigi Firpo. Trans. Daniel J. Donno. Berkeley: University of California Press, 1981.
———, and Tobias Adami. *Thomae e Realis Philosophiae Epilogisticae Partes Quatuor: Hoc Est De Rerum Natura, Hominum Moribus, Politica, (Cui Civitas Solis Iuncta Est) & Eoconomica*. Francofurti: Tampach, 1623. Print.
Campe, Joachim H. *Robinson der Jüngere: zur angenehmen und nützlichen Unterhaltung für Kinder. c'est-à-dire, Robinson le jeune, amusement utile pour les enfans*. Paris: L. T. Barrois, Fils, 1803. Print.
Canudo, Ricciotto. *La ville sans chef*. Paris: Édition Du "Monde illustré," 1910. Print.
Canzani, Lambro. *Uno sguardo all'avvenire*. Fano: Società Tipografica Cooperativa, 1903. Print.
Čapek, Karel. *W. U. R.: Werstands universal Robots (utopistisches Kollektivdrama in drei Aufzügen)* [better known as *R. U. R.: Rossum's Universal Robots*]. Trans. Otto Pick. Berlin: Drei Masken Verl., 1921; Prag: Orbis, 1922.
Cardias (pseud. of Giovanni Rossi). *Un comune socialista. Bozzetto semi-veridico di Cardias*. Milano, 1878. Print.
Carlile, Richard. *The Gauntlet*. 1833. Westport, CT: Greenwood Reprint Corp., 1970. Internet Resource.
Carter, Alan. "Anarchism: Some Theoretical Foundations." *Journal of Political Ideologies* 16.3 (Oct. 2011): 245–264.
Casanova, Giacomo. *Jcosaméron, ou, histoire d'Édouarde et d'Élisabeth qui passérent quatre vingt un ans chez les Mégamicres, habitans aborigénes du protocosme dans l'intérieur de notre globe*. 5 Vols. Prague: Imperimerie de l'école normale, 1788. Print.
Castel, de S.-P. C.-I. [*Projet pour rendre la paix perpétuelle en Europe*]. Lieu de Publication Non Identifié: Éditeur Non Identifié, 1712. Print.
Catalde, de. *Le paysan gentilhomme, ou avantures de M. Ransav, avec son voyage aux isles Jumelles*. Paris: Prault, 1737. Print. Available from https://babel.hathitrust.org.
Cathelineau, Alexandre, and Gaston Tissandier. *Voyage à la Lune: d'aprés un manuscrit authentique projeté d'un volcan lunaire*. Paris: Librairie Achille Faure, 1865. Print.
Chesney, George T. *The Battle of Dorking: Reminiscences of a Volunteer*. Edinburgh, 1971. Print.
Chirac, Auguste. *Si, étude sociale d'aprés demain*. Paris: Albert Savine, 1893. Internet Resource.
Christoph, Hans. *Die Fahrt in die Zukunft: ein Relativitätsroman*. Stuttgart: Deutsche Verl.-Anstalt, 1922. Print.
Christopolis; Life and Its Amenities in a Land of Garden Cities. London: S.W. Partridge & Co., 1903. Print.
[Clauxel, J. C.]. *Le sort réservé aux empereurs et rois*. Bruxelles, 1878. Print.
Cless, A[lfred]. "Ein Zukunftsbild der Menschheit." Zürich: Verlags-Magazin, J. Schabelitz, 1893. Pamphlet.
Code de la nature, ou le véritable esprit de ses lois de tout temps négligé ou méconnu. Par-tout: Chez Le Vrai Sage, 1755. Internet Resource.

Coeurderoy, Ernest. *Hurrah!!! ou la revolution par les Cosaques.* Londres, 1854. Internet Resource.

———. *Jours d'exil.* Londres: J. Thomas, 1854–1855. Print.

Colerus, Egmont. *Antarktis: Roman.* Leipzig: Ilf-Verlag, 1920. Print.

———. *Der dritte Weg: Roman.* Leipzig: Wien, 1921. Print.

———. *Sodom: Roman.* Wien: E. Strache, 1920. Print.

———. *Weisse Magier: Roman.* Wien: Rokola, 1922. Print.

Conrad, M. G. *… in purpurner Finsternis; Romanimprovisation aus dem d reissigsten Jahrhundert.* Leipzig: C. F. Tiefenbach, 1895. Internet Resource.

Considerant, Victor. *Au Texas.* Bruxelles: Société de Colonisation, 1855. Internet Resource.

———. *Du Texas: premier rapport à mes amis.* Poitiers: Service Commun de Documentation de l'Université de Poitiers, 2009. Internet Resource.

———, and Raymond Brucker. *Publication compléte des nouvelles découvertes de Sir John Herschel dans le ciel austral et dans la Lune. Tr. de l'Anglais.* Paris: Masson et Duprey, 1836. Internet Resource.

Constant, Jacques. *Le triomphe des suffragettes: roman des temps future.* Paris: Librairie universelle, 1910. Print.

A Constitution for the Kingdom of Heaven on Earth. Melbourne: Johnston, Fear & Kingham, 1915[?]. Print.

Cooper, James Fenimore. *Mark's Reef; or, the Crater: A Tale of the Pacific.* London: Richard Bentley, 1847. Print.

Corbett, George. *New Amazonia: A Foretaste of the Future.* London: Tower Pub, 1889. Print.

Cornelius, Peter Z. Z. [pseud. of Peter Plockhoy]. *The Way to the Peace and Settlement of These Nations.* London: Ptd. for D. White, 1659. Print.

Costa, Andrea. *Un sogno.* Firenze: G. Nerbini, 1901. Print.

Couvreur, André. *Une invasion de macrobes.* Paris: P. Lafitte, 1910. Print.

Crozat, Henry. *La cité idéale; ou, l'urbanisme social rationnel: son plan sa construction, son organisation.* Paris: E. Besson & Cie., 1920. Print.

Cyrille, V., and B. Gastineau. *La liquidation sociale. Prophétie.* [*Par V. Cyrille, avec la collaboration de B. Gastineau*]. Bruxelles: Verrycken, 1872. Print.

Davis, Laurence, and Ruth Kinna, ed. *Anarchism and Utopia.* Manchester: Manchester University Press, 2009.

The Dawn of the Twentieth Century: 1st January 1901. London: Field & Tuer, 1888. Print.

de Jong, Rudolf. "Biographische und Bibliographische Daten von Max Nettlau, März 1940" (Biographical and Bibliographical Data for Max Nettlau, March 1940). *International Review of Social History* 14 (1969): 444–482.

de la Dixmerie, Nicolas Bricaire. *Le sauvage de Taïti aux Français avec un envoi au philosophe ami des sauvages.* Paris Chez Lejay, Libraire, 1770.

de la Rue, Joubert. *Lettres d'un sauvage dépaysé.* Amsterdam: Jean François Jolly, 1738.

de Puisieux, Philippe-Florent. *Les hommes volants, ou les aventures de Pierre Wilkins.* Londres: Veuve Brunet, 1763. Print.

Defoe, Daniel. *The Life and Strange Surprizing Adventures of Robinson Crusoe: of York, Mariner: Who Lived Eight and Twenty Years All Alone in an Un-Inhabited Island on the Coast of America, Near the Mouth of the Great River of Oroonoque; Having Been Cast on Shore by Shipwreck, wherein All the Men Perished but Himself. With an Account How He Was at Last as Strangely Deliver'd by Pyrates. Written by Himself. the Fourth Edition. To Which Is Added a Map of the World, in Which Is Delineated the Voyages of Robinson Crusoe.* London: Printed for W. Taylor at the Ship in Pater-Noster-Row, 1719. Internet Resource.

Déjacque, Joseph. *L'humanisphère.* Bruxelles: Bibl. d. "Temps nouv.," 1899. Print.

Delbruck, Georges. *Au pays de l'harmonie: beauté, harmonie, amour.* Paris: Perrin et Cie, 1906. Internet Resource.

Delisle, de S. J. *De la philosophie de la nature*. Amsterdam: Arkstée & Merkus, 1770. Internet resource.

Der Sieg bei Jena: Ein Beitrag zur "Geschichte" Preussen-Deutschlands. Die letzte Schlacht; eine zukünftige Begebenheit. Berlin: Verlag "Die Einigekeit," 1908. Print.

Descottes, G. *Voyages dans les planètes et découverte des véritables destinées de l'homme*. 1864. Print.

Desfontaines, Pierre-François G. *Le nouveau Gulliver, ou voyage de Jean Gulliver: fils du Capitaine Gulliver*. À Paris: Chez La Veuve Clouzier, et François Le Breton, 1730. Print.

Deslinières, Lucien. *Le Maroc socialiste*. Paris: M. Giard & E. Briere, 1912. Print.

———, and J. Marc-Py. *La résurrection du Docteur Valbel, ou le monde dans Un demi-siècle*. Paris: France-Édition, 1921. Internet Resource.

Desmarest, Henri. *La femme future*. Paris: Ed. du livre moderne, 1900. Print.

Despres, Marie. *La grève des femmes*. Paris: A. Savine, 1895. Print.

d'Hupay, Joseph Alexandre Victor. *Maison de réunion pour la communauté philosophe dans la terre de l'auteur de ce projet: plan d'ordre propre aux personnes des deux sexes de tout âge & de diverses professions: suivi des exemples des nouveaux troglodites, par M. de Montesquieu, des Moraves, article de l'encyclopédie & d'une institution de vie commune religieuse & philosophique décrite par le P. Lami*. A Euphrate: Chez Les Associés Freres Dumplers, 1779. Print.

Dide, Noémie. *Fantaisie anticalviniste: notes humoristiques d'un voyageur*. Lausanne: Impr. F. Ruedi, 1909. Print.

Dixie, Lady Florence. *Isola; or, the Disinherited: A Revolt for Woman and All the Disinherited [a Drama in Verse] ... with Remarks thereon by G.J. Holyoake*. London: Leadenhall Press, 1903. Print.

Dolgoff, Sam, ed. *The Anarchist Collectives: Workers' Self-management in the Spanish Revolution 1936–1939*. New York: Free Life Editions, 1974.

Doni, Anton F. *I mondi celesti, terrestri, et infernali, de gli academici pellegrini*. Vinegia: Appresso Gabriel Giolito, 1562. Internet Resource.

Donnay, Charles M., and Lucien Descaves. *La clairière: Comédie en cinq actes, en prose*. Troisième édition. Paris, 1900. Print.

———. *La clairière: pièce en quatre actes*. S. l: S. n., 1900. Print.

Donnay, Maurice. *Lysistrata: comédie en quatre actes en prose*. Paris: P. Ollendorf, 1893. Print.

Donnelly, Ignatius. *Caesar's Column: A Story of the Twentieth Century*. Chicago: F. J. Schulte & Co., 1891. Print.

Draper, Christopher. "The Torch of Anarchy 1891–1896." https://radicalhistorynetwork.blogspot.com/2018/02/the-torch-of-anarchy-1891-1896.html.

Du Laurens H.-J. *Étrennes aux gens d'église, ou La chandelle d'Arras*. Bernes: Aux dépens de l'Académie d'Arras, 1765. Print.

Dupin, Gustave. *Les Robinsons de la paix*. Paris: Clarté, 1920. Print.

Durey, Michael. "John Lithgow's Lithconia: The Making and Meaning of America's First 'Utopian Socialist' Tract." *William and Mary Quarterly* 3rd ser. 49.4 (Oct. 1992): 675–694.

Dwight, Theodore W. "Harrington and His Influence on American Political Institutions and Political Thought." *Political Science Quarterly* (Mar. 1887): 1–44.

E R. V. F. L. *Relation du voyage de l'isle d'eutopie*. Delft: H. Van Rhin, 1711. Internet Resource.

Earwaker, J. P., ed. *Local Gleanings relating to Lancashire and Cheshire*. Manchester: Cornish and Day, n.d. Vol. 1 (Apr. 1875–Dec. 1876): 123.

Empereur, de C. *Étrennes de l'empereur de la Chine aux souverains de l'Europe pour l'année 1782: avec un plan de pacification proposé par le monarque Chinois & ses instructions au Mandarin Chou-King, lettré de la première classe ... son ambassadeur dans toutes les cours de l'Europe*. Constantinople: Publisher Not Identified, 1782. Print.

Enckell, Marianne. "Nettlau, Max." *Les Anarchistes. Dictionnaire biographique du mouvement libertaire francophone.* Ivry-sur-Seine: Les Editions Ouvrières, 2014. 371–372.

———. "Sept theses sur Max Nettlau" (Seven Theses about Max Nettlau). *Bulletin du CIRA (Centre international de recherches l'anarchisme)* [Lausanne] (1972) no. 24: [4]–5.

The English Catalogue of Books. 1864–1921.

Erbal, Jean. *En l'an 2050!!!* Paris: Bibliothèque du phare littéraire, 1889. Print.

Erskine, Thomas. *Armata: A Fragment.* London: John Murray, 1817. Print.

Estève, Louis. *La nouvelle abbaye de Thilème.* Toulouse: Bibliothèque de poésie, 1906. Print.

Etymonia. London: S. Tinsley, 1875. Print.

Etzler, John A. *The Paradise within the Reach of All Men Without Labor, by Powers of Nature and Machinery: An Address to All Intelligent Men. in Two Parts.* Pittsburgh, Pa: Etzler and Reinhold, 1833. Print.

Eulenberg, Herbert. *Die Insel: Ein Spiel.* Berlin: Gurlitt, 1918. Second ed., 1919. Print.

Fabien, Jacques. *Paris en songe, essai sur les logements à bon marché, le bien-être des masses, Etc.* Paris, 1863. Print.

Farrère, Claude. *Les condamnées à mort: roman.* Paris: Flammarion, 1920[?]. Print.

———, and Hans Reisiger. *Die Todgeweihten: Roman.* München: Drei Masken Verlag, 1921. Print.

Faure, Sébastien. *Encyclopédie anarchiste. A-C.* Paris: Editions des équateurs, 2012.

———. *Mi comunismo (la felicidad universal).* Buenos Aires: Editorial La protesta, 1922. Print.

———. *Mon communisme (le bonheur universel).* Paris: Impr. "La Fraternelle," 1921. Print.

Fazy, James. *Les voyages d'ertelib: conte traduit de l'arabe du poète Edbensahirad.* Genève: Manget et Cherbuliez, 1822. Print.

Fénélon, François S. M. *Les avantures de Telemaque fils d'Ulysse, ou suite du quatrième livre de l'Odyssée d'Homère.* À La Haye: Chez Adrian Moetjens, 1699. Internet Resource.

Fichte, Johann G. *Der geschlossene Handelsstaat. Ein philosophischer Entwurf als Anhang zur Rechtslehre.* Tübingen, 1800. Print.

Flammarion, Camille. *Les mondes imaginaires et les mondes réels.* Paris: S. n., 1865. 23rd ed., 1905. Print.

Fleischmann, Hector. *L'explosion du globe: roman d'aventures.* Paris: Albin Michel, 1910[?]. Print.

Florian, Jean-Pierre C. *Numa Pompilius, second roi de Rome: 1.* Paris: Didot, 1786. Print.

Flürscheim, Michael. *Deutschland in 100 Jahren, oder die Galoschen des Glücks: ein soziales Märchen.* Bubenheim: J. Schmitt, 1887. Print.

Foigny, Gabriel. *La terre australe connue: c'est à dire, la description de ce pays inconnu jusqu'ici, de ses moeurs & de ses coûtumes par Mr Sadeur: avec les avantures qui le conduisirent en ce continent, & les particularitez du sejour qu'il y fit durant trente-cinq ans & plus, & de son retour.* À Vannes [i. e., Genève]: Par Iacques Vernevil, 1676. Print.

Folingsby, Kenneth. *Meda: A Tale of the Future* [Glasgow, Scot.]: Ptd. [by Aird & Coghill] for Private Circulation, 1891. Rpt. London: H. F. Mitchell, 1892. Print.

Follin, H.-L. *Le révolution du 4 Septembre 19…* Paris: Aux Éditions "Liber," 1921. Print.

Fontenelle, de. *La république des philosophes: ou, histoire des Ajaoiens, ouvrage posthume de M. De Fontenelle.* on y a joint une lettres sur la nudité des sauvages. Genève: n.p., 1768. Genève: EDHIS, Éditions d'histoire sociale, 1970. Print.

Forrest, Henry J. *A Dream of Reform.* London: J. Chapman, 1848. Print.

Fourier, Charles. *Théorie des quatre mouvements et des destinées générales.* Leipzig, 1808. Print.

Fournière, Eugene. "Le rêve de Pierre Davant." *Revue socialiste* 30.175 (July 1899): 36–58.

France, Anatole. *La révolte des anges*. Paris: Calmann-Lévy, 1914. Internet Resource.
———. *L'île des pingouins*. Paris: C. Lévy, 1908. Print.
———. *Sur la pierre blanche*. Paris: Calmann-Lévy, 1903. Print.
Francé-Harrar, Annie. *Die Feuerseelen: phantastischer Roman*. 1920. Print.
Franklin, Alfred. *Les ruines de Paris en 1875: documents officiels et inédites*. Paris: L. Willem, 1875. Print.
Freiheit. Ed. Johann J. Most, and John E. Mueller. New York: [Publisher Not Identified], 1879–1910. Print.
Friederich, Johann K. *Dämonische Reisen in alle Welt*. Tübingen: Verlag Nicht Ermittelbar, 1847. Print.
Garnier, Charles-Georges-Thomas. *Voyages imaginaires, songes, visions et romans cabalistiques*. 39 vols. À Amsterdam: Rue et Hôtel Serpente, 1787–1789. Print.
Gastine, Louis. *Énigme dans l'espace*. Paris: La France Automobile et aérienne, 1909. Internet Resource.
———. *Le roi de l'espace*. Paris: La Maison du Livre Moderne, 19??. Print.
———, and Léon Perrin. *Dans l'azur: adventures d'un aviateur Français*. Préface de Gabriel Voisin. Paris: "Monde Illustré," 1909. Print.
Gégout, Ernest. *Jésus*. Paris: P.-V. Stock, 1897. Print.
Gehrke, Dr. A[lbert]. *Communistische Idealstaaten*. Bremen, Ger.: Verlag von C. Schünemann, 1878.
Geiger, Carl Ignaz, and Wilhelm G. Sommer. *Reise eines Erdbewohners in den Mars*. Sommer, 1790. Archival Material.
Gelardi, G. Cartella. *I naufraghi del sogno*. Rome, 1920. Unlocated.
Gesù Cristo avanti un consiglio di guerra. Genova: Tip. Delle-Piane, 1850. Print.
Gibbs, Rowan. "Who Wrote the First New Zealand Novel?" *Kite* (New Zealand) 7 (Dec. 1994): 8–9.
Gibelin, Antoine E. *Tulikan, fils de Gengiskan: ou, l'asie consolée*. Paris: Huet, 1803. Internet Resource.
Gilbert, Claude. *Histoire de Calejava; ou, de l'isle des hommes raisonnables: avec le paralelle de leur morale & du christianisme*. Dijon: J. Resayre, 1700. Print.
Godin, Jean B. A. *Solutions sociales*. Paris: A. Le Chevalier, 1871. Internet Resource.
Godwin, Francis. *The Man in the Moone or a Discourse of a Voyage Thither. Domingo Gonsales. The Speedy Messenger*. London: Printed by Iohn Norton for Iohn Kirton and Thomas Warren, 1638. Internet Resource.
Goethe, Johann W. *Wilhelm Meisters Lehrjahre: Roman*. Berlin: Unger, 1795. Print.
———. *Wilhelm Meisters Wanderjahre oder die Entsagenden*. Stuttgart: Verlag nicht ermittelbar, 1821. Print.
Gori, Pietro. *La leggenda del primo maggio*. Roma: Serantoni, 1905. Print.
Goudar, Ange. *Le proces des trois rois: Louis XVI. de France-Bourbon, Charles III. d'espagne-Bourbon, et George III d'hanovre, fabricant de boutons. Plaidé au tribunal des puissances-Européennes. Par Appendix, l'appel au Pape*. Traduit de l'anglois. Londres [i. e., Paris?], 1781. Internet Resource.
Gould, Frederick J. *The Agnostic Island: [A Novel]*. London: Watts for Propagandist Press Committee, 1891. Print.
Graham, Robert. "(Mis)Conceptions of Anarchism." *Anarchist Studies* 26.2 (2018): 32–55.
Gratacap, L. P. *The Evacuation of England: The Twist in the Gulf Stream*. New York: Brentano's, 1908. Internet Resource.
Grave, Jean. *Les aventures de Nono*. Paris: Stock, 1901. Print.

———. *Terre libre (les pionniers)*. Paris: Librairie des "Temps nouveaux," 1908. Print.
Gregorovius, Emil. *Der Himmel Auf Erden in Den Jahren 1901 bis 1912 V.* Leipzig: F. W. Grunow, 1892. Print.
Grimm, Jacob, and Wilhelm Grimm. *Kinder- und Hausmärchen*. Berlin: Realschulbuchh., 1812.
Grimmelshausen, Hans J. C. *Der abenteuerliche Simplicissimus Teutsch*. Mompelgart, 1669. Print.
Grousset, Paschal. *Le rêve d'un irréconciliable*. Paris: Madre, 1869. Internet Resource.
Grove, W[illiam]. [pseud of Reginald Colebrooke Reade]. *The Wreck of a World*. Fifth ed. London: Digby and Long, 1889. Print.
Gueudeville, Nicolas. *Dialogues ou entretiens entre un sauvage at le Baron de Lahontan; voyages du baron de Lahontan en Portugal et en Danemarc*. Amsterdam: Vve de Boeteman, 1704.
Guillaume, James. *Idées sur l'organisation sociale*. Chaux-de-Fonds: Impr. Courvoisier, 1876. Print.
Hall, Joseph. *Mundus alter et idem*. London: Lownes, 1605. Print.
Haller, Albrecht. *Alfred König der Angel-Sachsen*. Göttingen, 1773. Print.
———. *Usong*. Bern, 1771. Print.
Hamilton, Cicely, and Christopher St. John. *How the Vote Was Won: A Play in One Act*. [London]: Woman's Press, 1909. Print.
Hardt, Hans. *Im Zukunftsstaat*. Berlin: Hüpeden & Merzyn, 1905. Print.
Harrington, James. *The Commonwealth of Oceana*. London: Printed for D. Pakeman, 1656. Internet Resource.
Harris, Thomas L. *The Great Republic: A Poem of the Sun*. New York: Brotherhood of the New Life, 1867. Second ed. London: E. W. Allen, 1891. Print.
Harting, Pieter. *Anno 2066: ein Blick in die Zukunft*. Weimar: Herman Böhlau, 1866. Print.
Haushofer, Max. *Planetenfeuer: ein Zukunftsroman*. Stuttgart: Cotta, 1899. Print.
Havelock Ellis, Henry. *The Nineteenth Century; a Dialogue in Utopia*. London: Grant Richards, 1900. Print.
Hawel, Rudolf. *Im Reiche der Homunkuliden: Roman*. Wien: Huber & Lahme Nachfg, 1910. Internet Resource.
Hawthorne, Nathaniel. *The Blithedale Romance*. Boston: Ticknor, Reed, and Fields, 1852. Print.
Hayes, Frederick W. *The Great Revolution of 1905: Or, the Story of the Phalanx: With an Introductory Account of Civilization in Great Britain at the Close of the Nineteenth Century*. London: Robert Forder, 1893. Print.
Heinse, Johann J. W. *Ardinghello und die glückseeligen Inseln. Eine Italiänische Geschichte aus dem sechszehnten Jahrhundert*. Lemgo, 1787. Print.
Heliomanes. *A Journey to the Sun*. London: James Cornish, 1866. Print.
Hellenbach, Lazar. *Die Insel Mellonta*. Wien, 1883. Print.
Hemyng, Bracebridge. *The Commune in London: Or, Thirty Years hence: A Chapter of Anticipated History*. London: C. H. Clark, 1871. Print.
Henlau, A. *Ambisexia: Das Land der entjochten Frauen. Lustspiel in vier Aufzügen*. Leipzig: H. Fritzsche, 1848. Internet Resource.
The Hermit of Prague. "What Will Posterity Say of Us? An Address Delivered in the Darwin Hall, on Oct. 1st, 1912." *Bedrock* (London) Oct. 1912: 361–370.
Hertzka, Theodor. *Eine Reise nach Freiland*. Leipzig: P. Reclam, 1893. Print.
———. *Entrückt in die Zukunft: sozialpolitischer Roman*. Berlin: Dümmler, 1895. Print.
———. *Freiland: Ein sociales Zukunftsbild*. Leipzig: Duncker & Humblot, 1890. Tenth ed. Dresden: E. Pierson, 1896. Print.

Herzl, Theodor. *Der Judenstaat: Versuch einer modernen Lösung der Judenfrage.* Leipzig – Wien: M. Breitenstein's Verlags-Buchh., 1896. Print.
Hobbes, Thomas. *Leviathan.* London: Printed for A. Ckooke [i. e., Crooke], 1651. Print.
Hoffmann, François B. *Lisistrata, ou, les Athéniennes: comédie en un acte et en prose, mêlée de vaudevilles, imitée d'Aristophane; dont les représentations ont éte suspendues par ordre.* Paris: Chez Huet, 1802. Internet Resource.
Holberg, Ludvig. *Nicolai Klimii Iter Subterraneum: Novam Telluris Theoriam Ac Historiam Quintae Monarchiae Adhuc Nobis Incognitae Exhibens E Bibliotheca B. Abelini.* Hafniaae: Sumptibus Iacobi Preussii, 1741. Print.
Holland, Jan. *Darwinia.* Deventer, 1878. Print.
Horacek, C. "B. B. und seine Utopie *Vom besten Staat.*" *Archiv für die Geschichte des Sozialismus* 2 (1911): 68–97.
Howard, Ebenezer. *Tomorrow: A Peaceful Path to Real Reform.* London: Swan Sonnenschein, 1898. Print.
Howells, William D. *A Traveler from Altruria: Romance.* New York: Harper & Bros, 1894. Print.
Hudson, W. H. *A Crystal Age.* London: T. F. Unwin, 1887. Print.
Hugo, Victor. *Le Christ au Vatican.* Londres: London, 1862. Print.
Hume, David. *Political Discourses.* Second ed. Edinburgh: Printed by R. Fleming for A. Kincaid and A. Donaldson, 1752. Print.
Hunink, Maria. "Das Schiksal einer Bibliothek: Max Nettlau und Amsterdam" (The Fate of a Library: Max Nettlau and Amsterdam). *International Review of Social History* 27.1 (1982): 4–42.
Inchofer, Melchior, Giulio C. Scotti, and Europaeus L. Cornelius. *La monarchie des solipses.* Amsterdam: Publisher Not Identified, 1721. Print.
Ishill, Joseph, ed. *Elisée and Elie Reclus: In Memoriam.* Berkeley Heights, NJ: Oriole Press, 1927.
———, ed. *Peter Kropotkin, the Rebel, Thinker, and Humanitarian.* Berkeley Heights, NJ: Free Spirit Press, 1923.
Jacques, Norbert. *Piraths Insel: Roman.* Berlin: S. Fischer Verlag, 1917. Print.
Jahrbuch für Socialwissenschaft und Socialpolitik: sozialreformerische Zeitschrift. Zürich: Körber, 1879. Print.
Jameson, Fredric. *Archaeologies of the Future: The Desire Called Utopia and Other Science Fictions.* London: Verso Books, 2005.
Jaunez-Sponville, Pierre I., and Nicolas Bugnet. *La philosophie du Ruvarebohni, pays dont la découverte semble d'un grand intérêt pour l'homme, ou récit dialogué des moyens par lesquels les Ruvareheuxis, habitans de ce pays, ont été conduits au vrai et solide bonheur: par P. j. j.-S*** [Jaunez-Sponville] et Nicolas Bugnet.* Paris: Impr. de Le Normant, 1809. Print.
———. *Le Ruvarebohni: (le vrai bonheur).* Paris: Librairie Sandoz et Fischbacher, 1881. Internet Resource.
Jókai, Mór. *A jövő század regénye. IV-V.* Budapest: n.p., 1873.
———. *Der Roman des künftigen Jahrhunderts: in acht Büchern.* Pressburg: C. Stampfel, 1879. Internet Resource.
Joll, James. *The Anarchists.* Boston: Little, Brown-An Atlantic Monthly Book, 1964.
Joncquel, Octave, and Théo Varlet. *L'agonie de la terre: roman planétaire.* Amiens: Malfère, 1922. Print.
Josua: ein frohes evangelium aus künftigen Tagen; nach einem alten französischen Manuskripte. Wien, 1912. Print.

Joubert, de R, and Jean-Baptiste B. Argens. *Lettres d'un sauvage depaysé: contenant une critique des mœurs du siècle, & des réflexions sur des matières de Religion & de politique.* À Amsterdam: Chez Jean Francois Jolly, 1638. Print.

Jullien, Jean. *Enquête sur le monde futur.* Paris: Bibliothèque-Charpentier, 1909. Print.

Junqua, François. *Luméne, ou la fille des grands martyrs.* Paris: E. Dentu, 1881. Print.

Juppont, M. "L'oeuvre scientifique de Cyrano de Bergerac." *Mémoires de l'Académie des Sciences: Inscriptions et Belles-Lettres de Toulouse.* Tenth ser. 7 (1907): 312–375.

Kamidel de Lussefnoc (pseud.). *Dorotchim ou la gloire de Sodome*: *3e partie.* Nancy: Impr. Bertrand, 1909. Print.

———. *Les deux naufrages.* Nancy: Imprimerie Ouvriére, 1905. Print.

Kant, Immanuel. *Zum ewigen Frieden: ein philosophischer Entwurf.* Königsberg: F. Nicolovius, 1795. Print.

Kappus, Franz X. *Die lebenden Vierzehn: Roman.* 1918. Print.

Kateb, George. "Utopias and Utopianism." *The International Encyclopedia of the Social Sciences.* New York: Macmillan, 1968.

Kirchenheim, Arthur. *Schlaraffia politica: Geschichte der Dichtungen vom besten Staate.* Leipzig: Fr. Wilh. Grunow, 1892. Print.

Kleinwächter, Friedrich. *Die Staatsromane: ein Beitrag zur Lehre vom Communismus und Socialismus.* Wien: M. Breitenstein, 1891. Print.

Klopstock, Friedrich G. *Die deutsche Gelehrtenrepublik.* Hamburg, 1774. Print.

Koehler, Oswald. Der *sozialdemokratische Staat: Grundzüge einer muthmälichen ersten Form sozialdemokratischer Gesellschafts-Verfassung nebst einleitender Schilderung des bestehenden Systems.* Nürnberg: Wörlein, 1891. Print.

Kolney, Fernand. *L'amour dans cinq mille ans.* Paris: F. Kolney, 1928. Print.

Korf, Georg. *Die andere Seite der Welt.* Fourth ed. Stade: Zwei Welten-Verl., 1921. Print.

Krimerman, Leonard I., and Lewis Perry. *Patterns of Anarchy: A Collection of Writings on the Anarchist Tradition.* Garden City, NY: Anchor Books, 1966.

Kropotkin, Petr A. *Fields, Factories and Workshops, or, Industry Combined with Agriculture and Brain Work with Manual Work.* New York: G. P. Putnam's Sons, 1901. Print.

———. *La conqûete du pain.* Paris: Tresse & Stuck, 1892. Print.

———. *Le révolté: organe socialiste.* Genève: Le Révolté, 1879. Print.

———. *Paroles d'un révolté/Pierre Kropotkine; ouvrage publié, annoté et accompagné d'une préface par Élisée Reclus.* Paris: C. Marpon et E. Flammarion, 1885. Internet Resource.

Kuhn, Gabriel. "Editor's Note." *Revolution and Other Writings: A Political Reader.* By Gustav Landauer. Ed. and trans. Gabriel Kuhn. Oakland, CA: PM Press-Merlin, 2010. 10–17.

———, and Siegbert Wolf. Introduction. *Revolution and Other Writings: A Political Reader.* By Gustav Landauer. Ed. and trans. Gabriel Kuhn. Oakland, CA: PM Press-Merlin, 2010. 18–60.

Kumar, Krishan. *Utopia and Anti-utopia in Modern Times.* Oxford: Basil Blackwell, 1987.

———. *Utopianism.* Minneapolis: University of Minnesota Press, 1991.

La Hire, Jean de. *Le Mystere de XV.* 1911.

———. *L'homme qui peut vivre dans l'eau.* 1908; 1909. Sceaux: Impr. Charaire, 1925.

La Vieillard Abyssin. London: Chez J.F. Bastien, 1779. Internet Resource.

La voz del chauffeur: organo de la union chauffeurs. Buenos Aires: n.d. Print.

Laboulaye, Édouard. *Paris en Amérique.* Paris: Charpentier, 1863. Internet Resource.

———, and Hermann Pemsel. *Paris in Amerika.* Second ed. Erlangen: E. Besold, 1868. Print.

Labour Copartnership. London: At the Office of the Labour Association, 1894–1908. Print.

Laby, Jean de. *La société future: constitution idéale de la société des nations et constitutions nationales.* Paris: Librarie-Édition de La Place Clichy, 1920. Print.

Lahontan, Louis Armand de Lom d'Arce. *Dialogues ou entretiens entre un sauvage et le Baron de Lahontan: voyages du Baron de Lahontan en Portugal et en Danemarc.* Amsterdam: Veuve de Boeteman, 1704. Print.
Landauer, Gustav. *Aufruf zum Sozialismus.* Berlin: Sozialistischen Bundes, 1911. Second Ed. Berlin: P. Cassirer, 1919.
———. "Dreissig sozialistische Thesen." *Die Zukunft* (1 December 1907): 56–67.
[———]. *Ein Weg zur Befreiung der Arbeiter-Klasse.* Berlin: Marreck, 1895. Print.
———. Letter to Max Nettlau. 7 June 1911. IISH.
Lasswitz, Kurd. *Auf zwei Planeten. Roman.* Weimar, 1897. Print.
———. *Sternentau: Die Pflanze vom Neptunsmond.* Elischer, 1909. Archival Material.
Laurens, H. J. *Imirce, ou: la fille de la nature.* Berlin, 1765. Print.
Lawrence, James. *The Empire of the Nairs; or, the Rights of Women: An Utopian Romance, in Twelve Books.* London: Printed for T. Hookham, Jun. and E. T. Hookham, 1811. Print.
Le Diable à Paris: Paris et les Parisiens: moeurs et coutumes, caractères et portraits des habitants de Paris, tableau complet de leur vie privée, publique, politique, artistique, littéraire, industrielle, etc., etc. Paris: Michel Lévy Frères, libraires-éditeurs, 1845. Print.
Le Drimeur, A. *La cité future.* Paris: Nouvelle Librairie Parisienne, 1890. Print.
Le Mercier de la Rivière, Pierre-Paul. *L'heureuse nation, ou, relations du gouvernement des Féliciens; peuple souverainement libre sous l'empire absolu de ses loix.* Paris, 1792. Print.
Le monde des emiles, ou, l'éducation sociale. Paris: L. Colas, 1820. Print.
Lee, Thomas. *Falsivir's Travels: The Remarkable Adventures of John Falsivir, Seaman, at the North Pole and in the Interior of the Earth; with a Description of the Wonderful People and the Things He Discovered there.* 1886. Internet Resource.
Lehning, Arthur. See A. L.
L'en dehors. Orleans/Paris. Vols. 1–18. Nos. 1–335 (1922–1939).
Léo, André. *La commune de Malenpis: conte.* Paris: Librairie de la bibliothèque démocratique, 1874. Print.
Lesconvel, Pierre de. *Idée d'un regne doux et heureux: ou relation du voyage du Prince de Montberaud dans l'île de Naudely. Premier [Sic] partie enrichy de figures en taille douce.* À Caseres, capitale de l'île de Naudely: Chez Pierre Fortané, 1703. Print.
Lesguillon, Hermance. *Les femmes dans cent ans.* Paris: A. de Vresse, 1859. Internet Resource.
L'Estrange, Henry. *Platonia: A Tale of Other Worlds.* Bristol: J.W. Arrowsmith, 1893. Print.
Leszczyński, Stanislas. *Entretien d'un Européan avec un insulaire du royaume de Dumocala.* 1752. Print.
Lévis, Gaston. *Les voyages de Kang-Hi ou nouvelles lettres chinoises, par M. De Lévis.* Paris: L'Imprimerie de P. Didot l'ainé, 1810. Second ed. Paris: A. A. Renouard, 1812. Print.
Levitas, Ruth. *The Concept of Utopia.* Syracuse, NY: Syracuse University Press, 1990.
Levy, J. H. *An Individualist's Utopia.* London: Lawrence Nelson, 1900. Print.
Lewis, George C. "On Ideal Models in Politics." *A Treatise on the Methods of Observation and Reasoning in Politics.* 2 vols. London: Parker, 1852. 2: 236–309. Print.
Lichtenberger, André. "Notes on a Precursor of Socialism: Pechméja." *International Review of Sociology* 1 (1893).
Lichtneckert, Josef. *Der sozialdemokratische Welt-Staat mit Gemeineigentum und Eigenproduktion Als universalmittel zur Beseitigung aller Armut, Ausbeutung, Kriege, Seuchen, Not, kurz alles Elendes und zur Herbeiführung der dauernden Glückseligkeit und Friedens der Allmenschheit auf Erden.* Papiermühle S.-A: F. Engelke, 1912. Print.
Linton, E. Lynn. *The True History of Joshua Davidson.* London: Strahan, 1872. Print.

[Lithgow, John?]. *Equality, or, a History of Lithconia*. Philadelphia: Liberal Union, 1837. Print.
The Llano Colonist. Llano, CA. 1910s-1922. Internet Resource.
Llanos y Torriglia, Felix. *Como se hizo la revolución en Portugal*. Madrid: S. n., 1914. Print.
London, Jack. *The Iron Heel*. London: Grosset & Dunlap, 1907. Print.
Lucian. *Lucian's Dialogues of the Gods*. Ed. Nicholas Jeeves. Trans. H. and F. Fowler, and W. Tooke. N.p.: The PDR Press, 2016.
Luitjes, T. *Over de grondprincipen van christendom en anarchie als tegenstellingen*. Bussum: Grentzebach, 1902. Print.
Lytton, Edward B. L. *The Coming Race*. Edinburgh: W. Blackwood and Sons, 1871. Internet Resource.
Mackay, John H. *Der Freiheitsucher: Psychologie einer Entwicklung*. Berlin-Charlottenburg, 1920. Print.
———. *Gesammelte Werke in acht Bänden. Die Anarchisten: Kulturgemälde aus dem Ende des XIX Jahrhunderts*. Berlin: Bernhard Sacks Verlag, 1911. Print.
Magnus, Leonard A. *A Japanese Utopia*. London: George Routledge & Sons, 1905. Print.
Maillot, Abbé. *Voyage mystèrieux à l'isle de la vertu*. N.p.: n.p., 1788. Print.
Mantegazza, Paolo. *L'anno 3000*. Milano: Fratelli Treves, 1897. Internet Resource.
Manuel, Frank E., and Fritzie P. Manuel. *Utopian Thought in the Western World*. Cambridge: Harvard University Press-Belknap Press, 1979.
Maréchal, Pierre S. *Viaggi di Pitagora in Egitto, nella Caldea, nell'Indie, in Creta, a Sparta, in Sicilia, a Roma, a Cartagine, a Marsiglia e nelle Gallie: seguiti dalle sue leggi, politiche e morali*. Venezia: Andreola (Tip.), 1827. Print.
Maréchal, Sylvain. *Dictionnaire des athées anciens et modernes*. Paris: Chez Grabit, 1799. Internet Resource.
———. *L'age d'or: recueil de contes pastoraux*. A Mytilene: Chez Guillot, 1782. Internet Resource.
———. *Le jugement dernier des rois: prophétie en un acte, en prose*. Paris: De l'imp. de C.-F. Patris. Une et Indivisible, 1793. Print.
———. *Premières leçons du fils aîné d'un roi. Par un député préesomptif aux futurs états-généraux*. Bruxelles, 1789. Print.
Marivaux. Pierre. *L'île des esclaves: comedie, représenté pour la première fois par les comédiens Italiens du roi, le Lundi 5. Mars 1725*. À Paris: Chez Briasson, 1725. Print.
Marriott, Joseph. *A Catechism on Circumstances, or, The Foundation Stone of a Community*. London: Published by the "Association of All Classes of All Nations," at the Office, [1840?].
———. *Community: A Drama*. Manchester [Greater Manchester]: A. Heywood, 1838. Internet Resource.
———. "Community: A Vision." *The New Moral World, and Manual of Science*. 1837. Vol. No. 138–140, 143, 145–146, 148–155.
Masson, Emile. *Utopie des iles bienheureuses dans le Pacifique en l'an 1980*. Paris: Reider, 1921. Print.
Mathéma. *L'île d'Eve*. Autun (S.-et-L.): Dépôt central, 1907. Print.
Maubert, de G. J. H. *Lettres iroquoises*. Lausanne, 1752. Internet Resource.
"Max Nettlau – A Biography." *A Contribution to an Anarchist Bibliography of Latin America*. By Max Nettlau. 1926. Trans. Paul Sharkey. London: Kate Sharpe Library, 1994. [i–ii].
"Max Nettlau historien anarchiste" (Max Nettlau Anarchist Historian). Paris: Centre de Documentation Anarchiste, "Max Nettlau," Dec. 1981. Pamphlet. 15 pp.
Max Nettlau Papers. IISH. 42 metres. www.iisg.amsterdam/en.

Mazade, André. *Au pays de liberté.* Paris: E. Flammarion, 1900. Print.
McIver, G. M. *Neuroomia: A New Continent. A Manuscript Delivered by the Deep.* London: G. Robertson, 1894. Print.
M'Crib, Theophilus. *Kennaquhair: A Narrative of Utopian Travel.* London: Chapman and Hall, 1872. Print.
Mehring, Franz. *Herrn Eugen Richters Bilder aus der Gegenwart: eine Entgegnung.* Nürnberg: Wörlein, 1892.
Meléndez-Badillo, Jorell. "The Anarchist Imaginary: Max Nettlau and Latin America, 1890–1934." Ch. 10 of *Writing Revolution: Hispanic Anarchism in the United States.* Ed. Christopher James Castañeda and M. Montserrat Feu López. Urbana: U of Illinois Press, 2019. [173]–193.
Mella, Ricardo. *La nueva utopía.* 1890. Piedra Papel Libros, 2017. Print.
Mercier, Louis-Sébastien. *L'an deux mille quatre cent quarante: rêve s'il en fut jamais.* Londres [i. e., Paris?], 1771. Internet Resource.
Mereschkowsky, C. *Das irdische Paradies: Ein Märchen aus dem 27. Jahrhundert; eine utopie.* Berlin: Gottheiner, 1903. Print.
Mettais, Hippolyte. *L'an 5865, ou Paris dans 4000 ans.* Paris: Librairie Centrale, 1865. Print.
Meunier, Victor. *Jésus Christ devant les conseils de guerre.* Paris: Librairie philanthropique, 1849. Print.
Meyern, W. F. *Dya-Na-Sore: oder die Wanderer.* Wien: Bei Joseph Stahel, 1789. Print.
Michel, Louise. *Le monde nouveau.* Paris: E. Dentu, 1888. Print.
Miller, George N. *The Strike of a Sex, a Novel, with Author's Preface.* New York: Twentieth Century Pub. Co., 1891. Print.
Moeller, Otto M. *Gold und Ehre: Roman.* Stuttgart: J. Engelhorn, 1896. Print.
Moilin, Tony. *Paris en l'an 2000.* Paris, 1869. Print.
Montesquieu, Charles-Louis S. *Lettres persannes.* À Amsterdam et À Leipzig: Chez Arkstée et Merkus, 1761. Print.
———. *Persidskija Pis'ma.* V Sanktpeterburge, 1789. Print.
Monticelli, Carlo. *Il primo giorno del socialismo.* Roma: Mongini, 1904. Print.
———. *Socialismo popolare.* Fourth ed. Florence: C. Nerbini, 1902.
More, Thomas. *Life in Utopia.* Boston: Directors of the Old South Work, 1891. Print.
———. *Utopia: Libellus Vere Aureus.* Louvain: Thierry Martens, 1516. Print.
Morelly, Étienne-Gabriel. *Naufrage des isles flottantes, ou basiliade du célèbre Pilpai:poème héroïque.* Messine [i. e., Paris]: Société de Libraires, 1753. Print.
Morris, William. *News from Nowhere, or, an Epoch of Rest: Being Some Chapters from a Utopian Romance.* London: Reeves & Turner, 1891. Print.
———. *The Tables Turned, or, Nupkins Awakened: A Socialist Interlude as for the First Time Played at the Hall of the Socialist League on Saturday Oct. 15, 1887.* London: The Commonweal, 1887. Internet Resource.
———, and Edward C. Burne-Jones. *A Dream of John Ball; and a King's Lesson.* London: Reeves & Turner, 1888. Print.
Mosneron, de L. J.-B. *Le vallon aérion, ou, relation du Voyage d'un aéronaute dans un pays inconnu jusqu'à present; suivie de l'histoire de ses habitans et de la description de leurs moeurs.* Paris: J. Chaumerot, 1810.
Most, Johann J. *The Social Monster: A Paper on Communism and Anarchism.* New York: Bernhard & Schenck, 1890. Internet resource.
Mouhy, Charles F. *Lamekis ou les voyages extraordinaires d'un Egyptien dans la terre intérieure: 1.* Paris: Dupuis, 1735. Print.

Mumford, Lewis. *The Story of Utopias.* New York: Boni & Liveright, 1922. 100th Anniversary ed. Great Barrington, MA: Berkshire Publishing Group, 2022. Print.

Muñoz, Vladimiro. *Anarchists: A Biographical Encyclopedia.* Series 1. Trans. Scott Johnson. History of Anarchism series. New York: Gordon Press, 1981.

———. *Max Nettlau: Historian of Anarchism.* Trans. by Lucy Ross of *Una Cronologia de Max Nettlau* (A Max Nettlau Chronology). Men and Movements in the History and Philosophy of Anarchism. New York: Revisionist Press, 1978.

———. "Una Cronologia de Max Nettlau" (A Max Nettlau Chronology). *La Paz Mundial y las condiciones de su realización.* 1950. Second ed. Revised and augmented by Eugen Relgis and V. Muñoz. Montevideo, Uruguay: Ediciones "Solidaridad," 1972. 13–21.

Nariota [or Nariosa]. *Riflessioni di un uomo delle caverne rivenienete nel secolo XX.* Spezia, *Il Libertario,* 1916.

Nettlau, Max. *Bibliographie de l'anarchie.* Brussels: Bibliothèque des "Temps Nouveau," 1897.

———. *A Contribution to an Anarchist Bibliography of Latin America.* 1931. Trans Paul Sharkey. London: Kate Sharpley Library, 1994.

———. *De la crisis mundial a La anarquía: eugenesia de la sociedad libre.* Barcelona: Solidaridad obrera, 1933. Print.

———. "Death of Karl Marx." *The Commonweal* 4.113 (Mar. 10, 1888): 79.

———. *Die historische Entwickelung des Anarchismus.* New York: Freiheit, 1890.

———. *Élisée Reclus. Anarchist und Gelehrter (1830–1905).* Berlin: Verlag "Der Syndikalist," 1928.

———. *Eliseo Reclus, la vida de un sabio justo y rebelde.* 2 Vols. Barcelona: Publicaciones de "La Revista blanca," 1929. Print.

———. *En torno al pensamiento de Merlino* Barcelona: n.p., 1938.

———. *Ernest Coeurderoy.* Leipzig: Hirschfeld, 1911.

———. *Errico Malatesta. Das Leben eines Anarchisten.* Berlin: Verlag "Der Syndikalist," 1922.

———. *Eugenik der Anarchie.* Ed. Rudolf de Jong. Wetzlar: Büchse der Pandora, 1985.

———. "The Evolution of Anarchism." *Freedom* 9.96 [93] (May 1895): 6–7.

———. *Geschichte der Anarchie.* Vol. 1: *Der Verfrühling der Anarchie.* Berlin: Verlag "Der Syndikalist," 1925. Vol. 2: *Der Anarchismus von Proudhon zu Kropotkin.* Berlin: Verlag "Der Syndikalist," 1927. Vol. 3: *Anarchisten und Sozialrevolutionäre.* Berlin: ASY-Verlag, 1931. Vol. 4: *Die erste Blütezeit der Anarchie: 1886–1894.* Vaduz, Liechtenstein: Topos Verlag, 1981. Vol. 5: *Anarchisten und Syndikalisten, Part 1.* Vaduz, Liechtenstein: Topos Verlag, 1984.

———. *La paz mundial y las condiciones de su realización.* Montevideo: Ediciones "Humanidad," 1950.

———. *La Première Internationale en Espagne (1868–1888).* 2 vols. Ed. Renée Lamberet. Dordrecht: D. Reidel, 1969.

———. "La vida de Gustavo Landauer según su correspondencia." *La protesta—suplemento quincenal* (Buenos Aires) 8.309 (31 July 1929): [353]–392.

———. *La vida de Gustavo Landauer segun su correspondencia.* Buenos Aires, 1929. Print.

———. Letter to Emma Goldman. 14 April 1928. https://libertarian-labyrinth.org/anarchist-beginnings/suggestions-for-discussion/.

———. "L'idée anarchiste. Son passé – son avenir." *L'idée anarchiste* (Paris) 1 (13 Mar. 1924); 4–13 (24 Apr.–15 Nov 1924).

———. Max Nettlau Papers (1870–1944). 42 metres in extent. International Institute of Social History. ARCH01001. See https://www.yumpu.com/en/document/read/7005741/max-nettlau-papers-search-home-international-institute-of-social- for an easy-to-access catalogue of the Papers. This list was last updated 11 November 1989.

———. *Michael Bakunin. Eine Biographie*. 3 vols. Privately printed, 1896–1900. Rpt. Milan: Feltrinelli, 1971. Mimeographed ms. 1290 fl.

———. *Michael Bakunin. Eine biographische Skizze*. Berlin: P. Pawlowitsch, 1901.

———. *Responsibility and Solidarity in the Labor Struggle*. London: Freedom Office, 1900.

———. *Revival of the Inquisition. Details of the Tortures Inflicted on Spanish Political Prisoners*. London: J. Perry, 1897.

———. *A Short History of Anarchism*. Ed. and trans. Heiner M. Becker. London: Freedom Press, 1996. Originally published in Spanish in 1935.

———. *Why We Are Anarchists*. London: Office of "The Commonweal," 1894.

Neulif. *L'uthopie* [sic] *contemporaine: notes de voyage*. Paris: Libraire de La Société des Gens de Lettres, 1888. Print.

Neupauer, Josef. *Oesterreich im Jahre 2020: socialpolitischer Roman*. Dresden: Pierson, 1893. Print.

Newbrough, John Ballou. *Oahspe, a Light of Kosmon. in the Words of the Creator through His Angel Ambassadors*. Letchworth: "Oahspe Home," 1910. Print. First edition: *Oahspe. A New Bible in the Words of Jehovih and His Angel Embassadors* [sic]. London: Oahspe Publishing Association, 1882. Print.

North, Delaval. *The Last Man in London*. London: Hodder & Stoughton, 1887. Print. Available at https://data.historicaltexts.jisc.ac.uk/view?pubId=bl-002672868.

Norton, Seymour F. *Ten Men of Money Island, or, the Primer of Finance*. Chicago: Chicago Sentinel, 1891. Print.

Noyes, John Humphrey. *History of American Socialism*. Philadelphia: J. P. Lippincott, 1870.

Nyst, Ray. *La caverne, histoire pittoresque d'une famille humaine de vingt-neuf personnes, filles et garçons, petits et grands, à l'époque des luxuriantes forêts tertiaires et des saisons clémentes dans l'Europe centrale: roman précédé d'une introduction documentaire*. Bruxelles: L'auteur, 1909. Print.

"Observations and Comments." *Mother Earth* 1.1 (Mar. 1906). https://www.gutenberg.org/files/26600/26600-8.txt.

Offenbach, Jacques, and Hector Crémieux. *Orphée aux enfers: opéra-buffon en 2 actes*. Paris, 1858. Print.

———, Henri Meilhac, Ludovic Halévy, and Léon Roques. *La belle Héléne: opéra bouffe en 3 actes*. Paris: E. Gérard et Cie, 1865. Musical Score.

Oppenheimer, Franz. *Freiland in Deutschland*. Berlin: W. F. Fontane & Co., 1895. Print.

Otto, Berthold. *Der Zukunftsstaat als sozialistische Monarchie*. Berlin: Puttkammer & Mühlbrecht, 1910. Print.

Owen, Albert K. *A Dream of an Ideal City*. London: Murdoch & Co., 1897. Internet Resource.

Paepe, Cesar de. "Silhouette d'une societe collectiviste." *La revue socialiste* (Paris) 46 (Oct. 1888): 383–391.

Paine, Thomas. *The Age of Reason*. Paris [i.e., London?]: Printed by Barrois, 1794. Internet Resource.

———. *Rights of Man*. London: For J. Johnson, 1791. Print.

Panizza, Oskar, and Michael G. Conrad. *Meine Verteidigung in Sachen "Das Liebeskonzil": nebst dem Sachverständigengutachten des Dr. M. G. Conrad und dem Urteil des K. Landgerichts.* Zürich: Schabelitz, 1895. Print.

Paoloni, Francesco. *Una visita di Gesù Cristo.* Roma: Mongini, 1908. Print.

Parny, Évariste. *La guerre des dieux anciens et modernes: poème en dix chants.* Paris: Didot, 1799. Print.

Pataud, Émile, and Émile Pouget. *Comment nous ferons la revolution.* Paris: Jules Tallandier, 1909. Print.

Pechméja, Jean. *Télephe: en XII livres.* Londres [Paris?]: Et se trouve à Paris, chez Pissot, 1784. Print.

Pellerin, Georges. *Le monde dans deux mille ans.* Paris: Dentu, 1878. Print.

Pemberton, Max. *The Impregnable City: A Romance.* London: Cassell & Co., 1900. Print.

Pemberton, Robert. *The Happy Colony.* London: Saunders and Otley, 1854. Internet Resource.

Périer, Camille. *La grève des amoureux.* Paris: A. Faure, 1866. Print.

Petzler, Johann [Aloys]. *Die Sociale Baukunst: oder Gründe und Mittel für den Umsturz und Wiederaufbau der gesellschaftlichen Verhältnisse: besonders wie solche sich in neuester Zeit in England, dem grossen Musterstaat der modernen Civilisation, ausgebildet haben.* Hottingen-Zürich: Schweizerische Volksbuchhandlung, 1879. Internet Resource.

———. *Grosse Jubiläumsfeier und imposanter Triumphzug in Erinnerung des hundertjährigen Bestehens de social-demokratischen Staatseinrichtung in Britannien.* Nürnberg: Selbstverlag des Berfassers, 1897.

———. *Life in Utopia: Being a Faithful and Accurate Description of the Institutions That Regulate Labour, Art, Science, Agriculture, Education, Habitation, Matrimony, Law, Government, and Religion, in This Delightful Region of Human Imagination.* London: Authors' Co-operative Pub., 1890.

———. *Social Architecture; or, Reasons and Means for the Demolition and Reconstruction of the Social Edifice.* By an Exile from France [pseud.]. London: Samuel Tinsley, 1876. Print.

Petzold, Alfons. *Sevarinde: Ein alter Abenteurer-Roman.* 1923. Print.

Pezzl, Johann. *Faustin, oder das philosophische Jahrhundert.* Zürich, 1783. Print.

Pflüger, Paul. *Der schweizerische Sozialstaat: eine Umschau im Jahre 1950.* Zürich: Buchhandl. d. Schw. Grütlivereins, 1899. Print.

Pillot, Jean-Jacques. *Histoire des égaux, ou moyens d'établir l'égalité absolue parmi les mommes.* Paris: Aux Bureaux de La "Tribune Du Peuple," 1840. Print.

Piria, Francisco. *El socialismo triunfante: lo que será mi pais dentro de 200 años.* Montevideo: Impr. de Dornaleche y Reyes, 1898. Print.

Plato. *The Laws.* Ed. Malcolm Schofield. Trans. Tom Griffith. Cambridge Texts in the History of Political Thought. Cambridge: Cambridge University Press, 2016.

Plockhoy, Pieter C. *A Way Propounded to Make the Poor in These and Other Nations Happy: by Bringing Together a Fit, Suitable and Well Qualified People unto One Household-Government or Little Common-Wealth.* London: Printed for G. C., 1659. Internet Resource.

Poe, Edgar Allan. "Hans Phaall--A Tale." *Southern Literary Messenger* 1.10 (June 1835): 565–580.

Popper-Lynkeus, Josef. *Die Allgemeine Nährpflicht als Lösung der sozialen Frage: mit einem Nachweis der theoretischen und praktischen Wertlosigkeit der Wirtschaftslehre.* Dresden: C. Reissner, 1912. Internet Resource.

Posel'janin, Evgenij Nikolaevic. *Zwischen zwei Welten.* Leipzig: Verlag der Buchhandlung Klein, 1926.

Potonié-Pierre, Edmond. *Un peu plus tard.* Paris: L. Breton, 1893. Print.
Prat, J.-G. *Voyages et aventures d'Almanarre.* Paris: E. Leroux, 1876. Paris: Marpon et Flammarion, 1880. Print.
Příhoda, Marek. "Hledání Ideálního Státu. Cesta Do Ofírské Země M. M. Ščerbatova Mezi Historickým Mýtem a Utopií." *Historie--Otazky--Problemy* 2 (Dec. 2016): 78–89.
Quantin, Albert. *En plein vol: vision d'avenir.* Paris: A. Lemerre, 1913. Print.
———. *Histoire prochaine: roman socialiste.* Paris: Bibliothèque-Charpentier, 1910. Print.
Quérard, J.-M. *La France littéraire, ou dictionnaire bibliographique.* Paris: Firmin Didot Frères, Libraires, 1829.
Quiroule, Pierre. *En la sonada tierra del ideal.* Buenos Aires: Editorial Fueyo, n.d. Print.
———. *La ciudad anarquista Americana: obra de construccion revolucionaria con el plano de la ciudad libertaria.* Buenos Aires: "La Protesta," 1914. Print.
———. *Sobre la ruta de la anarquía. (novela libertaria).* Buenos Aires: Fueyo, 1909. Print.
Rabelais, François. *La vie tres horrificque du grand Gargantua, pere de Pantagrual.* Lyon: On Les Vend à Lyon Chez Francoys Juste, 1542. Print.
Ramsay, M. *Les voyages de Cyrus, avec un discours sur la mythologie. Par M. Ramsay. Tome premier.* À Paris: Chez Gabriel-François Quillau Fils, Imp. jur. lib. de l'université, Rue Galande, à l'annonciation, 1727. Internet Resource.
———. *The Travels of Cyrus.* London: Printed and Sold by T. Woodward and J. Peele, 1727. Print.
Rebmann, Andreas G. F. *Hans Kiekindiewelts Reisen in alle vier Welttheile und den Mond.* Leipzig: Heinsius, 1794. Print.
Reclus, Élisée. "Les colonies anarchistes." *Les temps nouveaux* 6.11 (July 7–13, 1900): 1–2.
Relgis, Eugen. "Prologo de la primera edicion: preliminares para una obra de Max Nettlau" (Prologue to the First Edition: Preliminaries for a Work by Max Nettlau). *La Paz Mundial y las condiciones de su realización.* Second ed. Revised and augmented by Eugen Relgis and V. Muñoz. Montevideo: Edicones "Solidaridad," 1972. 23–36.
Renard, Maurice. *Le péril bleu.* Paris: L. Michaud, 1911. Print.
———, Fritz Heubner, and Marta Karlweis. *Die blaue Gefahr. Roman. übertragen von Marta Karlweis. mit Zeichnungen von Fritz Heubner.* München: Drei Masken Verlag, 1922. Print.
Renouvier, Charles B. *Uchronie.* Paris: Bureau de la Critique Philosophique, 1876. Print.
———. *Uchronie. (l'utopie dans L'histoire).* Second ed. Paris: Alcan, 1901. Print.
Resnier, Guillaume. *République universelle, ou l'humanité ailée, réunie sous l'empire de la raison.* Genève[?], 1788. Print.
Retif de la Bretonne, Nicolas Edmé. *L' andrographe ou idées d'un honnête-homme, sur un projet de reglement, proposé à toutes les nations de L'Europe, pour operer une reforme générale des moeurs.* La Haie: Gosse & Pinet, 1782. Print.
———. *Le paysan perverti: ou les dangers de la ville, histoire récente, mise au jour d'aprés les véritables lettres des personages.* Imprimé à La Haye, et Se Trouve à Paris: Chés Esprit, Libraire, 1776. Print.
———. *Le thesmographe, ou idées d'un honnête-homme, sur un projet de règlement, proposeé à toutes les nations de l'Europe, pour opérer une réforme générale des loix. Avec des notes historiques.* 2 Pt. La-Haie [Paris], 1789. Print.
———, and Louis Binet. *La découverte Australe.* Imprimé à Leïpsick et se trouve À Paris, 1781. Print.

———, and Pierre Bourguet. *Les revies:suivi de "les converseuses."* Oxford: Voltaire Foundation, 2006. Print.

Rey-Dussueil, Antoine F. M. *La fin du monde: histoire du temps présent et des choses à venir.* Paris: Eugène Renduel, 1830. Print.

———. *Le monde nouveau: histoire faisant suite à la fin du monde.* Paris: Eugène Renduel, 1831. Internet Resource.

[Reynolds, James?]. *Equality, or, a History of Lithconia.* Philadelphia: Liberal Union, 1837. Print.

Richet, Charles. "Dans cent ans." *Revue scientifique (Revue rise)* 48–49 (Dec. 12 and 19, 1891; Jan. 30 and Mar. 12, 1892): 737–747; 779–785; 135–144; 321–333. *Dans cent ans.* Paris: P. Ollendorff, 1892. Print.

Richter, Eugen. *Sozialdemokratische Zukunftsbilder: frei nach Bebel.* Berlin: "Fortschritt," 1891. Print. English version: *Pictures of a Socialistic Future.* Authorised translation by Henry Wright. London: Swan Sonnenschein, 1893. Available from https://openlibrary.org/books/OL7212180M/Pictures_of_the_socialistic_future.

Rocker, Rudolf. *El herodoto de la anarquia.* México: Edicones Estela, 1950.

———. *Max Nettlau: Leben und Werk des historikers vergessener sozialer Bewegungen* (Max Nettlau: The Life and Work of a Forgotten Historian of Social Movements). Berlin: Karen Kramer, 1978. Spanish original, 1950. Swedish edition, 1956. French edition, 2015.

———. *The London Years.* Trans. Joseph Leftwitz. London: Robert Anscombe for the Rudolf Rocker Book Committee, 1956. 92–95.

Rockey, J. R. "An Australian Utopist: Robert Pemberton F. R. S. L., the Last of the Self-Confessed Owenites and the Last of the World Makers." *New Zealand JournL of History* 15.2 (Oct. 1981): 157–178.

Rondelet, Antonin. *Mon voyage au pays de Chimères.* Paris, 1875. Print.

Rosny, Joseph H. *Les Xipéhuz.* Paris: Savine, 1888. Print.

Rossi, Giovanni, and Alfred Sanftleben. *Utopie und Experiment: Studien und Berichte.* Zürich: A. Sanftleben, 1897. Print.

———, and Salvo Vaccaro. *Cecilia comunitá anarchica sperimentale: un episodio d'amore nella colonia "Cecilia."* Pisa: BFS, 1993. Print.

Rotter, Josef. *Im Jahre 1999.* Seifhennersdorf: Grömann, 1894. Print.

Rousseau, Jean Jacques. *Émile.* Paris, 1813. Print.

Rouzade, Léonie. *Le monde renversé.* Paris: Lachaud, 1872. Internet Resource.

———. *Voyage de Théodose à l'île d'utopie.* Paris: Lachaud, 1872. Internet Resource.

Ruedebusch, Emil F. *Die Eigenen: Ein Tendenzroman für freie Geister.* Berlin: Räde, 1903. Print.

———. *Freie Menschen in der Liebe und Ehe. Ein Versuch, die Menschen glücklicher und besser zu machen.* Mayville, WI: Selbstverlag des verfassers, 1895.

———. *The Old and the New Ideal: A Solution of That Part of the Social Question Which Pertains to Love, Marriage and Sexual Intercourse.* Second ed. Mayville, Wis., The Author, 1897. Internet Resource.

Russell, Bertrand, in collaboration with Dora Russell. *The Prospects of Industrial Civilization.* London: Century, 1923. Print.

Ryner, Han. *Les pacifiques.* Paris: E. Figuiere & Cie, 1914. Print.

Saint-Simon, Claude-Henri. *Lettres d'un habitant de Genève à ses contemporains.* Geneva: Barbier, 1802. Print.

Sainte-Foy, Philippe-August. *Lettres d'osman.* Constantinople [i.e., Paris]: n.p., 1753.

Sales, J. de. *Ma république*. France: Publisher Not Identified, 1800. Print.
Sand, George. *Les amours de l'age d'or*. Place of Publication Not Identified [1855?]. Internet Resource.
Santillán, Diego Abad de (pseud. of Sinesio García Hernández). "23 de julio de 1944: Muerte de Max Nettlau" (23 July 1944: The Death of Max Nettlau). *Reconstruir* 19 (July–Aug. 1962): 47–50.
Sargent, Lyman Tower. "Michael Flürscheim: From the Single Tax to Currency Reform." *Utopian Studies* 21.1 (2010): 139–161.
———. "The Three Faces of Utopianism." *The Minnesota Review* 7.3 (1967): 222–230.
———. "The Three Faces of Utopianism Revisited." *Utopian Studies* 5.1 (1994): 1–37.
Sarrazin, N.-J. *Le retour du siècle d'or, ou, rêve véritable et surprenant: suivi des moyens de rendre infaillible son accomplissement*. Metz: De l'Imprimerie de C. Lamort, 1816. Internet Resource.
Say, Jean B. *Olbie, ou, essai sur les moyens de réformer les mœurs d'une nation*. Paris: Deterville, 1800. Internet Resource.
Schaer, Roland. "Utopia: Space, Time, History." *Utopia: The Search for the Ideal in the Western World*. Ed. Roland Schaer, Gregory Claeys, and Lyman Tower Sargent. New York: New York Public Library, 2000. 3–7.
Scheerbart, Paul. *Die grosse Revolution: Ein Mondroman*. Leipzig: Insel-Verlag, 1902. Print.
[Scheierman, Nicolai]. *A Vision of the New Living Life by One Who Had It*. Berlin, 1923. Print.
Schnabel, Johann G., and Ludwig Tieck. *Die Insel Felsenburg; oder, wunderliche Fata einiger Seefahrer: eine Geschichte aus dem Anfange des achtzehnten Jahrhunderts*. 1732. Breslau: Josef Max, 1828. Print.
Schorr, S. *Zur Theorie des Zukunftsstaates*. Wien: Verl. d. "Deutschen Worte," 1896. Print.
Schrevel, Margreet with Ursula Balzer. "Max Nettlau." https://iisg.amsterdam/en/about/history/max-nettlau.
Seeliger, Ewald G. *Der Schrecken der Völker: ein Weltroman*. Berlin: Concordia Deutsche Verlags-Anstalt, 1908. Internet Resource.
Segundo certamen socialista: celebrado en Barcelona el día 10 De Noviembre de 1889 en el Palacio de Bellas Artes. Barcelona: Tip. La Academia, 1890. Print.
Seriman, Zaccaria. *Viaggi di Enrico Wanton alle terre incognite australi*. Ed. Al Paese delle Scimie. S. l: S. n., 1749. Print.
Shcherbatov, M. M. *Cesta Do Ofirské Země*. N. p.: N. p, [1784].
Sibbern, Frederik Christian. *Meddelelser af Indholdet af et Skrivt fra Aaret 2135*. Kjøbenhavn: C. H. Reitzel, 1862.
Sinclair, Upton. *The Industrial Republic: A Study of the America of Ten Years Hence*. New York: Doubleday, Page & Company, 1907. Print.
Sonnenfels, Josef. *Über die Abschaffung der Tortur*. Zürich: bey Orell, Gessner, Füesslin, 1775. Internet resource.
Souêtre, Olivier. *La cité de l'égalité*. Paris: Le Roy, 1896. Print.
Spence, Thomas. *The Constitution of Spensonia, a Country in Fairyland Situated Between Utopia and Oceana Brought from Thence by Captain Swallow (i.e. Thomas Spence)*. London: Author, 1801.
———. "The Marine Republic." *Pigs' Meat* 2.6 (1794): 68–72.
Spronck, Maurice. *L'an 330 de la république (XXIIe siècle de l'ère chrétienne)*. Paris: L. Chailley, 1894. Print.
Stamatov, Aleksandr. "The *Laozi* and Anarchism." *Asian Philosophy* 24.3 (2014): 260–278.

Stead, W. T. *If Christ Came to Chicago.* Chicago: Laird & Lee, 1894. Print.
Storch, Mathias. *En Grønlænders drøm.* Kjøbenhavn: Gyldendalske Boghandel, Nordisk Forlag, 1915. Print.
Strachey, John S. L. *How England Became a Republic; a Romance of the Constitution.* Bristol, England: J. W. Arrowsmith, 1891. Print.
Suleau, François L. *Voyage en l'air de M. S. Second réveil.* Balonnapolis [Paris], 1791. Print.
Sutherland, George. *Twentieth Century Inventions. A Forecast.* London: Longmans & Co., 1901. Print.
Suttner, Bertha. *Das Maschinenalter: Zukunftsvorlesungen über unsere Zeit.* Zürich: Verlagsmagazin, Schabelitz, 1889. Print.
Suvin, Darko. "Defining the Literary Genre of Utopia: Some Historical Semantics, Some Genology [sic], a Proposal, and a Plea." *Studies in the Literary Imagination* 6.2 (1973): 121–145.
Sweven, Godfrey [pseud. of John Macmillan Brown]. *Limanora: The Island of Progress.* New York: G. P. Putnam's Sons, 1903. Print.
Swift, Jonathan. *Travels into Several Remote Nations of the World: By Capt. Lemuel Guliver* [sic]. *Faithfully Abridged.* London: Printed for J. Stone, and R. King, 1727. Internet Resource.
Tarde, Gabriel. *Fragment d'histoire future.* Lyon: A. Storck, 1904. Print. *Underground Man.* Trans by Cloudesley Brereton; preface by H. G. Wells. London: Duckworth, 1905. Print.
Terrason, Jean. *Geschichte Sethos Königs in Egypten: 1.* Leipzig: Sommer, 1794. Print.
———. *The Life of Sethos. Taken from Private Memoirs of the Ancient Egyptians.* Trans. Thomas Lediard. 2 Vols. London, 1732. Print.
———. *Sethos, histoire ou vie tirée des monumens anecdotes de l'ancienne Égypte.* Paris, 1731. Print.
Terson, Jean. *Idéalie: voyage d'un rêveur dans le devenir de notre monde.* Paris: E. Leroux, 1882. Print.
Thirion, Emile. *Neustria, utopie individualiste.* Paris: Fischbacher, 1901. Internet Resource.
Thiusen, Ismar [pseud. of John Macnie]. *Looking Forward: Or, the Diothas.* New York: G. P. Putnam's Sons, 1890. Internet Resource.
Thomas, Chauncey. *The Crystal Button; or, Adventures of Paul Prognosis in the Forty-Ninth Century.* Boston: Houghton & Mifflin, 1891. Print.
Thomson, William. *Mammuth, or Human Nature Displayed on a Grand Scale: In a Tour with the Tinkers, into the Inland Parts of Africa.* London: Printed for J. Murray, 1789. Internet Resource.
———. *The Man in the Moon; or, Travels into the Lunar Regions, by the Man of the People.* London: Printed for J. Murray, No 32, Fleet-Street, 1783. Internet Resource.
Thoreau, Henry D. *Walden, or, Life in the Woods.* Boston: Ticknor and Fields, 1854.
Thornton, Cliff. "The Hunt for Hildebrand Bowman, Parts 1–4." *Cook's Log* 33.4–34.3 (Oct. 2000–July/Sept. 2001): 14–15; 34–36; 11–12; 6–9.
Thury, Marc. *Visite imaginative à un camp de travail le 1er Mai 1922: pour faire suite à une conférence du même auteur: la question sociale considéré dans son principe.* Genève: Henry Kündig, 1902. Print.
Tiphaigne de la Roche, Charles-François. *Histoire naturelle civile et politique des Galligenes antipodes de la nation Françoise, don't ils tirent leur origine: òu l'on développe la naissance, les progrés, les moeurs et les vertus singulieres de ces insulaires: les révolutions et les productions merveilleuses de leur isle, avec l' histoire de leur fondateur.* Genève: F. Cramer, 1770. Print.
Tolstoy, Leo. "Ivan, le sot et ses deux frères." 1886. Trans. Louise and Alymer Maude. http://www.revoltlib.com/anarchism/story-of-ivan-the-fool-translated-maudes-tolstoy-leo-1886/.

The Torch of Anarchy: A Monthly Revolutionary Journal. London: British Museum Microfilm Service, 1895. Print.
Touchatout (pseud. of Leon Bienvenu). *Le Trombinoscope*. Paris: Vallée, 1871. Print.
Tovar, Luis Gomez, and Almudena Delgado Larios. "Max Nettlau." *Esbozo de historia de las utopías*. Colección Investigación y Crítica [series] 8. Madrid: Ediciones Tuero, 1991. 23–30.
Trotter, John. *Travels in Phrenologasto*. Calcutta, India: Samuel Smith, 1825. Later ed. London: Saunders and Otley, 1829. Print.
Tyssot de Patot, Simon. *Peter Martons, eines gebohrnen frantzosen merckwürdige Lebens-Beschreibung worinnen viele wunderliche Begebenheiten enthalten die ihm in seinen Leben und auf Reisen zugestossen alles von ihm selbst wohl aufgezeichnet und seines Werths halben*. Trans. Johann F. Bachstrom. Leipzig und Görlitz: In der marcheschen Buchhandlung, 1737. Internet Resource.
———. *The Travels and Adventures of James Massey: Translated from the Original French Written by the Celebrated Monsieur Bayle. Being a General Criticism Upon Religion, the Several Arts and Sciences, Trade, Commerce, &c*. London: Printed for J. Watts, 1743. Internet Resource.
———. *Voyages et avantures de Jaques Massé*. À Bordeaux: Chez J. L'Aveugle, 1710. "L'Utopie," 1760. Print.
Ulbach, Louis, and Victor Hugo. *Paris Guide*. Paris: Librairie Internationale, 1867. Print.
Ulrich. *Euphorion* 16 (1909).
Vairasse, Denis. *The History of the Sevarites or Sevarambi, a Nation Inhabiting Part of the Third Continent Commonly Called Terræ Australes Incognitæ: With an Account of Their Admirable Government, Religion, Customs, and Language*. London: Printed for Henry Brome, 1675.
Varennes, de M. *La découverte de l'empire de Cantahar*. Paris: Chez P. Prault, 1730. Print.
Varlet, Théo, and Octave Joncquel. *Les Titans du ciel, roman planétaire*. Amiens: E. Malfere, 1921. Print.
Velde, Carl Franz van der. *Die Heilung der Eroberungssucht: ein Märchen in fünf Akten*. Dresden: Arnold, 1827. Internet Resource.
Verhaeren, Emile. *Les aubes*. Bruxelles, 1918. Print.
Vetsch, Jakob. *Die Sonnenstadt: ein Bekenntnis und ein Weg: Roman aus der Zukunft für die Gegenwart*. Zürich: Grütli-Buchhandlung, 1923. Print.
Veuillot, Louis. *Le lendemain de la victoire: vision*. Paris: J. Lecoffre, 1850. Print.
———. *L'esclave Vindex*. Bruxelles: De Mortier, 1849. Print.
Véron, Pierre. *En 1900*. Paris: Calmann-Lévy, 1878. Print.
Viganò, Francesco. *Viaggio nell'universo. Visioni del tempo e dello spazio*. Milano, 1838. Second ed. Milano: Zanaboni e Gabuzzi, 1885. Print.
Vilgensofer, A. *La terre dans cent mille ans: roman de mœurs*. Paris: H. Simonis-Empis, 1893. Print.
Villars, Nicolas-Pierre-Henri de Montfaucon, Abbé de. *M. le comte de Gabalis: ou, entretiens sur les sciences secretes*. Paris: C. Barbin, 1670. Print.
Villedeuil, Charles, Comte de. *Paris à l'envers*. Paris: Librairie Nouvelle, 1853. Full text available from https://books.google.com.
Villeneuve, Daniel Jost de. *Le voyageur philosophe dans un pais inconnu aux habitants de la terre*. À Amsterdam: Aux Dépens de l'éditeur, 1761. Print.
Vogel, Louis. *Delenda Austria!: Die Auflösung Österreichs als eine Nothwendigkeit unserer Zeit*. Herisau: M. Schläpfer, 1849. Print.
Vogt, Oskar. "Der goldne Spiegel und Wielands politische Ansichten." *Euphorion* 16 (1906): 616–620.

Voigt, Andreas. *Die sozialen Utopien: fünf Vorträge*. Leipzig: G. J. Göschen'sche Verlagshandlung, 1906. Print.

Voltaire. *Candide, ou l'optimisme*. Paris: Cramer, 1759. Print.

———. *Le Micromégas*. Londres: Imprimé Pour J. Robinson, 1752. Print.

———. *Zadig; ou, la destine: histoire orientale*. Lyon?: Publisher Not Identified, 1748. Print.

Voss, Julius, and Karl-Maria Guth. *Ini: ein Roman aus dem 21. Jahrhundert*. 1810; 2019. Internet Resource.

Vuilleumier, Marc. "Les sources de l'histoire sociale: Max Nettlau et ses collections" (Resources for Social History: Max Nettlau and His Collections). *Cahiers Vilfredo Pareto* (Vilfredo Pareto Reports) 2.3 (1964): 195–205. https://www.jstor.org/stable/40368656.

Vuilmet, V. *La cosmopolie ou la république universelle*. Bruxelles: Alliance Typographique M.-J. Poot et compagnie, 1869. Print.

Wallace, Edgar. *The Four Just Men*. London: Tallis Press, 1905. Print.

Wallace, Robert. *Various Prospects of Mankind, Nature, Providence*. London: Printed for Millar, 1761. Print.

Walter, Nicolas. *About Anarchism*. Anarchism 100 (1969). Oakland, CA: PM Press, 2002; 2019.

Ward, Colin. *Anarchism: A Very Short Introduction*. Oxford: Oxford University Press, 2004.

Waterhouse, Elizabeth. *The Brotherhood of Rest*. Reading: Langley, 1889. Print.

———. *The Island of Anarchy: A Fragment of History in the 20th Century*. Reading, England: Published by Miss Langley, Lovejoy's Library, 1887. Internet Resource.

Weitling, Wilhelm. *Garantien der Harmonie und Freiheit*. Vivis: Verl. d. Verfassers, 1842. Print.

Wells, H. G. *Anticipations of the Reaction of Mechanical and Scientific Progress upon Human Life and Thought*. London: Chapman and Hall, 1904. Print.

———. *The First Men in the Moon*. Indianapolis, IN: Bowen-Merrill, 1901. British ed. London: George Newnes, 1910. Print.

———. *The Food of the Gods: And How It Came to Earth*. London: Macmillan and Co., 1904. Internet Resource.

———. *In the Days of the Comet*. London: Macmillan, 1906. Print.

———. *The Invisible Man: A Grotesque Romance*. London: C. Arthur Pearson Limited, 1897. Print.

———. *Mankind in the Making*. London: Chapman & Hall, Ltd, 1903. Print.

———. *A Modern Utopia*. London: Chapman & Hall, 1905. Print.

———. *The Time Machine, an Invention*. London: Heinemann, 1895. Print.

———. *The War in the Air: And Particularly How Mr. Bert Smallways Fared While It Lasted*. Illus. A. C. Michael. London: G. Bell and Sons, 1908. Print.

———. *The War of the Worlds*. London: William Heinemann, 1898. Print.

———. *The World Set Free*. London, 1914. Print.

Westall, William B. *The Phantom City: A Volcanic Romance*. London: Cassell, 1886. Internet Resource.

———. *A Queer Race: The Story of a Strange People*. London: Cassell & Co., 1887. Print.

Wetstein, Jacob. *Lettres égyptiennes et angloises, ou, correspondance historique, philosophique, critique & littéraire, sur des sujets peu communs, entre un sage Égyptien et un savant anglois*. 1742. Print.

Whiting, Sydney. *Heliondé: or, Adventures in the Sun*. London: Chapman and Hall, 1855. Print.

Wichers, von G. O. *Krieg dem Kriege: dramatisches Zukunftsbild von Schluss des XIX. Jahrhunderts*. Zürich: Sozialdemokratischer Verlag, 1893. Print.

Wieland, Christoph M. *Der goldne Spiegel, oder, die Könige von Scheschian: eine wahre Geschichte. aus dem Scheschianischen übersetzt.* Leipzig: Bey M. G. Weidmanns Erben und Reich, 1772. Print.

———. *Geschichte der Abderiten.* Leipzig: Bey Weidmanns Erben und Reich, 1781. Print.

———. *Geschichte des Agathon.* Frankfurt und Leipzig: Verlag nicht ermittelbar, 1766. Internet resource.

Williams, Leonard. "Anarchism Revived." *New Political Science* 29.3 (Sept. 2007): 297–312.

Woodcock, George. *Anarchism: A History of Libertarian Ideas and Movements.* New York: New American Library, 1962. New Ed. Harmondsworth: Penguin, 1986; rpt. Peterborough, Ont., Can.: Broadview Encore Editions, 2004.

Wooldridge, C. W. *"The Kingdom of Heaven Is at Hand!" A Textbook of the Better Civilization within Reach, with* [sic] *Is Identical with the Kingdom of Heaven as It Was Proclaimed by Jesus of Nazareth.* Chicago: Kerr, 1900. Print.

Wright, Henry. *Mental Travels in Imagined Lands.* London: Trübner & Co., 1878. Print.

Zaets [also Zajac], Sten'ka. Как селените останали без началъство. Приказка. Sofia, 1923. Print.

———. *Kak Muziki Ostalis' Bez Nacal'stva. Skazka.* Peterburg i t.d: "Golos Truda," 1920. Sofia, 1923. Print.

Zamyatin, Yvgeny. *We.* 1920–1921. Trans. Gregory Zilboorg. New York: Dutton, 1924.

Zemmrich, Johannes. *Toteninseln und verwandte geographische Mythen.* Leiden: P. W. M. Trap, 1891. Diss. Universität Leipzig, 1890. Print.

Zilia et Agathide, ou, la volupté et le bonheur. À Madrid [Paris?]: Publisher Not Identified, 1787. Print.

Zisly, Henri. *Voyage au beau pays de Naturie.* Paris: L'auteur, 1900. Print.

Zola, Émile. *Fécondité.* Paris: Bibliothèque-Charpentier, 1899. Print.

———. *Travail.* Paris: Charpentier, 1901. Print.

Zollinger, Oskar. "Louis-Sébastien Merciers Beziehungen zur deutsche Literatur." *Zeitschrift für französische Sprache und Literatur* 25 (1903): 87–121.

Zschokke, Heinrich. *Das Goldmacher-Dorf.* Aarau: Verlag Nicht Ermittelbar, 1819. Print.

Żulawski, Jerzy. *Auf silbernen Gefilden: ein Mond-Roman.* [*Na Srebrnym Globie: Rękopis z Księżyca*]. Deutsch Von Kasimir Lodygowski. München: Georg Müller, 1903. Print.

———. *Stara Ziemia.* [*Die Alte Erde*]. Warsaw: "Bibljoteka Polska," 1921. Internet Resource.

———. *Zwyciezca.* [*Der Sieger*]. Krakow: Wydawn. Literackie, 1959. Print.

Zurbonsen, Friedrich. *Die Sage von der Völkerschlacht der Zunkunft "Am Birkenbaume."* Nach ihren Grundlagen dargestellt und untersucht, 1897. Print.

INDEX

This Index is deliberately limited in its scope given the range of material in the edition's Appendices and Bibliography. As is customary with scholarly editions, I have not indexed my own introduction. The Contents page makes clear what is covered there. Also, because of the sheer number of authors and works cited by Nettlau in his *Outline* (literally hundreds and especially in the later chapters), this Index is selective in its coverage of that work. It focuses on those utopians and works discussed by Nettlau and not merely mentioned.

Abbaye de Thélème (Rabelais) 16–17
Anarchism
   definition of 7–8
Andreae, Johann Valentin 17
Andrographe (de la Bretonne) 23
Aratus of Soli 10
Aristophanes 10
Aristotle 10

Bacon, Francis 17
Bakunin, Mikhail 2, 65
Bebel, August 43
Bellamy, Edward 42–45, 58
Berington, Simon 19
Blatchford, Robert 43
Blithedale Romance, The (Hawthorne) 34
Bulwer-Lytton, Edward 19

Cabet, Etienne 36
Campanella. Tommaso 17
Campe, Joachim 24
Candide (Voltaire) 24
Casanova, Giacomo 23
Cecilia colony 50
Cesta do Ofírské země
   (Shcherbatov) 23
Charlemagne 13

Charles Fourier: sein Leben und seine Theorien
   (Bebel) 45–46
Christianity
   as oppressive force 12–14
Civitas Soli (Campanella) 17
Claudel, J. C. 53–54
Clousden Hill 49
Coeurderoy, Ernest 37, 62
Coming Race, The (Bulwer-Lytton) 19
Commonwealth of Oceana,
   The (Harrington) 17
Communism
   failure in Russia 7
Como se hizo la revolucion
   (Donamaria) 67
Considerant, Victor 36–37
Constitution of Spensonia,
   The (Spence) 32, 33
Crystal Age, A (Hudson) 55
Cyrille, V. 38

d'Aulnoy, Madame 13
Das Liebeskonzil (Panizza) 11
de Bergerac, Cyrano 17
de la Boétie, Etienne 17, 25
de la Bretonne, Retif 22–23
de Parny, Evariste 11

Defoe, Daniel 18
Déjacque, Joseph 34–35
Der goldne Spiegel (Wieland) 24
Der Judenstaat (Herzl) 57
Deutschland in 100 Jahren
    (Flürscheim) 47
Dialogues of the Gods (Lucian) 11
Dickens, Charles 39
Dictionnaire des athées (Maréchal) 28
Die allgemeine Nährpflicht als Lösung der
    soziale Frage (Popper-Lynkaeus) 64
Die Frau und der Sozialsmus
    (Bebel) 43, 45–46
Die grosse Revolution (Scheerbart) 56
Donamaria, Pedro 67
Doni, Francesco 17
Dream of John Ball, A (Morris) 46
Du Laurens, Henri Joseph 11

Ecclesiazusae (Aristophanes) 10
Eine Reise nach Freiland (Hertzka) 46
El socialismo triunfante (Piria) 56
Emile (Rousseau) 24
Empedocles 10
Entretien d'un Européen avec un insulaire du
    royaume de Dumocala
    (Leszczyński) 22
Entrückt in die Zukunft (Hertzka) 46
Ephorus 10
Equality (Bellamy) 43, 45
Equality, or a History of Lithconia
    (Reynolds) 33
Étrennes aux gens d'église (Du Laurens) 11
Etzler, J. A. 33
Euhemerus of Messene 10
Evacuation of England,
    The (Gratacap) 57

Faure, Sébastien 62
Fécondité (Zola) 56
Fénelon, François 18
Fields, Factories and Workshops
    (Kropotkin) 48
Flammarion, Camille 43
Flürscheim, Michael 47
Foigny, Gabriel de 18
Follin, H.-L. 66
Fourier, Charles 36

Fourierists 36–37
Fragment d'histoire future
    (Tarde) 56
Free Life (Herbert) 51–52
free trade 41
Freiland in Deutschland
    (Oppenheimer) 47
Freiland, ein soziales Zukunftsbild
    (Hertzka) 46

Gabalis, Count of 13
Garden City movement 39, 48
Garnier, Charles 19, 24
Geschichte der Abderiten (Wieland) 29
Godwin, Francis 17
Goethe, Johann 24
Golden Age 4–5
Gratacap, L. P. 57
Guillaume, James 37–38
Gulliver's Travels (Swift) 18

Hall, Joseph 17
Harrington, James 17, 25
Hawthorne, Nathaniel 34
Hellenism 10–11
Herbert, Auberon 51–52
Hertzka, Theodor 46–47
Herzl, Theodor 57
Hesiod 10
Histoire de Calejava 18
History of Sevarites or Severambi,
    The (Vairasse) 18
Holberg, Ludvig 19
Howard, Ebenezer 47–48
Hudson, W. H. 55
Humanisphere (Déjacque) 34–35

I Mondi celesti, terrestri et infernali
    (Doni) 17
Iambulus 10
Icarie (Cabet) 36, 71
Icosaméron (Casanova) 23
Ini: Roman aus dem 21 Jahrhundert
    (Voss) 29
intentional communities 33–34, 47,
    49–50, 63–64
  newspapers by 52–53
interwar utopian literature 68–69

INDEX

Jesus Christ and social iniquity 57
Joncquel, Octave, and Théo Varlet 69
Jours d'exil (Coeurderoy) 37
Junqua, François 38

Kampffmeyer, Bernhard 48
Kautsky, Karl 17, 53
Kelly, Harry 48
King Arthur 13
Kropotkin, Peter 38, 41, 45, 48–50, 62

L'age d'or (Maréchal) 24
L'an de mille quatre cent quarante (Mercier) 22
L'autre monde ou histoire comique des états et des empires de la Lune (de Bergerac) 17
La belle Hélène (Offenbach) 11
La conquête du pain (Kropotkin) 38, 48
La découverte australe (de la Bretonne) 23
La Familistère 66
La guerre des dieux (de Parny) 11
La Jugement dernier des rois (Maréchal) 25
La Monarchie des Solipses 19
La protesta 62
La révolution du 4 septembre 19… (Follin) 66
La terre Australe connue (Foigny) 18
Landauer, Gustav 2, 48–49, 63–64
Lasswitz, Kurd 40, 44, 56
Laws (Plato) 10
Le sort réservé aux empereurs et rois (Claudel) 53–54
Le thesmographe (de la Bretonne) 22–24
Les états et empires du soleil (de Bergerac) 17
Les mondes imaginaries et les mondes reels (Flammarion) 44
Leszczyński, Stanislas 22
Looking Backward (Bellamy) 42, 43–44, 58
Lucian of Samosata 11
Lycurgus 10

Man in the Moone, The (Godwin) 17
Maréchal, Sylvain 13, 24–25, 28, 30
Mazzini, Giuseppe 72

Memoirs of Sigr Gaudentio di Lucca, The (Berington) 19
Mercier, Louis-Sébastien 22
Merlino, Francesco Saverio 54
Merrie England (Blatchford) 43
Moilin, Tony 36
Montaigne, Michel de 17
More, Thomas 15–16, 17, 25
Morelly, Étienne 21, 25
Morris, William 46
Mumford, Lewis 71–72
Mundus alter et idem (Hall) 17

Naufrage des isles flottantes (Morelly) 21
Nettlau, Max
    biographical sketch of, by IMAN 1–2
New Atlantis (Bacon) 17
Newbrough, John Ballou 65
News from Nowhere (Morris) 46
Nicolai Klimii iter subterraneum (Holberg) 19
non-socialist works 38–39, 66–67

Oahspe, A Light of Kosmon (Newbrough) 65
Offenbach, Jacques 11
Oppenheimer, Franz 47
Orpheé (Offenbach) 11
Owen, Robert 32, 34, 35

Panizza, Oskar 11
Paolini, Francesco 57
Paradise within the Reach of All Men, The (Etzler) 33
Pericles 4
Perrault, Charles 13
Phaleas of Chalcedon 10
Philemon and Baucis 12
Piria, Francisco 56
Plato 10, 15
Plockhoy P. C. 17, 22
Politeia (Phaleas) 10
Politeia (Plato) 15
Popper-Lynkeus, Joseph 64
Premières Leçons du fils aîne d'un roi (Maréchal) 25

Quiroule, Pierre 62, 82

Rabelais, François 16, 17, 18, 25
Rebmann, Andreas 18, 29
Reipublicae Christianopolitanae descriptio
    (Andreae) 17
Relation du voyage de l'isle d'Eutopie
    (E. R. V. F. L) 19
Renouvier, Charles 37
Republique universelle (Resnier) 23
Resnier, Guillaume 23
Reynolds, James 33
Richter, Eugen 58
Robin Hood 12
Robinson Crusoe (Defoe) 18
Robinson Jeune (Campe) 24
Rosny, J. H. 57, 68
Rossi, Giovanni 38, 50–51
Rousseau, Jean-Jacques 24
Russell, Bertrand 43, 61–62
Russian Revolution, the 69, 72

Sanftleben, Alfred 50, 51
Scheerbart, Paul 56
Servitude Volontaire (Boétie) 25
Shcherbatov, M. M. 23
Singnagtuyag (Storch) 67
Socrates 10
Sozialdemokratische Zukunftsbilder
    (Richter) 58
Spence, Thomas 31–32, 33
Statuts du bourg d'Oudun
    (de la Bretonne) 22
Storch, Mathias 67
Story of Utopias, The (Mumford) 71, 72
Swift, Jonathan 18

Tables Turned, The (Morris) 46
Tarde, Gabriel 56
Télémaque (Fénelon) 18
Thompson, William 35
Thoreau, Henry David 34
Tomorrow: A Peaceful Path to Real Reform
    (Howard) 48
Travail (Zola) 56

Uchronie (Renouvier) 37
Un comune socialista (Rossi) 50
Una visita di Gesù Cristo (Paolini) 57

utopia
  allegorical stories 24–25
  anarchist utopias 51
  animal fable 29–30
  anti-utopia 28
  attack on war 30
  definition of 3–8, 9
  educational novels genre 19–20, 24
  fantastic tales 67–68
  French Revolution 24, 27–28, 30, 31, 32
  German Republican movement 29
  isles genre 20–21
  novels about women's role 40, 56–57
  other planets 40
  pastoral genre 13–14
  peace 70
  pessimistic novels 56
  power of utopian thinking 72–73
  prophecy 70
  pure fantasy 55
  rise of capitalism 44–45
  satire 40–41, 58, 67
  scientific socialism 33
  socialism 25–26
  socialist utopias 53–54
  specialized 40
  study of 70–72
  uncorrupted savage genre 20
  Utopia (More) 15–16
  utopian newspapers 34
  Utopie und Experiment (Sanftleben
    and Rossi) 50–51

Vairasse, Denis 18, 21, 25
Verne, Jules 59
Viaggi di Pitagora (Maréchal) 28
Voltaire 24
Voss, Julius von 29
*Voyages imaginaires, songes, visions,
    et romans cabalistiques*
    (Garnier) 19, 24, 70, 77

Walden (Thoreau) 34
Wanderjahre (Goethe) 24
war 9, 10, 12, 17, 21, 30, 32, 41, 48, 57, 59,
    61, 63, 67, 68–69
Waterhouse, Elizabeth 41

Watteau, Jean-Antoine 13
Wells, H. G. 59–60
   MN's criticism of 59–60
"What 'Nationalism' Means"
   (Bellamy) 45
Wieland, Christopher 24, 29, 30
Wilhelm Meister's Lehrjahre (Goethe) 24
William Tell 12

Winstanley, Gerrard 17, 25
Wright, Henry 38

Xipéhuz (Rosny) 57

Zeno 10, 25
Zilia et Agathide 23–24
Zola, Emile 56